PRAISE FOR
STRONGER THROUGH ADVERSITY

Filled with wisdom, insights, and analysis, *Stronger Through Adversity* offers hope and practical tools to lead, inspire, and thrive. Through conversations with strategic leaders of some of the world's most recognized companies, Joseph Michelli reminds us all of the importance of leadership self-care, empathy, and compassion.

—CHIP CONLEY, Airbnb Strategic Advisor for Hospitality &
Leadership and Modern Elder Academy founder

I love this book. It doesn't offer tired and common suggestions but solutions learned from a diversity of leaders facing the biggest adversities of their lives. The insights are deep, but that doesn't make it difficult to read. Bravo on a much-needed book for the times.

—MARK SANBORN, speaker, author of *The Fred Factor* and
The Intention Imperative, and President, Sanborn & Associates, Inc.

With compelling stories and great writing, Michelli shares insights of top leaders dealing with one of the most profound worldwide crises of our time. This book reveals how major CEOs thrive under pressure and leverage their teams and organizations to remain agile and survive adversity.

—MARSHALL GOLDSMITH, *New York Times* #1 bestselling author
of *Triggers, Mojo*, and *What Got You Here Won't Get You There*

What if you could spend time with some of the world's most successful leaders? What if those leaders authentically shared their business tactics, setbacks, and successes? There's no need for "what-ifs." In *Stronger Through Adversity*, Joseph Michelli gives you exclusive access to leaders who will help you transform your business, strengthen your leadership, and maximize resilience. This is a much-needed book for our times.

—BRIAN WALSH, Founder and Chief Executive Officer,
The REAL Entrepreneur

Full of sage advice from top CEOs and powerful tools to implement their ideas, *Stronger Through Adversity* is exactly what you need to be a highly effective leader in difficult times and beyond.

—JOHN SPENCE, author of *Awesomely Simple*,
top business thought leader, and leadership development expert

Throughout the pandemic, leaders at all levels of business and society received a graduate-level crash course on leading through crisis and uncertainty. Joseph Michelli talked to prominent business, nonprofit, and public safety leaders at various stages of the health crisis and captured their insights in a highly applicable way. In good times or bad, *Stronger Through Adversity* is a leadership road map for resilience, productivity, and realistic optimism.

—DAVE WHITE, President, Global Client Services, AMCI Global

Good news from Joseph Michelli! America's foremost chronicler of successful enterprises gives us a simple but profound action plan to deal with the pandemic challenge. Although COVID-19 is unique, Michelli's interviews with leaders in the private and public sectors reveal that success comes from timeless values: empathy, authenticity, self-discipline, communication, adaptation, and innovation.

—ROBERT SPECTOR, author of *The Nordstrom Way to Customer Experience Excellence*

Joseph Michelli strikes the right balance between sound, pragmatic strategy and compassionate leadership. In the context of the pandemic, Joseph shares insights from extraordinary global leaders on how to provide physical and emotional safety for teams and customers. He offers direction and realistic optimism needed to navigate rattling economic environments. *Stronger Through Adversity* is a must-read for anyone seeking to thrive well beyond the pandemic!

—ELLEN ROHR, COO, ZOOM DRAIN, and author of *Where Did the Money Go?*

This is an extraordinary book that is loaded with lessons to help you and your business succeed. Get this book now. Let it change your life!

—BRIAN TRACY, author, speaker, and consultant

STRONGER
THROUGH
ADVERSITY

STRONGER

THROUGH

ADVERSITY

WORLD-CLASS LEADERS SHARE
PANDEMIC-TESTED LESSONS ON THRIVING
DURING THE TOUGHEST CHALLENGES

JOSEPH A. MICHELLI

NEW YORK   CHICAGO   SAN FRANCISCO   ATHENS   LONDON
MADRID   MEXICO CITY   MILAN   NEW DELHI
SINGAPORE   SYDNEY   TORONTO

1 2 3 4 5 6 7 8 9   LHN   26 25 24 23 22 21 20

ISBN 978-1-264-25739-3
MHID   1-264-25739-2

e-ISBN 978-1-264-25740-9
e-MHID   1-264-25740-6

Design by Lee Fukui and Mauna Eichner

Library of Congress Cataloging-in-Publication Data

Names: Michelli, Joseph A., author.
Title: Stronger through adversity : world class leaders share
   pandemic-tested lessons on thriving during the toughest challenges /
   Joseph A. Michelli.
Description: New York City : McGraw Hill, 2020. | Includes bibliographical
   references and index.
Identifiers: LCCN 2020040886 (print) | LCCN 2020040887 (ebook) | ISBN
   9781264257393 (hardback) | ISBN 9781264257409 (ebook)
Subjects: LCSH: Leadership. | Industrial management. | Crisis management.
Classification: LCC HD57.7 .M52523 2020 (print) | LCC HD57.7 (ebook) |
   DDC 658.4/056—dc23
LC record available at https://lccn.loc.gov/2020040886
LC ebook record available at https://lccn.loc.gov/2020040887

McGraw Hill books are available at special quantity discounts to use as premiums and sales promotions or for use in corporate training programs. To contact a representative, please visit the Contact Us pages at www.mhprofessional.com.

To my family, friends, and clients
May we emerge as the book's title suggests

Contents

PART III
MOVE WITH PURPOSE

PART IV
HARNESS CHANGE

PART V
FORGE THE FUTURE

Foreword

There is a proverb that says, "A smooth sea never made a skilled sailor."

As an 80-year-old, longtime owner of the World-Famous Pike Place Fish Market in Seattle, Washington, I know adversity is a most remarkable teacher.

Through my lifetime, I've experienced stiff challenges dating back to World War II when my family was forced to relocate from Seattle to Tule Lake and Minidoka internment camps. Under a presidential decree, as Japanese Americans, we were imprisoned in tarpaper huts surrounded by barbed wire. My parents lost their business (a produce stand in the Pike Place Market) and our home. We also faced significant prejudice upon returning to Seattle.

With those setbacks and others I've faced as a business owner (e.g., I was near bankruptcy in the 1980s), I've sought to take each breakdown and use it to create a breakthrough. Despite my challenges, I've led a business that became a destination for visitors who traveled to Seattle. We had multiple books written about us, and several training videos share our "fish philosophy." Fortune 500 companies extensively used our training materials. We were covered in *Fast Company* and *People* magazine and appeared on many television programs, including *Good Morning America*. Spike Lee included us in a television commercial that he produced for Levi's. *Dilbert* crafted a cartoon strip based on the Pike Place Fish Market, and *Wheel of Fortune* had a puzzle with our company name as the answer. My guys and I also have been in demand as speakers and trainers. My life is proof that you can become stronger through adversity.

Not only have I been fortunate to grow through life's many setbacks, but I've also had the privilege of watching my business achieve unimaginable financial success and community impact. Most importantly, I was able to hand the Pike Place Fish Market over to a new generation of owners—all of whom grew up in the business as employees. I've also watched the remarkable growth and adaptability of those leaders as they faced the challenges of this pandemic. All of that brings me to the importance of this book and to developing your mindset for overcoming adversity.

The author of this book, Joseph Michelli, is a friend I have worked with dating back more than 20 years. In 2004, we coauthored a book about the Pike Place Fish Market, titled *When Fish Fly*. Throughout his career, Joseph has helped countless leaders create engaging workplaces for their team members, deliver unique and memorable experiences for their customers, and manage through setbacks and adversity. Based on his work, it was no wonder that so many leaders from the world's most iconic brands answered his call for this book. Those leaders took the time to talk with him and share their lessons as they managed during one of the most challenging times in their professional lives.

In this book, Joseph skillfully captures and shares crisis leadership lessons that he collected from those conversations in areas like self-care, empathy, vulnerability, compassion, and personalization. Who wouldn't benefit from increasing each of these skill sets?

I am always learning on my journey to make a world-famous difference, and I trust you will also learn valuable lessons and practical tools in the pages ahead. Most importantly, I know you will walk away from this book inspired, hopeful, and more equipped to be *Stronger Through Adversity*.

JOHN YOKOYAMA
Owner of the World-Famous Pike
Place Fish Market (1965–2018)

Acknowledgments

So much has changed since 2019. In those "good old days," I took so much for granted—not least of which was hugging my grandchildren, having dinner with family and friends, and speaking in person for large audiences. I also didn't recognize the privileges I received growing up as an American male of Italian descent. While I have written acknowledgments in nine previous books, this one seems different. It feels more urgent in response to vulnerability.

Thanks to all essential service providers (healthcare professionals, delivery workers, food industry team members, information technology specialists, etc.). You have enabled my family to maintain health and safety. We should all be grateful for your willingness to put your lives in jeopardy, sacrifice family time, and endure unspeakable emotional strain so the rest of us can survive with only minor inconvenience.

On behalf of readers, I'm grateful to the 140-plus extraordinary leaders who took the time to share their challenges, setbacks, and insights. This book is your story.

Had it not been for clients who trusted me to help them navigate the pandemic, I wouldn't have been able to dedicate the time needed to bring this labor of love to fruition. The leaders of those organizations know who they are, and, hopefully, they also know how much their trust means to my team and me.

As it relates to that team, I am grateful for our adopted member— Donya Dickerson. Officially, Donya is the Associate Publisher of Business at McGraw Hill Professional, but she truly is a member of The Michelli Experience family. Hunkered down in a New York City borough, Donya navigated homeschooling, team leadership, and everything needed to expedite *Stronger Through Adversity*. Donya's guidance, trust, exacting standards, and nurturance have always been one of my life's greatest blessings.

The other remarkable members of my team are Kelly Merkel and Patti Michelli. Kelly is creative, calming, and the consummate multitasker. She fulfills needs and anticipates them. Her autonomous solutions exceed expectations for all she serves.

Jim Collins, the bestselling leadership author of books like *Good to Great*, suggests we should all have a personal board of directors of life. He describes that board as a handpicked group of about seven people you deeply respect and "who you would not want to let down." By that description, Patti Michelli is the chairman of my board. Patti is my wife, my partner, my COVID-19 quarantine companion, my life, and a constant source of remarkable wisdom, joy, and comfort. During the many 20-hour days involved in crafting this book, Patti's spirit was nothing short of life-giving. Her insights were keen, and her support unwavering. The words *thank you* are woefully insufficient!

To my children and grandchildren, I miss your physical presence. That said, please know how grateful I am for your continual outreach, love, and laughter. I am proud of each of you for the way you are navigating and making a difference in these challenging times.

As always, I thank you, the reader. I am grateful for the time you are taking to venture forward with me, as we all learn together. May we make this a safer, kinder, less divided, and better-led world.

STRONGER

T H R O U G H

ADVERSITY

CHAPTER 1

Leadership Forged Through Adversity

TAKING THE PUNCH

Ex-heavyweight champion Mike Tyson said, "Everybody has a plan until they get punched in the mouth."

In late 2019 and throughout 2020, virtually everyone across the globe took a full-frontal blow. A novel coronavirus, COVID-19, wiped out plans, disrupted livelihoods, and ended lives. The pandemic's force was swift and severe; particularly, for healthcare workers, students, parents, couples, people living alone, senior citizens, entrepreneurs, leaders, and small business owners.

Until COVID-19, most people hadn't encountered the jarring force of a submicroscopic infectious agent. Roughly 1/1,000 the width of a human hair, the tiny virus packed a walloping punch. It led to substantial death rates, widespread infections, a severe strain on healthcare resources, dramatic spikes in unemployment, business failures, school closures, event cancellations, extreme travel restrictions, and many other consequences.

Fortunately, as virus transmission surged, leaders and businesses responded with tenacity, adaptivity, and generosity. Healthcare providers endured grueling shifts exposed to high viral loads and isolated themselves from family members. Restaurant owners donated meals to frontline workers. Community leaders purchased and delivered items to homebound seniors. Many companies pivoted operations to produce hand sanitizer, ventilators, face shields, gowns, and masks.

At an individual level, people rapidly activated ingenuity and technology to address the need for human connection. Schoolteachers and principals augmented online learning by displaying banners with words of encouragement outside of students' homes. Automobile parades replaced birthday parties. Neighbors stepped onto their balconies and expressed solidarity and gratitude for frontline workers. High school and college graduates received support from strangers and watched commencement addresses from celebrities. Musicians live-streamed concerts for charitable causes. Friends socialized through virtual happy hours, game nights, shared movie-watching, and trivia contests. Where possible, work teams mitigated the business and social impact of COVID-19 through video conferences and collaboration tools. COVID-19 may have struck the first blow, but people counterpunched with empathy, self-discipline, adaptation, communication, and innovation.

This book outlines how business leaders and other individuals positively responded to and led through the challenges of COVID-19. Moreover, it is a book for anyone who seeks to lead (organizations, teams, communities, or families) long after the acute impact of the pandemic fades from memory.

GENEROSITY AND WISDOM SHARED

Before the pandemic, I had consulted with and wrote nine books about leaders at globally recognized companies like Starbucks, Mercedes-Benz, The Ritz-Carlton Hotel Company, Airbnb, UCLA Health Systems, the Pike Place Fish Market, and Zappos. Almost immediately, as COVID-19 spread, I was asked to participate on task forces for several high-profile brands. My role was to help leaders quickly adjust service delivery based on rapidly changing customer needs and regulatory constraints. Throughout those experiences, I marveled at the compassion, grittiness, team alignment, and leadership wisdom on display. I also began to realize that many textbook leadership concepts were proving ineffective in the face of this pandemic and that new approaches were driving success. For example, physical distancing and the need for rapid decisions (particularly at the outset of the pandemic) rendered participative management approaches impractical. The limitations of participative management were particularly evident when seeking consensus meant assembling all team members in a room to offer input or make decisions about workplace safety, methods of manufacturing, and work distributions. Conversely, command-and-control leadership tactics weren't particularly helpful if they prioritized performance over the feelings and innovative ideas of team members.

The leaders I saw succeeding in response to COVID-19 were authentically leveraging their strengths while rapidly adapting to the changing needs of their people and organizations. This blend of authenticity and adaptability was consistent with qualities shared by transformational leaders like Mahatma Gandhi, Mother Teresa, Abraham Lincoln, Nelson Mandela, and Franklin Roosevelt (FDR).

From the perspective of personality and leadership style, Mahatma Gandhi and President Roosevelt were vastly different. Gandhi leveraged his quiet, calm, and empowering approach to rally the liberation of India from British rule. FDR relied on his engaging yet extremely direct communication style to garner enthusiastic support during World War II. Gandhi led through silence; FDR led through dramatic oration. Yet both men led with an open mind and a strong sense of who they were.

I asked former Campbell Soup CEO and past president of Nabisco Douglas Conant about leadership strengths shared by Gandhi, FDR, and those who led well during COVID-19. Conant, now the Founder and CEO of ConantLeadership and the author of the book *Blueprint*, noted, "Professor Brené Brown has this powerful line. She says, 'You can either walk inside of your story and own it, or you can walk outside of your story and hustle for your worthiness every day.' My language around this is that your life story is your leadership story. Gandhi's life story is what led him to lead his way, and FDR's life story shaped his leadership. Knowing who you are and leading congruent with your story and your values is the key to success in times of calm and, more importantly, in times of crisis. That awareness, however, is only part of being an effective leader." Whether it was the strife faced by Gandhi, the war challenges experienced by FDR, or the uncertainties of COVID-19, effective leaders adopt a growth mindset. I suspect an inquisitive mindset has led you to this book.

Given the leadership extremes I observed during the pandemic, I felt an urgency to understand and capture insights and approaches that were having a transformational impact. As such, I started exploring how top leaders were not only leading with authenticity and adaptability during COVID-19 but how they were positioning their companies to succeed beyond the pandemic. I began reaching out to the most inspirational and effective leaders in my network. What started as in-person conversations quickly shifted to virtual discussions (most of which occurred via video-conferencing). During those meetings, my colleagues shared what they were affirming or learning anew in the face of the pandemic. Those discussions included the specific actions each leader was taking to both endure current challenges and position their teams and organizations to be stronger beyond COVID-19.

Early on, I expected to gain insights from 30 or 40 clients, possibly sharing their perspectives for a series of articles. However, the response for input was immediate and overwhelming. Not only did my clients engage the conversations, but they also introduced me to their colleagues. Unexpectedly, other leaders heard of my project and reached out to share their leadership lessons. In short order, I had interviewed more than 140 leaders from across the globe. It is the candid insights of those generous, thoughtful, and passionate leaders that fill the pages of this book.

DIVERSE CONTRIBUTORS

Most of the individuals who contributed to *Stronger Through Adversity* hold a title such as board member, founder, CEO, president, C-suite leader, or vice president of a highly recognizable brand. To balance the perspective of these talented for-profit leaders, I reached out to an equally impressive group of senior leaders at nonprofit organizations, academic institutions, and public safety agencies.

To avoid partisanship or divisiveness, I chose not to engage political leaders. I am certain historians and pundits will sufficiently critique the decisions and actions of politicians. By contrast, *Stronger Through Adversity* provides actionable insights from individuals who rose above self-interest in the service of their stakeholders (e.g., teams, organizations, shareholders, families, and communities).

While I've included a full list of all 140-plus contributors at the end of this book, a small subset of the organizations represented include:

Corporate Leaders

- Airbnb
- Barron's
- DHL Supply Chain
- Goldman Sachs
- Kohl's
- Mercedes-Benz
- Microsoft
- Panasonic
- Quest Diagnostics
- RBC
- Roche Diagnostics
- Siemens
- Southwest Airlines
- Starbucks
- Target
- Verizon
- Volkswagen

Nonprofit and Academic Leaders

- American Red Cross
- Direct Relief
- Feeding America
- Goodwill

- Human Rights Watch

- Humane Society of the United States

- St Jude's Children's Research Hospital

- Salvation Army

- United Way

- University of Arizona

- University of Tennessee

- Yale University

Public Safety Leaders

- Albany, Oregon Police Department

- Lealman, Florida Fire District

- Overland Park, Kansas Police Department

- Pinellas Park, Florida Fire Department

- Pinellas County, Florida Emergency Medical Services

- San Marino, California Police Department

- Spokane, Washington Fire Department

- Vancouver, Washington Police Department

As you will see in the pages that follow, contributors openly shared both their constructive actions and missteps as they moved through initial and sustained elements of the pandemic. All contributors provided their input without compensation. They engaged in the project with the hope that their honest perspective will serve as a gift to you and future generations of leaders who will invariably face crises, threats, obstacles, uncertainty, and unwanted changes.

The book's contributors offer insights geared toward effectively leading a work team as well as a large or small organization. While geared toward business leadership, the lessons and tools that follow apply to self-management, care for family, and contributions to a community.

The collective leadership themes that emerge from this impressive group of leaders have been tested globally (as many contributors managed operations that accommodated widely varying needs and regulations across continents). These contributors also represent a broad swath of economic sectors, including but *not* limited to:

- Agriculture

- Air travel

- Arts and entertainment

- Automotive

- Banking and finance

- Construction and homebuilding

- Durable and nondurable manufacturing

- Education

- Healthcare and insurance

- Hotel and short-term accommodations

- Retail

- Sports

- Technology

- Wellness

Contributors shared their insights, knowing a portion of the book's proceeds are being donated to *Direct Relief* (see box for information on the mission of this nonprofit) in support of first responders across the globe. By purchasing *Stronger Through Adversity* for yourself and colleagues, you are also contributing to those who have and will continue to address the health and economic consequences of the pandemic.

Direct Relief is a humanitarian aid organization, active in all 50 US states and more than 80 countries. Direct Relief's mission is to improve the health and lives of people affected by poverty or emergencies. The organization serves its purpose without regard to politics, religion, or ability to pay. Throughout the pandemic, Direct Relief coordinated with public health authorities, nonprofit organizations, and businesses in the United States and globally. The nonprofit provided personal protective equipment and essential medical supplies to health workers. Direct Relief continues to tailor its assistance to the world's most at-risk and vulnerable populations.

SHARED CHALLENGES

Unlike prior crises such as the global financial market crash in 1980 or the September 11, 2001, terrorist attacks in New York City and Washington DC, COVID-19's effects were universal. It was as if we were all in different boats facing the same storm. In a symbolic sense, gale-force winds or swirling currents did not spare any individual, family, or business. Irrespective of our unique health, operational, economic, and emotional challenges, we all endured similar conditions.

While your adversities were invariably unique to you, your family, and your business—the leaders interviewed for this book faced many familiar hardships including but not limited to:

- Decreased sleep and increased anxiety

- Mounting childcare and eldercare responsibilities

- Constantly evolving health guidelines and regulations

- Office and business closures

- Rapid transitions to a predominantly remote workforce

- Substantial staff reductions and furloughs

- A need for changes in policies and procedures affecting sales, products, and service delivery

- The infection and death of team members

Despite these challenges, the leaders I had the privilege of interviewing sought consistently to be *Stronger Through Adversity*. When I spoke with Lior Arussy, a consultant with whom I'd worked as part of customer experience transformation at Mercedes-Benz USA, he shared his perspective on facing COVID-19. Lior, who is now President of WordCreate Inc., suggested, "If you think of this pandemic like it was a race, there were three types of runners. Some did not make it to the finish line. Some made it to the finish but were broken when they arrived. Finally, some not only finished but positioned themselves to thrive. From the onset of the pandemic, I sought to be in the third group. For me, that meant I had to do things such as change my language and my thinking. For example, I didn't use the word 'unprecedented' because it implied defeat. Hurricane Katrina was unprecedented and terrorist attacks on 9/11 were unprecedented. Every new event could be described as unprecedented since its unique elements never merged before. I wanted this challenge to be an opportunity to become stronger and more resilient, so I chose language and actions that wouldn't lead to paralysis."

To Lior's point concerning the word *unprecedented*, most of us have not faced health or economic disruptions of this magnitude. People and businesses have, however, bounced back from pandemics and high levels of unemployment throughout history. For example, the bubonic plague killed more than 200 million people. Smallpox and the Spanish flu shortened the lives of 56 million and 40 million people, respectively. HIV/AIDS killed more than 30 million in recent history. Despite those devastating diseases, humanity and businesses rebounded. Similarly, Franklin Roosevelt faced 25 percent unemployment when he became president in 1931. Rather than decrying a lack of precedent, this is an optimal time to look for leadership tools that enable us to mount an unprecedented recovery and sustained success. This book offers practical leadership tools needed to not only weather the health and economic effects of a pandemic but also to thrive in all "storms" large and small.

UNIVERSAL THEMES, EXAMPLES, AND CALL TO ACTION

The chapters that follow highlight 20 lessons on how to prevail through challenges and setbacks. All teachable lessons come to life through leadership stories of those interviewed for the book. Their examples demonstrate how leaders navigated the ongoing impacts of COVID-19 (and, in some cases, the social unrest that followed from the murder of George Floyd). In each chapter, you will see how leaders positioned themselves and their organizations for success in a postcoronavirus world. Each chapter reflects the candid introspection of contributors and offers their insights on teachable lessons born from their accomplishments and missteps.

Throughout the book, you'll find spotlighted quotes referred to as "A Breath of Insight," chapter summaries referred to as a "Resilience Recap," and a closing call-to-action section titled "Your Strength Plan." That planning section poses questions for self-reflection and discussion with colleagues. It also provides an opportunity for you to apply lessons you are learning in the context of your leadership skills, your family, and your business. Each chapter covers an independent content area. In the final chapter, you will have the opportunity to continue to grow, develop, and share the insights you gained from this book.

SEEDS FOR A STRONGER FUTURE

Author Napoleon Hill once observed that "every adversity, every failure, every heartache carries with it the seed of an equal or greater benefit." COVID-19 led to widespread adversities like the death of a family member, a layoff, the loss of one's business, protracted anxiety, debilitating depression, and immobilization. It also carried "seeds for an equal or greater benefit."

Leaders like Edward Mady, a past recipient of *Hotels* Hotelier of the World award and Regional Director and General Manager of The Beverly Hills Hotel, notes, "Crisis is humbling. It can help us realize that there is so much that needs to be done and that no one has all the answers. It can help us value the importance of collaboration to achieve greatness. Adversity can foster an appreciation of the importance of serving first and worrying about what's in it for me later. It can also help us embrace change—partly because we lose the choice not to change. For me, a crisis is not only a test of leadership but a catalyst for personal and organizational growth. While I would not wish a pandemic or other adversity on anyone, I view it as a time for community and leadership growth." No matter the adversity or heartache you faced during COVID-19 or any future challenge, this book is structured to be a catalyst for you to grow your:

- Self

- Team

- Business culture

- Leadership communication

- Ability to collaborate to solve significant problems

- Innovation

- Ingenuity

- Resilience

One of the transformational leaders I referenced early in the chapter, Mahatma Gandhi, put it this way, "Strength does not come from winning. Your struggles develop your strengths. When you go through hardships and decide not to surrender, that is strength." It's time to dive in, learn from hardships, refuse to surrender, and be inspired by insights and tools to help you be *Stronger Through Adversity*.

PART I

SET THE FOUNDATION

A house built on granite and strong foundations,
not even the onslaught of pouring rain, gushing torrents
and strong winds will be able to pull down.
—HAILE SELASSIE,
former emperor of Ethiopia

The following four chapters explore the importance of setting a firm leadership foundation in times of adversity by:

- Prioritizing self-care
- Seeking assistance and maintaining a growth mindset
- Placing your people first
- Focusing on safety

CHAPTER 2

Put Your Mask on First

*If your compassion does not
include yourself, it is incomplete.*
—JACK KORNFIELD,
author and educator

SELFLESS, SELFISH, OR SELF-CARE?

We've all heard that part of an airline safety briefing where the flight attendant advises passengers to put on their oxygen mask before assisting others. While that guidance is sound, it can seem both counterintuitive and in opposition to other messages about leadership. Blockbuster movies like *Sully* celebrate leaders who demonstrate remarkable courage and a commitment to remove others from harm before they seek safety for themselves. Similarly, bestselling author Simon Sinek has titled one of his books *Leaders Eat Last*. While we might agree that leadership is *not* about power, prestige, or title, many of us who practice servant leadership do so at the expense of self-care. It is as if true leaders need to put an oxygen mask on as many people as possible before the leader loses consciousness.

In the early days of the pandemic, many of the leaders with whom I spoke reported that they had lost perspective on self-care. They were running on adrenaline, caffeine, and a shortage of sleep. They struggled to find time to attend to their emotional or physical well-being. Their desire to drive solutions often compromised their health, solitude, and self-reflection. Many of them were not "eating last," they forgot to eat at all. Faced with acute and unrelenting threats to the physical and perceived well-being of their teams, their customers, and the economic viability of their businesses, leaders often ignored warnings concerning their health, stamina, and mental sharpness. While they were attacking business problems, leaders faced disruptions to their work environments and also encountered upheaval in the lives of their partners, children, parents, and others who relied upon them.

Randy Keirn, District Fire Chief at the Lealman Fire District in St. Petersburg, Florida, reported that he saw many fellow leaders deny their own needs in pursuit of their mission—not always with the best of results, "I worked with a lot of leaders during the pandemic and was struck by how many were literally spending every day in meetings and virtual conferences. That left them with only the evenings to do the work generated during those meetings. Many of these people were absolutely exhausted. One person told me they hadn't slept in days." Leadership is difficult, but sound decisions are almost impossible without sleep.

LEADERS NEED CARE TOO

Unfortunately, while most leaders understand the importance of self-care, understanding doesn't necessarily translate into self-directed action. Despite an extensive background in human resiliency and vast experience as a healthcare leader, Chris Recinos found herself pulled into a leadership spiral where self-care was an afterthought. Chris holds a PhD in nursing, is the CEO of the Nurse Leader Network, and is also the Chief Nurse Executive at a major healthcare system in Los Angeles. She noted, "Like other senior leaders, I felt like I couldn't leave the hospital or step away from patient care. For example, I worked 52 consecutive days with no days off. It was hard to take time away when so many people came to me for solutions. It was also difficult to express weakness—so I put on my emotional armor to seem strong." This intense external focus seemed to be working for Chris until she could no longer ignore the large price she was paying for poor self-care. According to Chris, "Everything took a backseat except what was happening in the hospital. I was no longer teaching, recording my regular podcasts, or running my Nurse Leader Network. Since my husband also works at a hospital, our kids struggled in school. It was like *Lord of the Flies* at my house—with our children virtually stranded on an uninhabited island."

Well into this downward self-care cycle, Chris realized she needed to make a change. Sparked by a spontaneous and vulnerable conversation among nursing supervisors, Chris noted, "One leader said she felt like she should get the Worst Mother of the Year award and every other leader with a child at home expressed that same feeling. In that moment we knew we hadn't taken care of ourselves or our broader priorities. So we assigned accountability partners to make sure we were all taking respite. Every week we'd talk to our partner about what we did to re-energize, and they would make sure we were taking days off and truly disconnecting from the work. It's amazing how we as leaders can get so pulled into the importance of our work that we can lose ourselves and deprioritize our families in the process."

Assistant Dean of Executive Education and Professor of Strategy at the University of Arizona, Joe Carella, has spent more than 20 years helping executives and corporations like Chevron, Intel, and Hershey enhance their leadership effectiveness. The University of Arizona, founded in 1885, is a public research university in Tucson, Arizona. Joe succinctly shared his perspective that leading others cannot be viewed as weathering a specific situation: "Leadership shouldn't be event-driven, since true effectiveness involves consistency over time. To deliver consistent leadership for others, you have to first practice consistent care and self-leadership across times of calm and times of crisis." Burning oneself out in the face of crisis is not a sign of quality leadership. Leadership is steady and steadying—which means leaders must first steady themselves. This self-stabilizing component of leadership is essential when change is coming at you with harrowing speed.

RUNNING ON EMPTY—BUT STILL RUNNING

During a crisis, self-care can seem like just another set of tasks to complete in an already crammed day. The perceived burden of self-care behaviors increases when those behaviors are not part of a habit or routine. Erica Coletta, Global Vice President of People and Organization at Mars Petcare, believes self-care should be a leadership ritual—not an optional add-on.

Erica currently leads People and Organization (HR) for Mars Petcare—the largest segment of Mars—taking care of half of the world's pets through nutrition, care, and services. With more than 2,500 veterinary hospitals globally, Mars Petcare is also proud of their beloved household brands like

Pedigree, Cesar, Iams, and Royal Canin. Employing more than 85,000 associates—senior leaders like Erica feel a substantial responsibility to assure the well-being of their diverse Petcare team members across veterinary, sales, services, digital, and manufacturing among many other functions. Particularly as the Petcare business remained operational and quite busy taking care of pets and their owners throughout the pandemic. Erica honestly acknowledged: "At first, it was tough to continue the self-care rituals I had in place before the pandemic. Quite frankly, I seldom paused or took a deep breath. Like many other leaders, I am driven and solution-focused. Those qualities can become vulnerabilities when we seem to be tackling new and complex problems every day, especially during the pandemic. I can't say I did a great job of pacing my passion and energy in those early days of the pandemic. I still have my challenges. However, I was able to maintain my ritual of meditating and walking. By consciously taking the time to walk in nature and use a range of reflective practices, I stayed grounded, and I was more effective as I worked long hours and collaborated on building a new normal. Like many other leaders at Mars, I also gained strength from those around me and my family and friends who I love. These were the things that kept me grounded."

Stephanie Linnartz, Group President Consumer Operations at Marriott International, echoed the critical importance of developing and maintaining self-care rituals, particularly when leaders face waves of crises. Stephanie, a 23-year veteran leader at Marriott International, reflected on the challenges she and her colleagues faced at the height of the pandemic, "We operate in 134 countries and almost overnight, starting in China and moving to our properties around the globe, our business plummeted down nearly 90 percent. Of our roughly 7,500 hotels, 2,000 needed to be closed. This forced us to quickly figure out how we're going to cease operating those properties and empathically furlough tens of thousands of associates globally. At the same time, we had to quickly enhance cleaning protocols at our other 5,000-plus hotels. We also committed to serving our communities by providing a place for first responders to stay as they traveled to provide care or as a way not to expose their family members to risk. All of that had to and did get done at the same time."

During those daunting work challenges, Stephanie added, "I was also adjusting to working from home by converting a picnic table and my attic into a home office. As a mother, I had to adjust to my kids doing school online while being in my work space, to a husband working from home, and to a barking dog." Stephanie adds, "Despite the chaos swirling around me, I was intentional about taking care of myself, so that I could be there for my family at home and my family at Marriott. Even before this crisis hit, I'd been very focused on prayer and meditation and on running. I had to tell myself that self-care was not selfish and that I needed to permit myself to keep running at least five days a week. It took effort, but I couldn't let those coping tools go by the wayside."

WITH SO MUCH AT STAKE

I can imagine that as you are reading this, you might be thinking, *I would love to take time to walk or meditate, but the projects I'm working on are too vital and too time-sensitive.* Alternatively, you might be thinking something like, *Try telling my crying child, ranting teenager, or hyperactive dog that I need to pause to meditate.* Stacy Salvi, Senior Director of Strategic Product Alliances at Fitbit, shared similar thoughts given that many people turned to technology companies like Fitbit for strategic, tactical, and social assistance during the pandemic. For example, Fitbit developed, received FDA approval for, and manufactured a low-cost, easy-to-operate ventilator designed for emergency use—which they named Fitbit Flow.

The company also partnered with Stanford Medicine to apply algorithms to data collected from wearers of Fitbit devices who wished to have their body temperature and heart rate used as an indicator of a possible infection. In those cases, the device could issue an instant alert to the wearer. Given the significance of Fitbit's projects, Stacy noted, "My days started at 6:30 in the morning and ended at 9:30 or 10:30 at night. There were a lot of back-to-back video conferences crammed into those days. I am fortunate in that my husband takes on the bulk of childcare, but he also has a full-time job." As more and more worthwhile projects surfaced, Stacy reported the line between work and home virtually vanished. "Weekends weren't the same as they had been. It wasn't sign off on Friday night and sign back in on Monday. I found myself working through the entire weekend, and I had to be vigilant to take more breaks throughout each day. I work for a company that helps people stay active and track their movement, and here I was, needing to lead myself to prioritize my movement and to take mental breaks far more regularly."

While many leaders might not have time for long meditation sessions or extended walks, most (no matter the importance of their work or the urgent nature of their demands) can take short mental and movement breaks.

ATTEND TO AND
SHARE YOUR FEELINGS

Many leaders identified a self-care technique that was not only effective but also did not add to their daily task list. Their approach involved attending to, labeling, and expressing their feelings. Through those simple actions, leaders processed fear, anxiety, and frustration and more effectively connected with the feelings of others. For example, Ronnell Higgins, Director of Public Safety and Chief of Police at Yale University, noted, "Often leaders, particularly in law enforcement, project an image that nothing fazes them. Unfortunately, if they don't stay on top of their emotions, their feelings will build up over time, and those emotions come out in ways they don't expect or want. I see the labeling and expression of feelings as a necessary part of self-care and as a leadership strength, not as a sign of weakness. To that point, during the pandemic, I took a moment to cry."

Ronnell continued, "I'd just been informed that an officer who retired from our force about five years ago had lost his life battling COVID-19. I spoke by phone with his wife. She was also a retired police officer from our department. I thought about my peer and his family and considered the impact of the virus on so many people. I reflected on how much I cared about and wanted to keep my family and our community safe. As a result, I began feeling sadness, grief, and fear. So on a day filled with conference calls, I took time to close my door and cry." By expressing his emotions constructively, Ronnell was able to get back to work and take the lead on crucial public safety and property protection tasks. Not only did Ronnell benefit from his emotional expression, but he also felt comfortable talking about his sadness with the hope his story would normalize and encourage similar cathartic experiences.

Similarly, Brett Schlatterer, Fire Chief for the Pinellas Park Fire Department in Florida, shared the importance of tracking emotions so leaders can connect with others. Brett suggested, "I was afraid during this pandemic. My fear usually involved the health of my family. My wife is a nurse practitioner with an office on her hospital's COVID floor. She also has autoimmune challenges. I have an 86-year-old mother that lives with us, and I have a daughter with an autoimmune condition. So I got worried, nervous, and scared for them. As a leader, I had to acknowledge and face my fear. For example, the first time I interacted with a known COVID positive patient, I needed to recognize my fear, experience it, and work through it so I could do my job. That encounter occurred during a nursing home inspection with the Department of Health. As I interacted with the patient, I paid particular attention to my uneasiness and the anxiety I experienced as I touched items near the patient. For me, it was no different than the way I've dealt with past fear—whether it was the first time I dealt with bloodborne pathogens or I worried about hepatitis or HIV." With time, training, and a willingness to recognize his emotions, Brett reported that he became comfortable with the way he was protecting himself and his team. He furthered suggested that by recognizing his fear and anxiety, he could empathize more effectively with those he led and served.

SELF-CARE APPLIES TO YOU

It might seem obvious, but it is important to highlight that self-care applies to every leader and manager in an organization. CEOs and frontline managers are not exempt. Tash Elwyn is the President and CEO of Raymond James & Associates. Raymond James Financial manages approximately $775 billion in client assets across a network of about 8,100 financial advisors. Tash shared that the pandemic taught him "the importance of self-care while being focused on the well-being of those we serve. This pandemic has been the proverbial 'it's a marathon, not a sprint' situation. It has led me to conclude that we, as leaders in every level of the organization, need to view ourselves almost as if we are professional athletes, focusing on pacing ourselves such that we can perform at peak levels for a sustained period of time. This requires proper sleep, diet, and exercise, no matter how difficult that may be amidst handling everything else the pandemic presents." When it comes to professional athletes, we refer to self-care as preparation and training. That training builds stamina and sustains elite performance levels.

RESILIENCE RECAP

➤ Servant leaders must practice self-care. Leaders may want to "eat last," but they still need nourishment.

➤ Crises activate leaders to address seemingly endless organizational threats and opportunities. Unfortunately, leaders can become so absorbed in crisis management that they neglect their well-being.

➤ Leaders may think they can operate without sleep, physical activity, and mind-clearing breaks. Ultimately, however, they pay the price in decision-making, health, and life balance.

➤ Self-care is fundamental to self-leadership, and self-leadership is fundamental to leading others.

➤ Self-care is a discipline that needs to be practiced and ritualized. Like all other disciplines, it benefits from social support and partner accountability.

➤ No matter how busy you become, you should be able to get up, move, and take a short mental break.

➤ Increased awareness and expression of feelings provide self-care benefits and opportunities to understand the emotions of others.

➤ Leadership effectiveness is the byproduct of a marathon, *not* a sprint.

YOUR STRENGTH PLAN

1. When have you seen leaders neglect their self-care?

2. What specifically were the consequences to those leaders and their businesses when self-care wasn't prioritized?

3. When have you neglected your self-care in the service of others?

4. What factors or situations put you at risk for trying to lead others while neglecting yourself?

5. What examples do you have of leaders who serve others well without sacrificing their well-being in the process?

6. What specifically do you do to take care of yourself? If, in the words of Professor Joe Carella, leadership effectiveness is about the consistency of care provided to yourself and others, how consistently do you sustain self-care behaviors in times of calm and in times of challenge?

7. Do you have an accountability partner who helps you stay on track with self-care behaviors in the context of your overall leadership skills? If not, who might serve that role for you? For whom might you serve a similar function?

8. What's your self-care training plan to drive professional athlete level performance?

CHAPTER 3

Leave the Island, Follow the Terrain

*Asking for help does not mean you are
weak or incompetent. It usually indicates an
advanced level of honesty and intelligence.*
—ANNE WILSON SCHAEF,
author and psychologist

A TIME FOR GROWTH

In the preceding chapter, we explored ways leaders practiced self-care and "put their masks on first." Unfortunately, many leaders lose perspective on their limitations and carry an inordinate responsibility for the success of their organization, team, family, community, or family. They fail to heed the wisdom of poet John Donne when he wrote, "No man is an island, entire of itself." This chapter is about asking for help, seeking guidance, and staying open to new ideas.

Ironically, many of the leaders I spoke with credited the pandemic for fueling substantial personal and organizational growth. I heard statements like, "COVID-19 gave me a harsh wake-up call," or "The pandemic forced my team and me to dive into learning. As soon as we figured out operating in a lockdown, 'Bam,' we had to knit together a reopening plan."

Given the scale and fury of change during the pandemic, leaders reported being disoriented, perplexed, and at times—rudderless. To mount an effective response, they actively engaged colleagues outside of their normal work groups, reached out to professional networks, tracked the course of other leaders, and participated in collaborative sessions outside of their organizations. In essence, they searched their networks widely for ideas and solutions to adjust to unrelenting volatility.

I titled this leadership chapter "Leave the Island, Follow the Terrain." As you've likely surmised, "leaving the island" refers to seeking assistance. "Follow the terrain" is a phrase I first heard when I began mountain climbing. A more advanced climber said, "When the map doesn't match the terrain, always go with the terrain." The crisis nature of the pandemic made strategic and tactical road maps irrelevant. Accordingly, successful leaders quickly abandoned their prepandemic maps and closely tracked the evolving customer and business landscape. Let's look at how leaders left their islands and followed the terrain.

RESISTANCE IS NATURAL

From my perspective, there is a link between growth and resistance. Seedlings must break through the resistance of the earth, and bodybuilders need to resist hefty weights to build their muscles. Leaders must also push through habits and emotional resistance to grow themselves and their teams. Such was the case for a leader with whom I've worked across many settings—Dan Sills. Dan is a General Manager and Senior Vice President at Bauer Hockey. Bauer manufactures ice hockey equipment, skates, apparel, and other recreational and fitness gear. During the pandemic, leaders at Bauer adapted their business to produce and distribute more than 2 million face shields directly to frontline workers. The company also published online instructions for manufacturing face masks so that other companies could fulfill the critical need for personal protective equipment (PPE). Given the pandemic's shock waves, Dan candidly shared, "I wish I could say I was open and accepting of what was happening around me in the earliest days. I think I was experiencing Kubler-Ross's first stage of grief—denial. I remember sitting in a strategy session in Miami in February 2020. We were reviewing budgets that would go into effect in June, and we were planning for a sales team meeting in Germany that was to take place in March. Others around the table were discussing whether our Germany trip would be canceled and how the emerging virus would impact the game of hockey in the United States. I was certain people were overreacting, and, at worst, the virus would be a small speed bump for our business."

Dan's initial resistance is well-understood by cognitive psychologists and behavioral economists. They refer to it as "optimism bias." My mother would have called it "wishful thinking." Crises bring out a unique form of optimism bias, which researchers call a "normalcy or normality bias." This tendency underestimates the likelihood of a disaster and potential adverse effects when one occurs. Amid pandemics or natural disasters, studies have shown about 70 percent of people display varying degrees of a normality bias. We want to assume that disasters won't happen to us, and if they do, we want to believe the consequences will be mild. We also overestimate the speed and degree to which our lives will return to a precrisis state.

For Dan, staying engaged with team members helped him move swiftly through his resistance, "I was fortunate to be in regular contact with other leaders at Bauer. They helped me speed past my denial. I also tracked trends in related industries, which forced a shift in my perspective. For example, I sensed that when the National Basketball Association paused its season, the National Hockey League was soon to follow. All of that enabled my team and me to find ways to make a swift and meaningful course correction that maximized Bauer's substantial business and social impact." The perspective of other leaders was a powerful antidote to Dan's denial, and outside viewpoints will likely also nudge you through natural resistance.

REACHING OUT BROADLY

Dr. Bill Barrier, and other leaders, reached out beyond the walls of their businesses to assure they weren't on a leadership island. In the process, they saw how peers were coping with business turbulence. Bill is the Chief Strategy Officer at Pecan Deluxe Candy Company. This international food manufacturer provides ice cream, pralines, cookie dough, beverages, and other items to premium brands, other manufacturers, and restaurants. Bill shared, "I immediately started contacting people in my network, many of whom weren't in my industry. I wasn't looking for specific guidance for Pecan Deluxe, but I wanted to see how other leaders were approaching shared challenges. I found great value in simply connecting, listening, and being heard." Reaching out across industries can mitigate isolation risks and avail perspectives that wouldn't surface among peers or industry colleagues.

Kevin Washington, President and CEO of the YMCA, was able to engage, support, plan, and collaborate rapidly with a leadership consortium that formed well before the pandemic. The YMCA is active in 10,000 neighborhoods across America and focuses on "strengthening the community by connecting all people to their potential, purpose, and each other." Kevin noted, "I have a long history as a nonprofit leader, and I can think that I've seen it all before. The pandemic, however, was a monumental learning opportunity. I am fortunate to be part of an alliance of CEOs representing nonprofit and faith-based organizations. The alliance is called Leadership 18. Collectively, our group, which includes the American Cancer Society, the American Heart Association, the American Red Cross, and the Girl Scouts, employs more than 12 million people. During the pandemic, most of these organizations needed to find ways to serve communities with housing, food, recreation, and other essential services. Leadership 18 began meeting a couple of years ago, which enabled us to support one another quickly as COVID-19 emerged. It also gave us a chance to be stronger through our collective experiences and leverage greater scale. We wouldn't have been able to achieve the things we did had we not worked alongside one another on behalf of our communities and our people."

One way Leadership 18 banded together was to spearhead a request for government funding to offset the nonprofits' highest expenditure—employee salaries and benefits. On March 18, the leadership of this alliance collectively signed a letter asking for emergency assistance since charities have "payrolls exceeding those of most other U.S. industries, including construction, transportation, and finance. The largest expenditures for most of America's charitable organizations are personnel costs. Unfortunately, in multiple disaster relief laws in the past, Congress has approved employment-related tax credits that fail to recognize that we are significant employers."

Kevin concluded, "We knew that we couldn't fundraise our way out of our looming economic crisis. There was no scenario where the philanthropic pipeline could meet our growing needs. I feel blessed to have a community of like-minded leaders to whom I was able to turn for support, guidance, collaboration, and effective outcomes. Leadership can be lonely if you aren't willing to reach out and work together for shared growth." According to the National Council of Nonprofits, on March 25, Congress approved loan support for large nonprofits. By reaching out, Kevin

Washington received the benefits of a leadership community and leveraged the political power of other similar organizations. Other successful leaders engaged communities that were less industry-based and more regional.

FINDING INSIGHTS IN YOUR COMMUNITY

Jim Mortensen credits a community leader for including him in a cross-industry, regional action group called Challenge Seattle. Jim is the President and Chief Executive Officer at Ste. Michelle Wine Estates—the parent company for the Chateau Ste. Michelle winery. Based in Woodinville, Washington, Chateau Ste. Michelle is the state's oldest winery and a recipient of *Wine Enthusiast*'s designation as American Winery of the Year. Jim shared, "I was fortunate to be invited by former Washington state governor, Christine Gregoire, to participate in Challenge Seattle—an alliance of about 20 of our region's largest employers. I am grateful for the support participants gave one another during the pandemic, and more importantly, I am amazed by the magnitude of issues we collectively addressed."

Challenge Seattle's leadership community included CEOs, presidents, and board members from companies like Alaska Airlines, Amazon, the Bill & Melinda Gates Foundation, Boeing Commercial Airplanes, Costco, Microsoft, Nordstrom, REI, Starbucks, and Zillow. Jim noted, "In the CEO role, you try to make well-informed decisions driven by data and analysis. Early on, other than Johns Hopkins University data on global infections and fatalities, there wasn't a lot of information my team and I could use to identify patterns or anticipate the future. It was a gift for me to be involved in Challenge Seattle because it was like being in a forest surrounded by massive trees. Thanks to former Governor Gregoire's leadership, we challenged each other to see and understand different perspectives, share data, offer analyses, contribute ideas, think deeper, and make recommendations." Functionally, Jim described a process where leaders crowdsourced information and fostered a deep understanding of pandemic-related problems facing customers, communities, and the alliance's respective businesses. The group offered a safe environment for discourse, debate, and disagreement.

Through the group's meetings and homework assignments, leaders stayed data-driven and benefitted from insights of brands with a global perspective. For example, a Microsoft team member living in China called into a group meeting as the virus was just emerging in Washington state. Jim concluded, "The work done in Challenge Seattle allowed us as employers to take action on behalf of our teams, customers, and other stakeholders well in advance of guidance or regulation from our political leaders. In our case at Ste. Michelle Estates, it allowed us to be on our toes, not on our heels. It helped us anticipate the protocols and procedures we needed before we had a COVID-19 positive case in one of our production facilities in eastern Washington and before we reopened our tasting room to our 400,000 annual visitors."

The notion that leaders are "self-made" or "self-sufficient" is illusory. Crises, by their nature, serve as great equalizers, often forcing people to come together to grab a foothold on rapidly changing terrain.

A Breath of Insight

Leadership is a constant state of learning, it's also something we can't do on our own. Leaders work together. So today, who are you going to ask for help to create a healthy, inclusive, and prosperous future for the world?
—**Silver Feldman,** Manager, Business Systems at FOX Sports

ONLY ASK IF YOU ARE READY TO HEAR

Dave Pace was quick to note that many leaders are willing to ask for help only when things get dire; however, even in those situations, it becomes challenging to stay open to novel ideas. Dave has been a senior leader for many companies. For example, he has been the President/CEO of Jamba Juice and the President of Carrabba's. Presently, he serves as a Board Member for the Ownership Advisory Group of the Dallas Stars, the founder and owner of the Circle Double J Ranch, and the Chairman of the Board for Red Robin Gourmet Burgers. Dave noted, "Success as a leader in times of crisis means asking for guidance and listening to the wisdom you can collect from that input. It is a time to challenge yourself to learn as much as you can and to dig in to find information as well as people who will challenge old approaches with new ideas. It's not easy to abandon our entrenched assumptions. It's more comfortable to cling to the way things have always been or to the way we want them to be. Leadership, however, requires a constant commitment to developing your intellectual and tactical agility." Reaching out will help assure you are not on your leadership island, but it doesn't guarantee you are accepting the guidance of others concerning new possible paths.

David Chiem is the Founder and CEO of MindChamps—Singapore's leading early education provider, with more than 100,000 graduates across 83 centers in seven countries. MindChamps is a company I know well as I profiled them in a 2019 book titled *The MindChamps Way: How to Turn an Idea into a Global Movement.* In the context of the pandemic, David shared, "Before setting up our first preschool, my team and I researched factors that contribute to the resilience and adaptivity of sports champions and exceptional leaders. We've built those qualities into our curriculum and in the way we select and develop leaders. The pandemic reinforced the importance of maintaining what we call a 'learning mind,' which is fundamental to realizing champion-level potential. Working across continents, we've had to learn and adapt to minute-by-minute changes so we could continue to provide service to the children of essential workers. The worst thing you could do during the pandemic was close your mind to information and ideas, or be unwilling to try new things. Without that hunger for learning, you risked irrelevance or defeat." While many leaders acknowledge the importance of staying open to new ideas and soliciting the input of others, many trudged through the pandemic without the benefit of helpful teams, diverse networks, or preestablished alliances.

STAYING OPEN THROUGH PERSONAL DISCOVERY

Operating without the resources of leaders in large companies, a client of mine diligently tracked, studied, and applied effective actions he saw other leaders taking. James Giacopelli holds CEO positions for several small to midsize organizations, including Giacopelli Accounting and Tax Services and Complexions Dance Academy. Complexions is a world-renowned performing arts brand with training and performance elements that typically engage more than 300,000 people annually across more than 20 countries. James noted, "I doubled down on my study of other leaders.

Everywhere I turned, there were examples of terrific and less than stellar leadership on display across various levels of government and business. Our performing arts company was navigating some rather harsh cancellations and disruptions, so I systematically analyzed the actions of other CEOs as if I were in a learning lab. I wanted to benefit from being a fast follower of the best and most productive actions taken by leaders who were mounting creative responses. I looked at Fortune 500 companies to see what they were doing with their wealth of resources, and I also studied smaller businesses to learn how they were leveraging their agility. Our leadership team then adapted and incorporated the most promising actions into our operational and financial tactics. We also adjusted or scrapped efforts that weren't getting us our desired outcomes."

It is a natural human response to "pull inward" during a crisis. We narrow our focus to improve the likelihood we will find safety. In the process of narrowing our options and putting on armor for battle, leaders can form resistance in the context of a normalcy or optimism bias or get swept into the belief that they carry an inordinate responsibility to win the battle on their own. Even when leaders humble themselves to ask for help, they aren't necessarily willing or prepared to act on the input they receive. Leaders who prevail across uncertain and more predictable times continue to develop their abilities to "leave the island and follow the terrain."

RESILIENCE RECAP

➤ No woman, man, or leader is an island entire of itself.

➤ Leaders can carry an inordinate responsibility for the success of their organization, team, community, or family.

➤ Resistance is a natural element in growth.

➤ Teams can nudge one another through periods of denial and minimization.

➤ Optimism and normalcy biases are empirically validated tendencies that make it harder to accept the need for assistance or prompt action.

➤ Seeking input and assistance can serve to break through a leader's sense of isolation.

➤ Reaching out to colleagues outside of your industry provides a unique perspective on shared leadership challenges.

➤ By establishing constructive leadership alliances and leveraging them within or across industries, you are likely to garner support, share data, offer analyses, contribute ideas, and think deeper.

➤ While it can be challenging to ask for input, listening to that input can be an even more significant hurdle.

➤ Athletic champions and extraordinary business leaders possess a growth or learning mindset.

➤ Track and learn from the leadership actions of others. You don't always have to be an innovator. It often pays to be a fast follower instead. Consider traditional media, social media, and case studies to be your learning lab and adapt those lessons to your business.

YOUR STRENGTH PLAN

1. How often, in your leadership role, do you turn to others for input or assistance?

2. In what areas are you most inclined to ask for help? Where are you least likely?

3. Think of a time when you should have asked for help but didn't. What got in the way? How did your resistance impact the situation? Conversely, can you think of a time when an outcome improved due to your outreach?

4. When have you demonstrated an optimism bias or a normalcy bias? How did you work through it?

5. Do you turn to others outside your organization or industry for leadership support or advice? If you do, what value do they provide? If you don't, what prevents you from doing so?

6. Who turns to you for leadership advice or support?

7. Is it more comfortable to ask or be asked for assistance?

8. Individuals with open mindsets tend to share a few characteristics, rate yourself on each statement below using a scale from 1 to 5—with 1 being "not at all true for me" and 5 being "extremely true for me." Consider working on areas that will expand your open mindset.

   - I don't give up when things don't go easily: _____
   - I eagerly seek challenges: _____
   - I am quick to ask for input and constructive feedback: _____
   - I see setbacks as terrific learning opportunities: _____
   - I enjoy and am inspired by the success of others: _____

   The goal of an open-mindset assessment isn't to get 5s. Instead, it is to gain a greater understanding concerning areas of strength and opportunity. Your strengths can be enhanced, and your opportunity areas supplemented—it's a matter of being open to continual growth.

9. Where do you look to study the leadership practices of others? What have you learned and or applied lately as part of your information seeking?

CHAPTER 4

Practice Employee Obsession

Everyone talks about building a relationship with your customer.
I think you build one with your employees first.
—ANGELA AHRENDTS,
former Senior Vice President,
Retail, Apple

THE DEBATE SHOULD END

In the previous two chapters, we explored the importance of self-care, asking for assistance, and fostering a growth mindset. In the pages ahead, we shift focus from introspection and taking care of yourself and encourage a laser focus on employee well-being.

I realized when I titled this leadership chapter "Practice Employee Obsession" that I was a bit provocative. In its most negative connotation, *obsession* can be interpreted to mean "practice a disturbing employee preoccupation"—clearly that isn't what the leaders I interviewed would recommend. In a broader sense, *obsession* implies "compelling motivation." The word is used frequently in the context of customer experience design and customer care. For example, four main principles guide Amazon:

1. Customer obsession (not competitor focus)

2. Operational excellence

3. Passion for invention

4. Long-term thinking

A quick Google search on the phrase "*customer* obsession" produces approximately 49,600,000 results, and related search phrases include "how to measure customer obsession," "why is customer obsession important," and "customer obsession and technology." However, the phrase "*employee* obsession" produces about a fifth of the results, and many of those explore how employee engagement contributes to "customer obsession."

As a certified customer experience professional and leadership consultant, I have had a front-row seat to raging debates about whether companies should aspire to put the customer or the employee first. As you might guess from Amazon's guiding principles, Jeff Bezos consistently says, "put the customer first," while the founder of the Virgin Group, Sir Richard Branson, believes, "Clients do not come first. Employees come first. If you take care of your employees, they will take care of the clients."

Not liking these "either/or" debates, I favor wording like "human-centric" or "human-obsessed." Shouldn't equal importance be given to the team member (internal customer) experience *and* the experience of someone who purchases your products and services (external customer)?

The pandemic changed the way many leaders think about and value their team members. With so many people working from home, leaders experienced their team members in their employees' home environments; thus, interacting with them in a more personal setting. They also relied on their teams for survival, especially when they needed them to innovate solutions to serve and retain customers quickly. Many leaders also realized they were asking people to take risks on behalf of a company and its customers. Given all these factors, the leaders I spoke with resoundingly shared the significance of and methods needed to "practice employee obsession."

THE TIMES THEY ARE A CHANGING

John Gainor is a leader I worked with when he was President and CEO of International Dairy Queen. He currently serves as Public Board Director for Saia Inc. and is a member of the Board of Directors at Jack in the Box Inc. Saia is a leading interstate to international freight carrier that directly transports across the contiguous 48 US states while also serving Alaska, Hawaii, Mexico, and Puerto Rico through its partner network. Jack in the Box Inc. is a restaurant company that operates and franchises more than 2,200 restaurants in 21 states and Guam.

As it relates to employee obsession, John shared, "The pandemic has increased the awareness of my colleagues regarding the importance of team members. Generally, I've ascribed to the idea that all stakeholders hold equal importance, but the pandemic has exposed a new truth. Employees should take precedent. Leaders couldn't place their worries about economic viability above the needs of their team, and they couldn't place customers and shareholders above their employees." While John and I used to agree on the equal importance of customers and team members, his perspective shifted in favor of employees during the pandemic. From John's perspective, the crisis spotlighted high-functioning teams, without which many brands couldn't adapt and engage customers.

CARING FOR AND CARING ABOUT

Having been a consultant for Mercedes-Benz USA and the author of *Driven to Delight*, a book that dives deeply into that company's customer experience transformation, I had the opportunity to work with then CEO Steve Cannon. Steve is presently the CEO of AMB Sports + Entertainment. In his current role, he leads all business operations of the National Football League's Atlanta Falcons, Atlanta United of Major League Soccer, Mercedes-Benz Stadium, and PGA TOUR Superstore. Steve viewed the pandemic as giving his leadership team a chance to both take care of (care for) his team members and get to know (care about) them as individuals. Steve noted, "I've been in continuous Zoom call mode, and it has given me the ability to have conversations with team members on a deeper and more personal level. In addition to weekly video calls with 400 to 600 people, I've engaged regular small video conference CEO lunches. I started each lunch by asking attendees to take 60 seconds and find something personal they can bring back to share with the group. People brought their wedding pictures, went and got their kids and had them sit on their lap, fetched a dog they'd rescued, and so much more." That sharing enabled Steve and his leadership team to see beyond what his people do at AMB Sports + Entertainment and provided insights into who they are.

While technology-facilitated meetings can get impersonal, Steve and leaders like him used the accessibility benefits of technology to reduce the gap between leaders and teams. Steve noted, "I've asked to be invited to marketing meetings, sales meetings, and others. Before the pandemic,

I wouldn't have attended those meetings when they were held in conference rooms all over our building. Fortunately, I've been able to drop in during the crisis—not to oversee progress but to make myself available and remove barriers or assist in any way that would make the group's work easier." Steve's leadership team, like that of many others I interviewed, also did regular check-ins with team members. Those phone calls or video chats were typically little more than asking how team members were doing and taking the time to listen. Steve concluded, "Across all of our interactions, we made sure to celebrate the joys of life—birthdays, anniversaries, and, in one instance, the excitement of the arrival of a first-born son."

For many leaders, technology allowed them to connect at all touch-points along the employment journey. Brien Convery is the National Director of Early Talent Acquisition at the Royal Bank of Canada (RBC). RBC is one of Canada's biggest banks and among the largest in the world based on market capitalization. RBC has 86,000-plus full- and part-time employees serving 16 million clients across Canada, the United States, and 34 other countries. Brien shared how leaders at RBC worked to strengthen relationships with prospects and new hires before and during the pandemic. "A couple of years ago, we defined the branded universal experience we wanted to provide to college students who we were recruiting, hiring, and bringing into our culture. By taking the time to lay out an optimal end-to-end journey (complete with the tools needed and the people who would be accountable), we identified gaps and technologies needed to digitally enhance relationships, growth, and the engagement of prospects and new hires." Brien reported, "The pandemic accelerated the use of digital platforms like our RBC Canada Student Café—a structured networking program where we emulate office collisions. Collisions are those moments in an office environment where new hires naturally come in contact with executives or other colleagues in the hallway or the lunch areas. We have been intentional with virtual coffees and office hours to connect our students and new hires with leaders who will get to know them, answer their questions, share our culture, and mentor them."

Brien and his team realized that in a physical office environment, new hires learn about a company's culture through formal activities like orientation training and informal interactions with the leaders they meet during hallway and cafeteria encounters. A senior leader can also make a point of stopping by a new hire's desk to welcome him or her. Since many of those naturally occurring interactions aren't possible in work from home settings, RBC coordinated those "collisions" in the form of virtual coffees and leader office hours. Effectively "caring for" and "caring about" team members requires leaders to think about the employee experience from the team members' vantage point. It then requires investment in tools and processes (like virtual coffees) to fill gaps and drive engagement. In the context of the pandemic, many of those gaps were technology-aided, but leader-powered.

TAKING IT OFF THE SCREEN

Given the amount of time many teams were meeting via video conferences, many leaders I interviewed looked for ways to care for and about their teams in unexpected ways. Scott Kendrick is the VP of Marketing at CallMiner, a technology solution company that provides advanced speech analytic tools to strengthen client interactions across varied communication platforms. You might think a technology company would rely solely on digital tools to bring leaders and team members together. CallMiner, however, supplemented team member experiences through an old-fashioned care package. Scott explained, "We wanted to show that we cared in a tangible yet fun way, so we sent a care package that included a Remote Together/Work from Home Warrior T-shirt, branded swag, hand sanitizer, a small whiteboard, and a deck of cards."

Care Package Sent to CallMiner Team Members Working from Home

The feedback that leaders at CallMiner received from this small gesture was overwhelming and included comments like "I received my surprise COVID-19 Care Package today. What an awesome thing for CallMiner to do for us! Swag is awesome, but the support . . . that we have experienced during this time has been even more amazing. I have never been more proud to work for a company . . . WOW!"

Other leaders wow their team members with simple acts of thoughtfulness. Cheri Perry is the President of Total Merchant Concepts, a credit card–processing company that *Seattle Business* magazine recognized as one of the best places to work in Washington. Cheri stated, "Long before COVID-19, we referred to Fridays in our office as 'love letter Fridays' because my team sends personal notes to a subset of our clients each week. The notes are simple handwritten messages that check in with and let our clients know they matter. It might seem odd that a financial service business sends personal letters to clients, but we believe those small loving acts are the right thing to do." Partway through the pandemic, Cheri realized that she needed to adopt the same behavior but direct her notes to her team. Cheri explained, "I started writing and sending personal letters home to my team members. Even in the dark cloud of the pandemic, I could see a silver lining where the care of team members could and should be elevated." As leaders, we can make employee rewards and recognition costly and complicated. By contrast, care packages and personal letters can be simple, low-tech ways to practice employee obsession. However, they do require leaders to set aside time for those kind and powerful actions.

BE WILLING TO ADJUST OR DECLINE WORK

For leaders who managed teams that couldn't work from home, employee obsession involved navigating needs. Frank Donchez, the Chief of Police in Overland Park, Kansas, explained, "Our officers had to be on the streets to maintain public safety. As leaders, we needed to do everything we could to conduct business in new ways. For example, we held roll calls outside and practiced social distancing wherever possible. We also encouraged our officers to back off self-initiated activity. That's where caring for our teams and our community required a hard balance. As speeding and other traffic offenses began to escalate, we had to rethink, redesign, and reengage some of those activities we previously relaxed."

Frank shared that caring for his officers is truly an obsession of his, and at times that care forced conflicting and anguishing choices. For example, he noted, "Tragically, we had an officer die in the line of duty during the pandemic. We made decisions that enabled our officers to grieve and honor our fallen brother at his funeral, while also restricting funeral attendance and potential virus transmission. As leaders, we faced painful challenges to secure our convention center, assure social distance, and limit attendance to immediate family and our officer's family. That meant not allowing our retirees, police spouses, and many other agencies to attend and fill the venue." Imagine being in a situation where you are grieving a loss, trying to take care of team members who are grieving, and having to limit the number of people who could come together for a funeral. The pandemic placed many leaders in untenable situations, where they used their best judgment to weigh the competing needs of those they served.

Ryan Hart, Managing Director of the PricewaterhouseCoopers (PwC) Tokyo Experience Center, explained how he also had to make difficult choices to care for his team. PWC is the world's second-largest professional services network and provides assurance, tax, and consulting services. Ryan noted that meeting the needs of a team during a crisis can be very complicated, "I've lived and worked throughout Asia for more than 20 years. As I watched how employees, clients, and governments across Asia-Pacific managed the pandemic, it reinforced my thinking that there is never a one-size-fits-all solution to any problem or crisis. Dealing with complex issues underpinned by cultural nuances, language barriers, and disparate value systems has forced me to slow down my decision-making, listen more, and think more efficiently before I act. By understanding each person's context more deeply, it's helped me adapt more accurately to changes in the work environment." Based on Ryan's methodical approach and slower decision-making, he noted, "The health and well-being of my team needed to supersede the needs of other stakeholders and our customers. If a customer request put one of my team members at potential risk, as a team, we needed to rethink the solution, redesign the delivery, or walk away entirely in the event a client couldn't accept our position on safety."

It's easy to say your employees come first, and it is difficult to actually terminate a client relationship because the client doesn't protect or respect your employees. Have you ever made such a choice? Practicing employee obsession isn't a "feel good" slogan. It is a call to action that requires rethinking, redesigning, and yes, even turning clients away if that's what it takes to meet your team members' needs.

ANTICIPATING NEEDS
DOESN'T MEAN CODDLING

Many leaders felt it was not enough to react to employee needs and that instead, they had to anticipate them. They also gave employees tools so their team members could take action on their own. Barbie Winterbottom is the Chief People Officer and Chief Human Resource Officer at BIC Graphic. The company is one of the largest suppliers in the promotional products industry with recognizable brands like BIC and Koozie. BIC Graphic operates five manufacturing facilities in the United States. Barbie shared how she and her team prepared for employee needs from the onset of the pandemic: "We knew caring for our people meant leaning in. So immediately, we created hubs to bring the best information possible to our team members. We tailored that information so they could readily see how it related to them. For example, we created a work from home resource hub and shared information on the emotional impacts of isolation. We created a private Facebook page where team members could connect." Barbie reported extensive use of coping resources and employee surveys that showed appreciation for and value from those tools.

Since furloughs were the best path forward for team members and the company, Barbie and her team provided ongoing information to furloughed workers on topics like how to apply for unemployment and garner other financial benefits. Additionally, BIC Graphic leaders anticipated and created resources for remaining team members to address their anxieties. Barbie and her team were conscientious always to be a source of empowerment, "As an HR leader, I wanted to make sure we didn't view this as a time to spoon-feed employees. It's a natural reaction to coddle when people panic, but we gave each individual what they needed in a way that allowed them to function as a whole person. If you don't believe that your employees are online shopping at Amazon and managing their lives outside of work in a digital age, then you are failing to see them fully. Given their digital resourcefulness off work, we provided information on benefits, payroll, and taxes that empowered them to research and take care of their needs on our payroll portal as opposed to us taking actions for them."

Leaders can expect that crises will create a sense of powerlessness for team members. As the saying goes, information is power, so providing helpful information in advance of a need is empowering. Waiting for those needs to surface and then addressing them when your team members can take care of the issues for themselves is disempowering. Despite the urge to "do for" employees, often the most significant way to care for them is to give them informational tools and then stand back.

BACKING GOOD INTENTIONS WITH POLICY AND MONEY

For many leaders like Hans Vestberg, CEO of Verizon, obsessing about employees meant turning positive intentions into policy changes and financial investments. Well into the pandemic, corporate communication firm SJR reported on positive and negative perceptions of CEOs. SJR rated CEOs based on an analysis of "online national and international news outlets, RSS feeds, 20+ social media sites, and additional publicly available data." Hans Vestberg ranked fourth amid the pandemic, moving up 36 positions from his prepandemic ranking. *Forbes* magazine placed Verizon atop their Corporate Responders list because the company provided "one of the most expansive sick leave policies of big employers. It also scored top marks for backup dependent care and efforts to help surrounding communities. As of early May 2020, the company had not laid off any of its roughly 135,000 employees."

When I asked Hans Vestberg why Verizon invested so much in team members during highly uncertain financial times, without hesitation, he said, "Because it is the responsibility of business leaders to do so. We launched a COVID-19 leave of absence policy that provided our team members with 100 percent of pay for 26 weeks if they were diagnosed with COVID-19 because it was the right thing to do. Additionally, we offered leave to caregivers and team members with underlying conditions at 100 percent of pay for 8 weeks of leave, and 60 percent of pay for an additional 18 weeks of leave. We also offered a similar leave to employees with a medical background who were responding to a community call for assistance in treating patients with COVID-19. We provided added compensation to team members in the field because they kept our customers connected at a time in history when connections were invaluable. While we made similar investments on behalf of our customers, in the end, we as leaders knew Verizon is nothing more than the collective effort and innovation of our people." Hans concluded, "As CEO, I often receive more credit than I deserve when things are going well. My job and the job of leaders at Verizon is fairly simple. Take care of your people, and they will create success for your customers, which will translate into success for our shareholders as well."

Could it be that simple? According to Hans Vestberg and many other successful leaders, the answer is a resounding: "Yes, practice employee obsession."

RESILIENCE RECAP

➤ The pandemic elevated the priority of the employee experience for many leaders.

➤ Employee centricity or employee obsession involves both caring *for* and caring *about* your team.

➤ Technologies like videoconferencing can make leaders more accessible and reduce the gap between them and their teams.

➤ Prioritizing team members requires intentionality and a willingness to take the time to listen on a personal level.

➤ Mapping the employee journey is a useful way to identify gaps and tools you can use to engage team members consistently.

➤ Often "low-tech" actions like care packages and personal notes can make a powerful connection with team members.

➤ Employee-obsessed leaders rethink, redesign, and turn clients away (if needed) to ensure leaders meet their teams' needs.

➤ While meeting employee needs is essential, anticipating them is likely more valuable.

➤ The job of a leader, in crisis and calm, is to offer team members tools and support that enables them to take action whenever and wherever possible.

➤ When leaders invest in their people, those team members create customer success, which fuels financial benefits for all stakeholders.

YOUR STRENGTH PLAN

1. Would the people you serve describe you as an employee-obsessed leader? Would they view you as more customer-centric or team member–centric?

2. When have you felt cared *for*, and when have you felt cared *about*?

3. How would you characterize the difference between caring *for* versus caring *about* someone?

4. In what ways do you care for your team members?

5. In what ways do you care about them?

6. How would your team members know they are a priority or that you obsess about their success?

7. Have you mapped your team members' journey to identify gaps and tools to help narrow those gaps?

8. How effectively do you use technology to increase your accessibility as a leader?

9. In what ways do you set limits on customers and others to ensure you meet your team members' needs?

10. How effectively do you anticipate team member needs?

11. To what degree do you coddle as opposed to enable your team? Where can you make improvements?

12. Where are you investing in your people so they can drive customer success and overall financial viability?

CHAPTER 5

Set Safety Supreme

The purpose is clear.
It is safety with solvency.
—DWIGHT D. EISENHOWER,
thirty-fourth president of the United States

AS TRUE TODAY AS IT WAS
TWO MILLENNIA AGO

The more things change, the more they stay the same or so it would seem from reading Marcus Tullius Cicero's writings. Cicero was a Roman statesman and orator who lived from 106–43 BC. Not only did Cicero's ideas impact the Roman Empire, but they resurfaced at the beginning of the Renaissance in the fourteenth century. One of Cicero's maxims remained keenly relevant for those leading during the pandemic, and the idea behind it resurfaced again and again during my interviews. Cicero observed, "Salus populi suprema lex," which translates from the Latin to mean "Let the (good or) safety of the people be the highest law."

Throughout this chapter, we will move from employee obsession to broad insights concerning the emergence of safety as a critical guiding business principle. We will explore how leaders drove safety for all stakeholders (team members, third-party service providers, customers, and, in the case of business-to-business providers, even their customer's customers). You will also see how leaders took a universal safety approach that included psychological and financial well-being. COVID-19 has forever changed the way leaders, employees, and customers view physical and emotional safety. Let's explore how you can apply insights gained throughout the pandemic to maximize the future physical and emotional well-being of those you serve.

INCREASING THE VISIBILITY

Most of the leaders with whom I spoke had safety and security plans in place for their businesses long before the pandemic. Few, however, consistently worked on safety issues like they did in the throes of the COVID-19 crisis. For the most part, safety considerations operated in the background and leaped to center stage with the outbreak of the novel coronavirus. Scott Burger, formerly the CEO of Pandora Jewelry Americas, is currently the CEO of Classic Brands. Scott's current company began manufacturing waterbeds in the 1970s. Its product line includes high-quality latex, memory foam mattresses; bed frames; pillows; and other sleep accessories. In 2018, Classic Brands also began producing and selling furniture.

In the context of the pandemic, Scott noted, "When you oversee manufacturing operations, safety is always operating in the background. However, COVID-19 elevated safety to the highest levels of importance not only in our manufacturing operations but in every aspect of our work. For example, we focused on preventative measures but still had an asymptomatic team member find out they had been exposed to someone who was COVID-I9 positive. In response, we immediately decided to close the entire facility where that exposed team member worked for a 48-hour period. We also brought in cleaners to do deep, deep sanitation. Our choice to shut down operations temporarily out of an abundance of caution hurt our business, but it was probably one of the easiest choices my leadership team and I have ever had to make."

Leaders like Scott acted swiftly to reduce the risk of COVID-19 transmission in their work environments. They did so, knowing that those actions would have a negative short-term economic impact. As such, safety became the visible driver of operational decision-making as leaders faced a pervasive and invisible challenge.

BEYOND YOUR TEAM

Whole Foods Market, a multinational supermarket chain that merged with Amazon in 2017, offered physical safety tools and resources to its team members and third-party providers. Andres Traslavina, Senior Director of Executive Recruiting at Whole Foods Market, noted, "The pandemic served to remind us all as leaders that our main job should be the care of everyone who serves customers on behalf of our brand. From my perspective, leaders should first and foremost be in the business of taking care of what Abraham Maslow referred to as physiologic and safety needs. Those needs include making sure everyone who takes care of your customers has food, water, and security."

At Whole Foods Market, leaders took a variety of actions to address the physiologic and safety needs of the company's team members and other outside service providers. Those actions included the facilitation of work from home where possible, designated shopping hours for their team members, face mask requirements for Whole Foods Market team members and third-party workers, and the provision of gloves and personal face shields.

Andres added, "Security also went beyond protecting our people from physical harm, and extended to the psychological and financial safety of team members and business partners." Specifically, Whole Foods Market provided unlimited call-outs, expanded paid sick leave benefits, and increased funding for its team member emergency fund—available to any team member facing an unforeseeable or critical situation.

EQUALLY APPLICABLE TO B OR C

Leaders at Whole Foods Market, like many other business-to-consumer (B2C) brands, created safety precautions to protect the customers who entered their stores. For example, Whole Foods Market regulated the number of customers allowed in the stores, operated under social distancing guidelines, and implemented mandatory daily temperature screenings for team members. Leaders in business-to-business (B2B) companies, like Classic Brands, had a less direct impact on the physical safety of the end consumer and focused more on the financial well-being of their business customers. As Scott Burger put it, "We needed to move beyond the vendor role we traditionally played for our brick and mortar retailers. With their physical stores closed, we literally helped them pivot to online sales. Rather than shipping our products to their stores, we shipped directly to their customers. In essence, we did what we could to help protect our traditional retailers' ability to conduct business and sustain operations."

Prioritizing and balancing team member and customer safety, in a B2B or B2C setting, created a paradigm shift for leaders. A thoughtful spokesperson for that change is Gerry Agnes, President and CEO of Elevations Credit Union based in Boulder, Colorado. Before the pandemic, Gerry and his leadership team stewarded their not-for-profit credit union of approximately 117,000 members to win the prestigious Malcolm Baldridge National Quality Award. Gerry observed, "Throughout my career, and I suspect the career of most leaders, I've thought of employment as a way to make the lives of our team better and more enriched. This pandemic forced me to see work as having a pervasive potential to produce harm and even death. That is a daunting realization, particularly because our credit union provides services that are essential for our credit union members. Without access to their money, our credit union members can't buy food, maintain shelter, or care for their families. Given the critical nature of our work, leaders acted swiftly to reduce the risk for our teams and for our credit union members.

"For example," added Gerry, "we modified operations to require appointments for branch visits and provided drive-up teller service. We also paid a 50 percent premium to those who worked in our branches. We called it heroic pay. That salary enhancement went to 120 of our 550-person workforce, and it received huge support and praise even from those who were able to work from home. We also instituted 14 business days of catastrophic pay if a team member was diagnosed with or cared for a family member with COVID-19. We provided other psychological and financial support." Gerry concluded, "The pandemic changed the way I looked at safety and security, and it helped me grow in my appreciation of what it means to be an essential provider of services during a time of tremendous health and economic uncertainty." During the pandemic, employment (usually the source of positive social, economic, and emotional outcomes) suddenly had the potential to cause widespread harm or death. Where possible, leaders responded to that danger by moving employees to the safety of a work from home setting. In cases where public need required employees to assume greater risk, leaders like Gerry mitigated the risk and compensated those team members for their bravery. Through it all, leaders maximized safety and expressed gratitude for the heroism of those who worked for them.

> ### A Breath of Insight
>
> Crises bring out the best and worst in people.
> I've learned to embrace the good and kind and do
> my best to ignore the negative. For the majority of
> people, you see a desire to be kind and stay united
> against a common enemy like COVID-19.
>
> **—Steve Weintraub,** Owner, Gold & Diamond Source Inc.

DEVELOPING A SAFETY FRAMEWORK

University of Denver (DU) Chancellor Jeremy Haefner offered his insights on how he crafted a decision-making framework to address increased safety concerns at his university. DU is the oldest private research university in the Rocky Mountain Region of the United States. Founded in 1864, its combined undergraduate and graduate student body is roughly 12,000. Jeremy noted, "I lead from some immutable values—be just, be compassionate, and demonstrate a healthy sense of humility. Early on during this pandemic, I also created a set of principles that would support my values while guiding the decisions that I knew would surface soon. Those principles were prioritized with the health and safety of staff, students, and faculty being primary. Other essential factors included the educational experience of our students, the livelihood of our staff and faculty, the long-term well-being of the university, social equity, and the public good." With that framework, leadership decisions could be made rapidly and in the context of guardrails. For example, Jeremy and his team watched how other universities, starting first with those in Washington state, responded to the virus.

"The health and safety principle enabled us to move all of our classes online swiftly," explained Jeremy. "Some decisions, however, had to be considered not only in the context of security but also by using other elements of my framework. Given classes had moved online from a safety perspective, I had to drop down to considerations of equity and fairness for decisions such as whether we should move to a pass plus, pass, no pass grading system during the pandemic." Chancellor Jeremy Haefner reviewed similar decisions made by other universities, the results of weeks of dialogue with faculty, and signatures secured on a student petition. He noted, "I decided to go forward with the modified grading system because online classes created the unintended consequence of an uneven playing field where students without high-speed internet or a home environment conducive to learning faced an academic disadvantage." Chancellor Haefner and other leaders like him placed safety and security at the top of a matrix, which they used as filters for decision-making. They watched how others faced safety challenges and carefully considered the input of those who would be most affected by their decisions. They also balanced the need for swift action with the risk of moving too rapidly. Any major decision, especially those involving health or safety, should be considered with similar diligence.

WORKING TOGETHER

Given the universal nature of security and safety issues, many leaders shared how they worked with others in their industry to elevate their collective success. Carolyne Doyon, President and CEO of North America and the Caribbean at Club Med, highlighted this collaborative approach within the travel industry. As the pandemic forced the closure of her resorts, Carolyne explained how the travel industry rallied with newfound "togetherness." From tourism boards and hotel operators to airlines and travel agencies, Carolyne explained the industry collaborated to set safety standards for future reopenings, "I've seen all sectors of the industry truly come together in ways we haven't before." Specifically, Carolyne noted that leaders at Club Med recognized they had "a responsibility alongside other hospitality brands to ensure all travelers who decide to book an all-inclusive getaway will feel confident that they'll have a safe, comfortable, and memorable experience. Each and every resort or hotel brand needs to stay true to its unique value proposition in the market, yet abide by a common denominator of strict hygiene and safety protocols. Health and safety have always been top priorities among travelers, and now they are key determining factors in a consumer's decisions to travel."

As soon as the pandemic gathered momentum and Club Med closed resorts, Carolyne and her team immediately began planning safety protocols that would need to be in place when the resorts eventually accepted guests again. Carolyne stated those protocols "were then implemented as our resorts reopened so we could meet the enhanced standard of what's considered clean and safe. To ensure the safety and comfort of travelers, we also continued to prioritize the safety of our employees, especially those who live in our resorts' neighboring communities. We've communicated with them consistently, remained open to their questions, and coordinated food donations to support financial security during the peak of the pandemic."

Opportunities for coordinated efforts to address safety also occurred across international borders within brands like Miele, a 120-year-old German manufacturer of premium commercial equipment and household appliances. Jan Heck, President and CEO of Miele USA, shared his perspective on safety and organizational unity: "During the throes of the pandemic, I regularly talked to leaders across Miele. All of my colleagues, whether they were in Australia or Germany, resoundingly focused on safety as their ultimate priority. Often in a global organization, you will see differing priorities at the country level, but safety was the great equalizer and company driver for Miele. For us, it became increasingly galvanizing as we experienced a COVID-19 death within our organization. That drove alignment to do everything needed to keep our people safe and to help our retailers maximize their financial safety. We also made decisions on a case-by-case basis to offer relief to those retailers who were suffering financially." Quite often, regional differences create variation in a company's "true north" or (in the words of Cicero) in its "highest law." Health, psychological, and economic challenges from the pandemic unified leaders across and within brands to support a clear priority—the safety and security of everyone the company serves.

I've watched how independent business owners partnered together to place decisions of safety above all other considerations. Those observations occurred as I participated on a COVID-19 leadership taskforce for Sonny's BBQ restaurants. James Yarmuth is the President and CEO of Sonny's Franchise Company, which oversees a restaurant chain with approximately 100 franchise locations across nine southeastern US states. James noted, "In the early days of the pandemic, our franchise leadership team, franchisee leaders, and the entire franchisee community unanimously supported our longstanding commitment to the well-being of our team members and customers—a grouping we call the Sonny's family. Leveraging data and tracking trends both internationally, and throughout the US, we had regular thoughtful conversations with our franchisees. That data and those discussions enabled us to agree to close all of our dining areas; even before governors in the states where we primarily operate instructed us to do so. Similarly, we agreed to reopen our dining rooms based upon stringent safety plans and infection rates in a given area." James added, "We weren't going to compromise team members' or our guests' safety just because political officials said we could start opening restaurants in their state."

As someone who has worked with many franchise operations, I can attest to regular and heated disagreements between the franchisors and franchisees and within the franchise community. Those disagreements can often become problematic over minor issues and extremely divisive when the revenue of franchisees is at stake. By aligning safety as the "highest law," Sonny's BBQ achieved extraordinary solidarity. Like many other leaders who chose to collaborate during the pandemic, leaders at Sonny's BBQ were not afraid to act prudently to take action on safety even before they were required to do so by outside forces.

RESILIENCE RECAP

➤ Whether running in the background or on center stage for your business, "Salus populi suprema lex" ("Let the safety of the people be the highest law").

➤ Actions demonstrate whether a leader prioritizes the safety and physical well-being of his or her team. That safety must also extend to individuals who partner with you to serve your customers.

➤ Physical safety is a piece of the overall safety equation; however, more comprehensive safety considerations must also consider psychological and financial security.

➤ Customer safety measures should parallel those provided to team members (and if you are a business-to-business provider, they should extend to helping your customer achieve financial security).

> ➤ As uncertainty increases, leaders need to invest their time and resources in developing processes, systems, and technologies that maximize safety for their team members and customers.

> ➤ As a result of COVID-19, leaders should reconceptualize the future role of safety in their businesses and develop decision-making frameworks that place safety as a top-level filter or principle.

> ➤ The prioritization of safety has the opportunity to drive alignment within your organization and across your industry.

YOUR STRENGTH PLAN

1. Irrespective of the pandemic, how important is the safety of your people and your customers?

2. What specifically are you doing to drive the physical and psychological well-being of your team members and customers?

3. If you were to give yourself a letter grade on your commitment to and leadership of team and customer safety, what letter grade would you give yourself and colleagues? Would that grade differ if you are rating psychological versus physical security? What would be required to improve your rating(s)?

4. How aligned is your organization on the importance of customer and team member safety? How do you incorporate physical and psychological safety into your business decision-making?

5. With whom can you partner to drive even greater physical and psychological safety across your business, your industry, and your community?

PART II

BUILD CONNECTIONS

*The ear of the leader must ring
with the voices of the people.*
—WOODROW WILSON,
twenty-eighth president of the United States

The following four chapters explore how extraordinary leaders build trust by:

- Listening for understanding and empathy
- Communicating with objectivity
- Attending to tone and communication cadence
- Being vulnerable and transparent

CHAPTER 6

Listen Beyond
the Words

*The most important thing in communication
is hearing what isn't said.*
—PETER DRUCKER,
management consultant

BEFORE WE SPEAK

During times of constant change, I take comfort in words of enduring wisdom. For example, in the last chapter, I shared Cicero's guidance to "Let the safety of the people be the highest law."

For this chapter, I want to turn to the Greek philosopher Epictetus, who, in the first century AD, provided an enduring observation that sets up the leadership insights that will be shared in this chapter. Epictetus noted, "We have two ears and one mouth so that we can listen twice as much as we speak." Epictetus's astute observation notwithstanding, many people (including leaders) focus more on what they want to say and less on what others are saying.

The pandemic and civil unrest across the world changed the way many leaders approach listening. For example, leaders reached out to team members and customers more. They regularly took a "pulse" on the emotional status, fears, and morale of their people. Leaders increased stakeholder listening through surveys. They spent more unstructured time with those they served to create space for meaningful conversations. They practiced active, continuous listening, and they "closed the loop" by taking action on what they heard. From Epictetus's perspective, during this time of extreme disruption, the most successful leaders listened twice as much as they spoke.

LISTENING WITH
NEWFOUND INTEREST

Anxiety, by its nature, affects the way people share information. For some people, talking helps reduce fear. For others, fear minimizes the desire to talk. Given those differences, the less communicative group can often get overlooked as their counterparts become more vocal. So how can you listen for the needs of both of those groups? The short answer is that you reach out comprehensively.

Ozlem Kilic, DSc, is the Associate Dean of Academic and Student Affairs at the University of Tennessee, Knoxville. Founded in 1794, the University of Tennessee is a public research institution with 10 undergraduate and 11 graduate colleges. In her role, Ozlem is quite accustomed to listening to student needs, but the pandemic expanded the scope and intentionality of that listening. Ozlem reported, "Leadership during a crisis required personal outreach to everyone. At the University of Tennessee, that involved our faculty and staff contacting each student. Collectively, we initiated 40,000-plus calls and Zoom sessions. It became so consuming that I would dream about video conferences."

Ozlem explained that the outreach was tiring, gratifying, and morale-building, "Many students needed solutions, others were just happy to know we cared. Everyone with whom I spoke was grateful for my concern. Most importantly, we demonstrated that our students mattered, and we learned what mattered most to them. For me, listening is the heart of leadership." Ozlem and her colleagues took immediate action whenever possible to resolve individual student needs. They also aggregated common concerns and created systemic solutions. Most importantly, they reached out and asked important questions, like "How are you doing?" and "What can I do to help?"

Throughout the crisis, Kia Croom was surprised by the increased availability and openness of those she contacted. Kia is the Nonprofit Fundraising Executive at Fund Development Solutions—a nonprofit community development company that addresses "critical social issues impacting un-derrepresented people in underserved communities." Kia noted, "As hectic as the pandemic has been, I sensed a shift in people's willingness to accept a call. I spoke with people by phone, whom I'd only communicated with via email for years. Individuals who were usually very transactional en-gaged in more relational conversations, and overall my calls lasted longer than they had at any other time in my 20 years of fundraising. I'm sure that the people I reached out to were more open to conversation, but I wonder if I also subtly changed the way I was listening. Maybe I was asking more questions, expressing a greater interest, or leaning in more with a listening ear. My takeaway from the pandemic involves a greater appreciation for how heartfelt listening can strengthen personal and professional relationships."

Unlike Kia, some leaders never consider how their actions contribute to customer or employee behavior. For example, when a team member is reluctant to share thoughts, feelings, disagreements, or ideas, the leader as-sumes it's because the team member is anxious or not willing to open up. In some cases, team members won't share because the leader has not of-fered the time or interest to enable that communication. To borrow from another source of timeless wisdom, when it comes to listening, leaders, may in part, "reap what they sow."

WHAT SHOULD I LISTEN FOR?

Leaders routinely reported that they enhanced both formal and informal listening for all stakeholders during the pandemic. Formal listening in-cludes such things as inviting customers to attend virtual feedback ses-sions (focus groups) or sending surveys to employees. Informal listening involves activities like asking team members how they are doing at the be-ginning of a video conference, encouraging employees to reach out via phone or email, and reading customer input that is shared across social channels. Using formal approaches like surveys can generate a large quan-tity of information quickly, while informal methods can produce rich qualitative insights that people share on their terms. To be effective, leaders like Cheryl Vescio relied on both formal and informal listening ap-proaches. Cheryl is the Senior Director of the Retail Sales Group at Zeiss—an international technology solutions company that provides lenses for glasses, cameras, binoculars, and other medical, research, and industrial applications. Cheryl described Zeiss's formal listening by noting, "In addition to published industry data, very early on, we conducted our own research to gauge the impact of the crisis and to identify what the most significant customer needs and concerns were. Based on our findings, we were able to rapidly pivot our marketing and communication strategies to address emerging needs. For example, we were able to respond to staff hygiene training, practice management tools, social media tips, how to practice sanitization for reopening, and other concerns."

From an informal perspective, Cheryl reported she and her colleagues became more accessible to customers and team members so both groups could express themselves when and how they desired. Cheryl explained she and her team increased their hours of availability and widened methods through which they could be reached to include "phone, email, text, and on whatever channel they wanted . . . accessibility has always been part of our culture, but we certainly put it to the test. I made sure I was visible via video but also kicked off many of the 60 hours of training events. Mostly, I was there to check in, hear the voices, and feel the energy. By taking this approach, I was able to respond to those who may be feeling down and work with the team to help them move back toward normal." Cheryl and her team supplemented industry data with formal customer surveys. The large quantity of information collected from Zeiss customers through those surveys was used to make important communication and service adjustments throughout the pandemic. Zeiss's leaders made themselves widely available to team members. Additionally, leaders reached out informally to prompt dialogue with their teams.

James Walker also sought objective and subjective input during the pandemic but relied more heavily on what people were sharing during conversations. James is Senior Vice President of Restaurants at Nathan's Famous, a company that sells more than 700 million hot dogs annually. Nathan's Famous, founded in 1916, is one of America's oldest quick-service restaurants. James noted, "While we tracked consumer sentiment, my team and I were less focused on the numbers generated from surveys and more focused on people's feelings. We paid special attention to what employees, franchisees, and customers were saying. We heard what each group was thinking, feeling, and planning to do throughout the crisis. For example, we had a strong gauge on the magnitude of stress on employees. We listened to their worries concerning their health, families, jobs, and even their concern for the financial impact on Nathan's Famous. The value of increasing our casual listening was twofold. We sought to strengthen our connections and needed to stay ahead of our stakeholders' concerns wherever possible—rather than reacting to them." For Nathan's Famous, listening helped leaders grasp the intensity and breadth of thoughts and feelings experienced by their franchisees, employees, and customers. That insight enabled leaders to be proactive as they built stronger connections with those they served.

Leaders who specialize in customer insights validated James' emphasis on informal listening (as opposed to survey data), especially during volatile times. Natasha Hritzuk is the Vice President and Head of Consumer Insights at WarnerMedia Entertainment. WarnerMedia is a multinational media conglomerate that includes brands like HBO, HBO Max, Warner Bros., Cinemax, TNT, TBS, and CNN. Natasha and her team were reluctant to seek input through a formal and impersonal survey during the early stages of the pandemic. Natasha noted, "In the first two months of our journey with COVID-19, we were concerned about a consumer survey being unwelcomed and receiving a low response rate. So, we initially engaged people in ways that were a bit unusual for us—through online focus groups and ethnography [descriptive or immersive studies using tools like customer journals]—before we returned to a survey approach."

Natasha and her team had some additional concerns about the quality of the input they would receive from surveys collected during a pandemic. "However, we didn't see a decline in quality," she said. "Instead, we saw significant changes from week to week, and that variability made it hard to provide meaningful insights for the business units. When we were two months into weekly surveys, we backed off on our survey frequency so consumer reactivity could settle out. Over time consumer feedback showed less volatility, and we could get a better gauge on how they were doing, thinking, and processing." Natasha summarized considerations for conducting surveys by noting, "My career and the success of our brands hinges on gaining customer insights at scale through formal listening. The key is to understand that trends can be hard to identify when stakeholders are extremely unsettled."

Based on the input of leaders like Natasha and my own experiences with employee and customer surveys conducted throughout the pandemic, I am a proponent of using short, intermittent (pulse) surveys to capture large samples of customer and employee sentiment. This approach creates an opportunity to repeat questions to assess changes in thoughts, feelings, and needs over time. It also enables you to insert questions tailored to a specific situation (e.g., readiness to return to work) and to evaluate perceptions based on prior feedback (e.g., willingness to dine in now that servers are wearing masks). These pulse surveys are useful in any rapidly changing situation, such as a public relations crisis, a major social disruption, or a major modification of products or service delivery.

A Breath of Insight

Communication is essential . . . informal communication is lacking when you aren't physically present with coworkers. This type of communication often is taken for granted but vital to the functions of a team.

—**Andy Farrell,** Special Assistant to the
Head Coach and Recruiting Coordinator,
Dayton Flyers Men's Basketball, and
Cofounder, Rising Coaches Elite

UNDERSTANDING IS NOT ENOUGH

Whether it's an informal conversation or a large-scale survey, your overall approach to listening should drive two outcomes—understanding and empathy. Understanding implies you are clear about what someone is saying, and empathy means you seek to connect with their feelings. For leaders like Alberto Brea, empathy and understanding are fundamental to all relationships—business and personal. Alberto is the Chief Growth Strategist at Rise Consultants, a privately held financial solutions company that helps companies become more productive and profitable. Alberto explained, "Leadership takes place on multiple levels including corporate, team, community, and home. To lead at every level, you need to listen actively. You have to have a genuine interest in others and believe that your interest can make a difference for them and you. You also have to give people space to speak and follow up with clarifying questions. Above all else, you have to want to understand the feelings behind people's words." When you listen for understanding and connect on a feeling level, all your relationships prosper, but that success requires active involvement in the listening process.

Kerop Janoyan, Dean of the Graduate School at Clarkson University, demonstrated the value of actively probing to discover unstated needs and emotions. Clarkson is a public research university founded in 1896, with three New York state campuses located in Potsdam, Schenectady, and Beacon. Kerop explained his approach to follow-up, "Even if you think you understand the needs of others, you're probably missing many of the details. For example, there were striking and subtle differences in what worried on-campus graduate students compared to our remote learners (usually professionals who are working and going to school). The needs of those groups differed from graduate students in hands-on professional programs like physician assistants or occupational therapists. Unless you ask a lot of questions, you will operate from assumptions or misunderstand. If you don't put yourself in the place of others, you will miss their unstated or deeper needs."

Kerop took the perspective of international students to identify an underlying fear they were experiencing. Kerop added, "I thought about what it was like to come from a foreign country before I engaged in follow-up questioning with an international student. Through that inquiry, I learned that he, and other students like him, were afraid that if they tested positive for COVID-19, they would not be entitled to care in the US." Listening intently and getting to the feelings behind the words is an essential leadership skill that takes on amplified importance during crises. It forces us to challenge our assumptions and reach out broadly to all those we serve.

STEPPING INTO THE SHOES OF OTHERS

Empathy is similar to a "sense of humor" in that many people overestimate the degree to which they demonstrate it. Having written about and trained leaders and frontline workers on ways to enhance empathy, I've found it crucial to create a shared understanding of the concept. Empathy is a component of emotional intelligence (EQ), a predictor of leadership success, and a trainable skill.

In its purest form, empathy reflects an awareness of the emotional state of others. In practice, it requires a person to assume another individual's frame of reference to understand their feelings, thoughts, and attitudes. Studies of pain transmission show that people have a deeply ingrained empathy response. For example, if you observe someone who is suffering and seek to "feel their pain," quite literally, your brain will activate the same neural pathways as if you encountered actual physical pain. Empathy enables actions that demonstrate compassion and personalization, which I'll cover in Chapters 12 and 19, respectively.

Like any other skill, empathic listening requires commitment and practice. Gary Bagley and his team provided an example of what it means to put empathy into action. Gary is the Executive Director of New York Cares, New York City's largest volunteer network. As part of the organization's response to COVID-19, New York Cares worked with more than 38,000 volunteers who delivered over 115,000 hours of service across 5,800 projects. Throughout the pandemic, those volunteers also delivered more than 22.6 million meals across all five boroughs of New York.

For the sake of driving empathy, Gary reported, "As a leadership team, we joined volunteers in making technology support calls to families, many of which were in transitional housing, who received an iPad to connect their children with online learning. Those calls put us in a position to understand what our volunteers hear, feel, and experience. They also gave us empathy for parents who were struggling with technologies that most of us take for granted. The calls ranged from helping someone use the iPad or learn how to access Google Classroom, to listening to the gratitude expressed by parents whose children hadn't been able to participate in school for over a month. Those experiences moved our team. We felt privileged to step into the shoes of our volunteers and experience their world."

Stepping into someone else's shoes is not merely an intellectual exercise. Sometimes it takes direct action to sit beside those you wish to understand. Cutting-edge leaders understand that when they make investments of time and emotional energy, they strengthen their empathy skills, engage a noble cause, and are given a privilege.

MAKING SURE LISTENING
ISN'T WASTED

Before I conclude a chapter on listening, I must note that listening can be either an end unto itself or a means to an end. Active listening creates understanding, and empathic listening produces connection. Both of those outcomes are worthwhile, but the ultimate value of listening is to foster improvements for the person speaking and for your business.

Many leaders talk about benefitting from stakeholder input by closing the loop on that feedback. In reality, two loops need to be closed when it comes to stakeholder listening—an inner loop and an outer loop. The inner loop involves sharing feedback with individuals that can effect change inside your organization. The outer loop consists of providing feedback to respondents that updates them on how you've taken action on their input.

Lindsay Jurist-Rosner, Cofounder and CEO of Wellthy, suggested that information collected from stakeholders is rocket fuel for organizational growth, particularly when it drives constant improvement. Wellthy is a company that helps families and individuals coordinate and manage care for aging, disabled, and chronically ill loved ones. Lindsay noted, "Our commitment to listening to all constituents is only as good as our ability to translate what we hear into rapid learning and innovation. Because New York City is our base, we were in a constant state of listening and learning during the pandemic. We collected information, shared it internally, innovated solutions, communicated resolution back to those that provided input, and repeated that process. For example, listening enabled us to respond to the emerging mental health needs of our team members. We innovated solutions, informed them of the mental health services we secured on their behalf, and announced a much-needed mental health day." Stakeholder listening is a critical component of a virtuous and continuous improvement loop. It is the foundation for understanding, growth, team engagement, customer service, and business refinement. Show me a leader who masters the art of listening, and I will show you a productive team.

Paul Tillich, the philosopher, once said, "The first duty of love is to listen." In my opinion, listening is also the first duty of leadership—with the second duty being to listen more. Persuasive and expressive leaders may receive notoriety, but active listeners lead change—especially those who *listen beyond the words.* I trust you're listening!

RESILIENCE RECAP

➤ In the words of Epictetus, "We have two ears and one mouth so that we can listen twice as much as we speak."

➤ In crises, leaders are well-served to increase informal listening (e.g., casual conversations) to assess the status, fears, attitudes, and behaviors of those they serve.

➤ Listening is the heart of leadership.

➤ The communication openness and flow of ideas within a team are often proportional to the listening skills of the leader.

➤ Formal listening tools (e.g., surveys) are invaluable for gaining stakeholder insights at scale. However, it can be challenging to identify trends when stakeholders are unsettled.

➤ Pulse surveys provide opportunities for repeated measurement, assessment of a current issue, or evaluation of progress made based on prior feedback.

➤ Understanding implies you are clear about something a person says.

➤ Empathy reflects an understanding of what a person is feeling and experiencing.

➤ Empathy is a trainable skill that predicts leadership success and is a component of emotional intelligence.

➤ Empathy requires an individual to assume another person's frame of reference to understand his or her feelings, thoughts, and attitudes.

➤ Compassion and personalization are actions that follow from empathy.

> ➤ In closed-loop communication, there is an inner loop (where feedback is shared inside an organization to effect change) and an outer loop (where respondents receive updates on actions taken based on their input).

> ➤ The first duty of leadership is to listen; the second duty is to listen more.

YOUR STRENGTH PLAN

1. Who listens to you well? What are the behaviors they demonstrate?

2. On a 1–10 scale, how would you rate yourself as a listener? (With 1 being extraordinarily inattentive and 10 being extraordinarily attentive.) What is the basis of your rating? If you think there is room for improvement in your listening skills, there are many free active listening tools available online. Some of those tools can be found at strongerthroughadversity.com. Once you brush up on those skills, it's essential to practice them until they become habitual.

3. How do you use formal and informal listening to gain actionable insights from your stakeholders?

4. How frequently do you use pulse surveys with your team members, customers, and other stakeholders? What have you learned from that listening approach? What have you changed based on that input?

5. What is the process you use to close internal and external feedback loops? Where can you make improvements in either your internal or external loop?

6. When have you felt someone effectively empathized with you?

7. When have you felt you effectively empathized with someone else? How do you know you were effective?

8. What steps have you taken to practice your empathy skills or to help your team enhance their empathy?

9. Do you agree that listening is the first duty of leadership? If so, why does that ring true for you? If not, why doesn't it resonate?

CHAPTER 7

Seek Carefully and Speak Truthfully

Transparency, honesty, kindness, good stewardship,
even humor, work in businesses at all times.
—JOHN GERZEMA,
CEO, Harris Insights and Analytics

DON'T SAY WHAT YOU DON'T KNOW

You are a leader. People look to you for answers.

In times of crisis, there is a heightened need for leaders to provide the information people are looking for so your teams, customers, and other stakeholders can maintain stability and move forward. But how can you do this when you don't have the information needed to paint a clear picture of what is currently happening, let alone offer guidance for the future?

In the first two chapters of this book, I highlighted how leaders could fall into a couple of traps—thinking they must sacrifice self-care and trying to handle all challenges alone. When it comes to possessing information and making judgments based on available data, leaders can fall into additional quagmires. One is the result of feeling pressure to be "the authority" on matters outside their sphere of knowledge or expertise. The other results from the unrealistic need to be clairvoyant so they can quell anxiety involving an uncertain future.

Even in times of calm, around 70 percent of people feel what researchers Pauline Clance and Suzanne Imes label as "imposter syndrome." That psychological phenomenon reflects a fear that our limitations render us unqualified for our role. John Steinbeck's diary provides candid examples of imposter syndrome. In 1938, while working on his Pulitzer Prize–winning novel *Grapes of Wrath*, Steinbeck wrote: "I'm not a writer. I've been fooling myself and other people. I wish I were. No one else knows my lack of ability the way I do." As a leader, many of us will connect with Steinbeck's perspective.

In a crisis, more than at any other time, it feels like all eyes are locked on leaders. Under that scrutiny, many feel like they are or will be exposed as an imposter—unless they can provide information that addresses current needs and guides the future. In this chapter, leaders explore the importance of sharing accurate and objective information in times of crisis. They also speak to the importance of being transparent as they offer that information. In Chapter 8, we discuss the appropriate cadence and alignment of information sharing. Chapter 9 shows why information transparency must be augmented by leadership vulnerability.

RESISTING THE FACADE

Chuck DiNardo is the President at Aesculap, Inc. Aesculap, a division of Braun, is the largest global manufacturer of medical devices, surgical instruments, and sterilization container systems. Chuck openly shared the responsibility he felt to have transparent communications with the organization during the pandemic and to create as much certainty for our employees during these uncertain times. Chuck noted, "During the pandemic, we focused on three fundamental pillars: the safety of our employees, meeting the critical needs of our healthcare customers, and understanding our responsibility to the broader community that we serve. Our financial performance took a back seat to what we believed, as a family-owned company, was truly important." Leaders can feel pressure to communicate with maximum certainty, but it carries more weight to focus on your fundamental pillars and invite your team to help you understand and address your most pressing gaps and challenges.

No leader can be all-knowing or offer guarantees in an environment of unrelenting change. Insecurities can create feelings of being an imposter, but leaders who act omniscient are likely the actual imposters. Han Fei, a Chinese philosopher who lived in the third century BC, put it this way, "He who claims to be sure of something for which there is no evidence is a fool, and he who acts on the basis of what cannot be proved is an imposter."

SAY YOU DON'T KNOW

Maxine Clark founded Build-A-Bear Workshop in 1997. Build-A-Bear is an experiential retail brand where customers interactively assemble and customize stuffed animals and toys. There are more than 400 Build-A-Bear Workshop stores worldwide. Maxine offered compelling guidance concerning leadership communication: "I've learned in my long time of being a leader that some of the most powerful words I can say are 'I don't know.' Leaders don't have all the answers, nor should they. Leadership is about helping people ask and find answers to questions that will position their people and their business for greatness."

Maxine continued, "Leaders don't need to prove how smart they are, we aren't in a competition. As I've matured as a leader, I've become increasingly aware of all the things I don't know, and I am incredibly comfortable letting people know when I don't have an answer. Fortunately, with maturity also comes more resourcefulness in finding information, answers, and solutions as well as a more extensive network of people with whom I can consult."

Let's explore Maxine's wisdom in the context of a hypothetical. Imagine it's early July 2020, and a frontline team member asks if you can provide him or her with a face shield to use as an alternative to a cloth mask. Let's also assume you don't know the availability of shields or the current status of fluidly changing Centers for Disease Control and Prevention (CDC) guidance regarding their use. Rather than offering your best guess, you tell the team member you will check out the possibility and get back to that person within 24 hours. In the interim, you determine face shields are readily available. However, just days before the request, the CDC advised it "does not recommend use of face shields for normal everyday activities or as a substitute for cloth face coverings." You and your team would have both benefitted from your honesty and your research. Leadership requires us to admit when our answers would be little more than guesses. It also requires the active pursuit of valid data to address important questions.

THE UNKNOWABLE AND THE QUEST

Can we become infected with COVID-19 by handling packages? How accurate is the information being reported by state health officials? How long does the virus linger in the air? Will a mask reduce my likelihood of being infected? Leaders faced so many questions during the pandemic, and many of those queries either were only partially answerable or had answers that later changed. Amid the blur of questionable information, leaders needed to take a serenity prayer approach to information reliability. As you'll recall, Reinhold Niebuhr's serenity prayer advises that we should seek divine intervention to accept the things we cannot change, the courage to change the things we can, and the wisdom to know the difference. When it comes to the pursuit of information during a crisis, a slight word change applies. Leaders have to accept the information they can't gather, rapidly find the information they can, and be granted the wisdom to know the difference.

Colin Mincy, the Chief People Officer at Human Rights Watch, described his approach to determine what was knowable during the crisis. Through its global membership, Human Rights Watch investigates and reports abuses happening around the world. Colin noted, "Leaders have to rectify a desire to know everything possible with the reality that not everything is knowable. Throughout the pandemic, there were many things I wanted to know to help make decisions, but there was a lot of contradictory information floating around. In some cases, you had to accept that the information you obtained wasn't optimal, but it could inform imminent decisions. You acknowledged the limitations of the available information, made the best decisions possible with it, and reversed course when more reliable information surfaced."

Colin's guidance to continually evaluate the quality of information you use for decision-making is both astute and essential to managing the fluidity of crisis. Waiting to get perfect data is paralyzing, being unable to make decisions with partial information slows progress, and being unwilling to shift when information changes can put your business in peril. The key to information acquisition, as Colin said, is the search for the "best available" information needed to sufficiently address pressing challenges coupled with the adaptability to change direction as better information surfaces. In essence, leaders must be vigilant about the quality of data on which we rely.

Jay Mason suggested that during the pandemic, actionable information could be challenging to access, but ingenuity and dedication produced results. Jay is the Vice President for Market Intelligence at the PulteGroup. That company is the third-largest homebuilder with operations in more than 40 major cities. Since 1950, the PulteGroup's subsidiary brands have built approximately 750,000 homes throughout the United States.

Jay observed, "The need for reliable and actionable data in a crisis shoots through the roof. Some decisions don't require a lot of data, and experts in our field make great decisions based on their own experience, knowledge, wisdom, and good judgment, but my job is to make sure they have as much data as possible for sound decision-making." According to Jay, leaders had many places to turn for actionable intelligence—even in a crisis. For example, he noted, "We found value in making some inferences based on prior recessions, real estate corrections, gluts of supply, and price drops. Still, we had to increase the frequency of our data reviews. We went from annual capital investment considerations to weekly ones. We also switched from watching weekly sales indicators to tracking numbers daily. Most significantly, we had to innovate ways to get data on our own. This innovation was required as some third-party data providers couldn't get us what we needed quickly enough." With determination, teamwork, and data mining, companies like PulteGroup were able to access information needed for business decision-making and leadership communication in the throes of crisis. However, even when you have valid information to communicate, how do you decide what to share?

A Breath of Insight

Leaders need help with not just their focus but focusing their teams. With children out of school, physical distancing, working from home, and disruptions all around us, focus is the ultimate currency in this climate. Many times, it's difficult to separate the urgent from the important.

—Makenzie Rath, President, Talent Plus, Inc.

SAY WHAT IS SO

Before the pandemic, it was not unusual for leaders to emphasize the positives and downplay negative elements of a message. Out of fear of decreasing morale or enthusiasm, leaders would lightly acknowledge a company's threats or opportunities while rallying teams behind their organizations' strengths and opportunities. During the pandemic, however, leaders acknowledged an increased willingness to share a more balanced picture. Moez Limayem, PhD, is Dean for the University of South Florida (USF) Muma College of Business. USF is the fourth-largest university in Florida, with roughly 51,000 students and three campuses in the Tampa area.

Moez noted, "In times of calm you are likely to see leaders emphasize optimistic forecasts and hit on trends that will inspire their teams. During the pandemic, it heartened me to see a greater willingness to share strengths and challenges. Leaders responded to the gravity of the situation with thoughtful consideration. They painted more complete pictures of current and future states, even if some of what they shared could be alarming." In non-crises times, leaders can take shortcuts with information and frame the future without sufficient detail. They also can err toward a more Pollyannaish view. Despite the urgency of the crisis, uncertainty fueled more direct sharing and shined a light on what was possible beyond the chaos.

Chaos does not begin to describe Charlie Cole's circumstance during the COVID-19 lockdown. Charlie is the CEO of FTD, one of the largest florist networks in the world with more than 30,000 floral shop partners in more than 125 countries. To understand Charlie's challenge, you'll need some context on events at FTD, which predated the pandemic.

In 2014, FTD assumed $200 million in debt to purchase a key competitor, ProFlowers. By June 2019, due to lagging sales, FTD announced bankruptcy. In August 2019, the private equity group Nexus Capital Management acquired FTD. An executive board chairman led the company before Charlie started his role on March 23, 2020—one day after the FTD team had sheltered in place.

Charlie picks up the story there. "I started when the pandemic had reached a crescendo. Usually, when you start as a CEO, you initiate a process of getting to know people and helping them get to know you. However,

I had to dive in and address immediate questions and concerns. For example, I got an email in my second week from a team member who asked, 'When do you think we're going back to the office?' My response was consistent with many I made during that time. I replied, 'I have no idea, and anybody that pretends to answer that question is lying to you.' Fortunately, there were many questions my leadership team and I could address. That email, however, exemplified the need to establish credibility as soon as I arrived by being direct and not speculating or trying to sugarcoat information." For Charlie, realism has emerged as a guiding communication principle. He noted, "I developed a leadership mantra. It sounds odd to say that I have a mantra given I've only been here a short time, but it goes like this, 'No hiding bad news, no hiding bad news, no hiding bad news.'" Not all the news has been good since Charlie arrived (e.g., the global supply of flowers was down going into Mother's Day). However, FTD has met strong demand from people who have wanted to connect with loved ones despite the inability to have physical contact.

Mark Miller, coauthor of the award-winning book *Legacy in the Making* and Chief Strategy Officer at Team One, believes leaders will be judged, in part, by the way they shared the truth. Team One is a digital, communications, and media agency that helps premium brands like Lexus and The Ritz-Carlton Hotel Company differentiate themselves and stay connected to prospects and customers. Mark observed, "People will remember how we as leaders communicated with them during crisis times. Did we tell the truth? Were we forthcoming with the positives and negatives of situations? Did we provide them with the information they needed to make informed decisions? Did we act out of self-interest or come from a place of sincerity, honesty, and decency? I think they will also watch to see if some of that behavior stays around when we aren't in a crisis. They will watch to see if leaders regress to a place that lacks information transparency."

While most people think of information transparency as a reflection of a leader's trustworthiness, Mark flips the concept to consider how honest communication sends the message, "My team needs this truth and can be trusted with it." Trust is reciprocal. If I don't communicate truthfully, I lose your trust. If I don't trust you, I am less inclined to communicate in a forthright manner. Put differently, to be trusted, you have to extend trust, and you have to offer information transparently.

THE BEST POLICY, ESPECIALLY IN A CRISIS

Howard Behar is a retired President of Starbucks International and part of the triumvirate who fueled the brand's meteoric rise. I first met Howard in 2005 while working on *The Starbucks Experience*. The architects behind Starbucks have been referred to as H2O—reflecting the first letters of their first names (Howard Schultz, Howard Behar, and Orin Smith).

Since Howard is a leadership treasure, I asked for his guiding principle on sharing good news and bad. Howard related a story from his first CEO position—long before his days at Starbucks. He shared, "That business was in trouble, so I wrote a letter to the board telling them how I would fix things if they appointed me CEO. To my surprise, they chose me. Unfortunately, that choice created a problem for them and me. They got a CEO without experience, and I stepped into a company with more issues than I could have ever imagined. No one was forthcoming with the truth when I considered the job, and officers of the company withheld the truth from one another. To cut costs, we were about to conduct a layoff, which would be the first of many over my career."

Howard continued, "Senior leaders met and discussed who we would layoff, and we put the names of those individuals on a sheet of paper. Unfortunately, on the day we met, someone left the original layoff list in the copy machine. Within two hours, my phone was ringing off the hook with questions about the rumored layoff. When I asked my leadership team how I should respond, the majority opinion was that I should say the list was just an exercise. I had visions of being the shortest tenured leader of that organization. Fortunately, my administrative assistant offered wisdom that ran contrary to the advice of the leadership team. She said, 'Only the truth sounds like the truth.'"

Howard completed the story by noting that he called a meeting with all 1,500 of the company's employees. At that meeting, he laid out a realistic, albeit daunting, picture of the company's plight. As you might imagine, Howard's truth-sharing was well-received, the company improved with time, and Howard advanced in his storied leadership career. To assure the lesson was never forgotten, Howard framed the saying, "Only the truth sounds like the truth." It hangs in his office today.

Leaders can buy into a myriad of distortions, including beliefs that they should be omniscient or clairvoyant, or they should withhold information for the good of those they serve. As noted throughout the chapter, leadership effectiveness necessitates an understanding that "only the truth sounds like the truth." Throughout the pandemic and for years to come, people need leaders to admit what they don't know, search for the best available information, share a balanced picture of the current and emerging circumstances, and trust them to handle the truth. Our teams and customers need us to "seek carefully and speak truthfully."

RESILIENCE RECAP

➤ Approximately 70 percent of people report having feelings consistent with "imposter syndrome."

➤ From a leader's perspective, the imposter syndrome might sound like, "Given what I know about myself, why should people follow me?"

➤ Despite pressure to have all the answers, no leader can live up to that expectation or offer guarantees in an environment of unrelenting change.

➤ Some of the most important words you can say as a leader are "I don't know." The next most important words should be "Let's look for a way to get that answer."

➤ While it may be more challenging to capture accurate information and data in times of swirling change, it is achievable with perseverance and innovation.

➤ Leaders typically respond to crises by sharing information that provides a more comprehensive picture of evolving circumstances, even if some of what they share might be alarming.

➤ Several mantras might prove helpful when considering information sharing. They include:

  • No hiding bad news
  • Honesty is the best policy
  • Only the truth sounds like the truth

YOUR STRENGTH PLAN

1. Have you had a situation where you should have answered a question with the words, "I don't know," but answered anyway? If so, what prompted you to come up with an answer?

2. Have you had a leader answer a question with a "best guess" response when he or she should have said, "I don't know"? How did it feel to receive that answer? What contributed to the leader's willingness to respond the way he or she did?

3. How do your insecurities or the knowledge of your shortcomings feed into an "imposter syndrome"? If the imposter syndrome does not resonate with you, what are you doing to keep your insecurities from affecting your leadership?

4. Have you had someone hide bad news from you or fail to disclose it to you? If so, how did you come to know the truth? How did it feel when you found out? What was the person's rationale for not being forthcoming? Flip the situation around. Can you remember a time when you withheld bad news? If so, explore the reasoning behind your choice.

5. Think of a time when you or another leader painted a comprehensive picture of evolving circumstances complete with the good news and the bad. How was the message received? Why is that situation memorable?

6. What information do team members need to hear that you may not have thought to share previously?

CHAPTER 8

Choose Words Wisely

*Take advantage of every opportunity to practice your
communication skills so that when important occasions arise,
you will have the gift, the style, the sharpness, the clarity,
and the emotions to affect other people.*

—JIM ROHN,

entrepreneur and author

OVERCOMMUNICATION IS NOT THE GOAL

Let's debunk a popular myth—you can communicate too much during a crisis!

While people need more communication frequency and different styles of communication during disruptive times, striving to overcommunicate is a sure way to lose the attention of your audience. In this chapter, leaders share how and why they increased communication frequency, relevance, inclusiveness, and purpose during the pandemic. They outline methods for leveraging stories, platforms, and targeted communication. You will also read how leaders focus on the tone of their messages and communicate through stories.

HOW MUCH IS ENOUGH AND
HOW MUCH IS TOO MUCH?

Author and former presidential speechwriter James Humes once said, "The art of communication is the language of leadership." Humes's sentiment resoundingly echoed in the words of those I interviewed during the pandemic, including Jason Bradshaw. Jason, bestselling author of

It's All About the CEX!, is the Chief Customer and Marketing Officer at Volkswagen Group Australia. The Volkswagen Group is a leading automobile manufacturer with 123 production plants and more than 670,000 employees worldwide.

Jason encapsulated the views of other interviewees by noting, "Communication is *everything*—frequent, transparent communication is essential for both employees and customers. Today the customer and employee experience are heavily influenced by the frequency and quality of their communication. Customers and employees are craving certainty in uncertain times."

While leaders differed in their approach to crisis communication, they universally emphasized the need to increase message volume and frequency. Penny Pennington is the Managing Partner at Edward Jones—one of the largest investment firms in the United States, serving approximately 7 million clients. From a cadence perspective, Penny noted, "We've dialed up the frequency of communication and talked directly about the issues on the minds of the people we serve. We openly shared how we were making decisions and the reasons behind the hard choices we faced, like wage freezes or the cancellation of major events."

Leaders like Penny cautioned that a failure to amp up messaging could result in a vacuum that customers and team members would fill with misinformation, rumors, and worst-case scenarios. Conversely, these leaders warned that too much communication could lead to message fatigue, disruptions in workflow, and less engagement when attention to a specific message was needed. They also emphasized the importance of communicating based on a plan as opposed to an impulse.

DANGER—YOUR LIPS ARE MOVING

Most of us understand the power of our words. We know that as our leadership platform and influence expand, responsible communication becomes increasingly important.

John Incontro is the Chief of Police for the city of San Marino, California, and the President of the Los Angeles County Police Chiefs Association. That Association's membership includes Police Chief Executives from 45 independent cities in Los Angeles County. John shared his perspective on official public safety communications, "In times of crisis, leaders have to be especially careful with the words they choose. They should ensure critical messages are briefed, discussed, and agreed upon. For my department, I evaluate official communications to make sure they are consistent with our department values and community standards. For the Los Angeles County Police Chief's Association, we increased the frequency of our meetings, shared lessons learned, identified roadblocks, and used the power of the group to advocate for our shared needs. To do that, we debated and aligned on cohesive messaging, which we adapted as conditions warranted. We were sensitive to the language we used in our communications and how our words might be perceived outside the audience for which they were intended."

John's insights remind leaders to assume every message you craft (even if it's a personal email, text, or private social media post) will become public. In times of crisis, careless words, off-color jokes, biased language, and baseless claims can bewilder, distract, and, worse yet, harm stakeholders. Conversely, well-chosen words can empower, rally, and inspire others. Of course, if we exert too much precision in everything we say and write, we can sound robotic and contrived.

Linda Rutherford, Senior Vice President and Chief Communication Officer for Southwest Airlines, is a cutting-edge thinker and extraordinary practitioner in areas of leadership communication and crisis specific messaging. As such, you will hear from her on a couple of occasions in this chapter. Southwest is one of the leading airlines in the United States and the world's largest low-cost carrier. The company's primary mission is to "offer the highest quality of service, with warmth, friendliness, self-pride, and company spirit."

Linda noted, "In times of crisis, people get anxious and crave information. So not only do we need to communicate more often, we must do it in a multi-channel way and be inclusive. At Southwest, that means engaging a variety of voices starting with our CEO." Linda added, "If you aren't organized, you can easily create confusion and distrust through your messaging. That distrust can escalate quickly, given how fast information changes. All communications must be aligned. Marketing, operations, and your communication teams need to stay in sync as they coordinate messages to their respective groups—customers, the media, and employees. That aligned messaging is something we work on 24 hours a day. Collaboratively, we are looking at each new communication to make sure it is purposeful, well-timed, congruent, and relevant for the audience to which it is directed."

Concerning inclusivity, leaders like Linda recommended involving team members from diverse perspectives to write, edit, and present text-based, videotaped, and live communications. They also recommended being sensitive to gender references or binary she/he pronouns. They emphasized the importance of evaluating and rooting out unconscious bias from messages. Those biases are often associated with race, ethnicity, nationality, age, socioeconomic background, or religion.

To Linda's point regarding multi-channel messaging, many leaders talked about how they varied message delivery platforms, so team members and customers didn't develop channel fatigue. Several leaders specifically talked about "Zoom fatigue," a term popularized in a *National Geographic* article written by Julia Sklar. Zoom fatigue not only applies to the videoconferencing application Zoom but all other video-call interfaces like Skype, FaceTime, and Google Hangouts. Put simply, Zoom fatigue reflects weariness, anxiety, or emotional resistance to engaging in more video conferences. Video calls are particularly demanding because team members can be on camera continually, and grow weary from tracking the expressions of others, across a steady day of video-based meetings. Leaders have reduced Zoom fatigue by having meetings where people don't turn on their cameras. Leaders also varied communication strategies by using short video clips, emails, business communication tools like Slack, company websites, intranets, and private community pages. In all cases, leaders helped stakeholders use available channels and guided them to find up-to-date information.

Jim Fitzpatrick, Cofounder and President of JBF Business Media, strongly advocated for the use of recorded video clips so team members and customers could view content when they wanted. Jim and his wife, Bridget, launched JBF Business Media in 2012. The company includes the CBT Automotive Network, CBT Studios Atlanta, and the Atlanta Small Business Network. Jim noted, "We saw extraordinary engagement from our audiences to the video content that we provided throughout the pandemic. As a result, we produced far more short video interviews for our clients than we had ever done before. Crises often pull for more video storytelling. A television network like CNN catapulted to significance with embedded reporters during Operation Desert Storm and the Gulf War."

People want to see and hear from their leaders and not only in the context of scheduled meetings. They want content they can consume when and how they want to view it.

Whether communication occurred via phone, text, or prerecorded or live video events, leaders recommended thoughtful, aligned, inclusive, and varied messaging platforms. They also suggested the person sending a message should think carefully about the purpose of each communication and the unique needs of the intended audience. They should tailor their messages based on what they learn from the listening skills discussed in Chapter 6.

BEFORE YOU SHARE

In a crisis, information bombards team members and customers. Customers receive troves of generic messages from companies with whom they have minimally interacted. These vacuous messages assure the customer that the brand is "taking the crisis seriously." Similarly, employees often receive updates and messages that are not well-targeted. In the height of crises, information, misinformation, contradictory information, and general communication noise abounds. To not contribute to that noise and to increase the likelihood people will pay attention to your communication, everything you share must have a clear purpose. Generally, leaders categorized two primary goals for expressive communication during a crisis—information-sharing or relationship-building.

Mike Bolland is the Director of Customer Insights at Discount Tire, the United States' largest independent wheel and tire retailer, operating more than 1,000 stores in 35 states. Mike noted, "Much of our communication was required to culturally and tactically manage rapid change. From an operations perspective, we had to ensure people understood the 'why' behind every change and direct them on how to deliver touchless processes and enhanced sanitization. We were careful to limit communication to essential elements whenever possible. At the same time, we kept the lines of communication going in two directions, so the field could dialogue with us to share ideas, problems, and best practices."

Mike continued, "I've worked for Discount Tire for 28 years. Over that time, I've learned the importance of change management communication. Well-planned strategic communication is especially critical when many things are shifting at once. As a leader, you must not only explain what needs to be changed but also provide the rationale for the change. When you offer those explanations, your teams can also communicate that rationale to customers. That entire process has to be a dialogue. It can't be corporate leaders pushing information, processes, or procedures out to the field." Mike highlights the importance of bidirectional conversations consistent with the closed-loop communication discussed in the previous chapter. He also demonstrates the purpose behind most of his organization's messaging—change readiness and conversations around operational initiatives.

Many leaders discussed corporate culture enhancement or team-building messages. They sought to replicate impromptu hallway conversations through online interactions and social communications. In Chapter 17, we explore team-strengthening communication strategies and community-building activities. For now, the primary takeaway is to know the purpose of every communication in advance of hitting send or inviting people to a video call. Are you reaching out to gather input, share information, connect, or promote team building? If you don't have an identified purpose, you may want to hold that communication and wait until you have a more purposeful message to deliver.

A Breath of Insight

It's important to have a succinct plan and communicate it repeatedly. And to always remember the humanity of the situation.
—**Sylvia Acevedo,** CEO, Girl Scouts of the USA

POSITIVE, RESPECTFUL, RELEVANT, AND RICH WITH STORIES

For leaders like Bill and Karolyn Barr, Owners of Spradley Barr Ford in Fort Collins, Colorado, the purpose of their communication was often to express comfort and positivity. Karolyn noted, "Everyone we serve, our members and customers, underwent extreme levels of stress, so we tried to communicate with additional kindness and optimism." Bill added, "Frightening messages filled the news media, and you could hear the fatigue and anxiety in people's voices when you talked to them. We committed to be realistic yet optimistic. We didn't dilute the truth; we just positioned it as a step toward better times. We also tried to keep messages thoughtful and brief. Out of respect, we tried to craft messages that got to the point quickly and ended positively." It's likely you've interacted with leaders who were not respectful of your time, lacked kindness, or didn't strike an optimistic tone. Remembering how it felt to deal with them should be sufficient motivation to invest extra effort in those areas for team members and customers alike.

Linda Rutherford, Senior Vice President and Chief Communication Officer for Southwest Airlines, reinforced the importance of message tone. She also suggested leaders infuse messages with brand-congruent emotion. Linda indicated that a brand's emotionality must be respectful of its audience and circumstance. Linda noted, "The emotionality of the Southwest brand is one of our most valuable assets. An element of our emotionality is humor. For example, many flight attendants sing and tell jokes during travel. That humor also shows up in our marketing messages and our brand advertising. During the pandemic and times of challenge, we appropriately dial down and mute humor. Leaders can't be tone-deaf in any environment but particularly not during a crisis."

Linda added, "The purpose of Southwest Airlines is to connect people to what's important in their lives through friendly, reliable, and low-cost air travel. We kept telling stories of how we live our purpose, and we built on that narrative, even in crisis communication." Linda shared stories of how Southwest continued to connect people to what was most important in their lives. She gave examples of Southwest flights that brought soldiers back to their final resting place or helped family members get to those who were ill and suffering, some from the coronavirus. She offered examples of Southwest moving medical supplies like ventilators to needed locations. Linda concluded, "Our people are the emotional force behind our brand. As communicators, we must tell their stories. They have been the face of the crisis."

Penny Pennington, Managing Partner at Edward Jones, also pointed to the importance of leadership storytelling, particularly when those stories spotlight team members living your company's purpose. Penny shared, "I'm always listening for stories from customers or team members and believe that part of my communication role is to share examples of our culture in action. During the pandemic, we focused on building and strengthening connections. I was scheduled for a broadcast message recently and shared this story. A number of our branch teams deliver meals to elderly clients respecting all guidelines to assure the client's safety. During one of those drop-offs, a client gestured from behind their screen door and said, 'Please pick up that rock on the porch.' When our colleague lifted it, they noticed the words 'you matter' written on the bottom. The client instructed them to bring the rock back to the branch as a reminder that their kindness matters."

Kindness does matter, as does leadership storytelling. In the words of marketing executive Chris Cavanaugh, "Storytellers, by the very act of telling, communicate a radical learning that changes lives and the world. Telling stories is a universally accessible means through which people make meaning." Aligned, positive, relevant, and purposeful storytelling is not only at the heart of crisis communication and leadership, but it has also fueled relationships since humans first wrote on cave walls.

RESILIENCE RECAP

➤ You can communicate too much or too little during a crisis.

➤ Failing to increase messaging during a crisis can create a vacuum that customers and team members fill with misinformation, rumors, and worst-case scenarios.

➤ Too much communication can lead to message fatigue, disruptions in workflow, and less engagement.

➤ Crisis communication should be purposeful, well-timed, congruent, and relevant to the intended audience.

➤ In times of crisis, leaders have to be especially careful with the words they choose and respect the power of their communication.

➤ Leaders should assume that every message they craft (even private texts and emails) will become public.

➤ At all times (but especially during crises) careless words, off-color jokes, biased language, and baseless claims can harm stakeholders.

➤ To increase communication inclusivity, leaders should involve team members from diverse perspectives to write, edit, and present text-based, videotaped, and live communications.

➤ Leaders need to screen for gender references or binary she/he pronouns. They should be aware of unconscious bias associated with race, ethnicity, nationality, age, socioeconomic background, or religion and take steps to rid messages of those biases.

➤ Leaders are encouraged to vary messaging across channels like email, business communication tools like Slack, company websites, intranets, and private community pages. This approach can drive engagement and reduce platform exhaustion (e.g., Zoom fatigue).

➤ Identify the purpose behind your message before you share it. Are you reaching out to gather input, share information, connect, or promote team building?

➤ Soften your tone and seek brevity.

➤ Remember to share purposeful stories infused with brand-congruent emotionality.

YOUR STRENGTH PLAN

1. When has someone communicated too little with you? How did you fill in the gaps when their communication was not forthcoming?

2. Has anyone overcommunicated with you? How did their messages interrupt your workflow, concentration, or productivity? How did you respond to their excessive communication?

3. When have the words of a business leader inspired you? When have your words inspired others?

4. How do you ensure your messages are inclusive?

5. What processes do you (or can you) use to discover your unconscious biases? How often do you help others find theirs? What do you do to remove those biases from your communications?

6. How do you ensure your message tone is sensitive to current social conditions and attendant to the needs of your audience?

7. How frequently do you collect and share positive stories with or about your team members, customers, and other stakeholders? When was the last time you shared a story? Why not share one now.

8. How would you describe the emotionality of your brand? To what degree do you infuse that emotionality into your messaging?

CHAPTER 9

Bring Yourself to Work

Vulnerability is a guardian of integrity.
—ANNE TRUITT,
artist and author

GHOSTS OF LEADERSHIP PAST

Not long ago, companies were substantially hierarchical and bureaucratic. Leaders evoked top-down authority, viewed employees as resources (not unlike raw materials, tools, or machines), and prioritized compliance over employee-generated ideas.

Over the past several decades, perspectives on leadership have shifted. Technological advances, global interconnectivity, and research on effectiveness have all contributed to a heightened focus on collaboration and relational leadership.

Before the pandemic, leadership training blended relational elements, including participative, servant, and transformational leadership approaches. Leaders were encouraged to engage team members in ways that would have been unacceptable just a generation ago. However, with a widespread crisis, would leaders demonstrate participative and servant type leadership, or would they revert to pockets of "old-school" thinking?

In earlier chapters, we addressed some outdated ideas that weren't suited for times of adversity. For example, you've read about leaders whose actions challenged "old-school" notions that a leader should:

- Be a hero

- Forgo self-care

- Figure out solutions on his or her own

- Never admit a lack of knowledge

In this chapter, leaders confront a subtle and entrenched old-school belief that harm will come from personal transparency and vulnerability. These leaders discuss how COVID-19 placed them in situations where transparency was critical and extremely beneficial. They share insights on why you need to add authenticity and emotionality to accurate information sharing (addressed in Chapter 7). Leaders explain the importance of asking for assistance from your team and supervisees (not just to peers—as discussed in Chapter 3). They offer examples of errors and missteps they made and why they shared those mistakes with their teams and others in their companies. You will also see how personal disclosure increased morale, community, innovation, and productivity.

DOES IT HAVE TO BE PERSONAL?

Pattie Cuen is a Vice President and Chief Marketing and Communications Officer at Cedars-Sinai. Cedars-Sinai is a Los Angeles–based, nonprofit multi-specialty academic health science center, which includes an 886-bed hospital. That hospital alone employs a staff of more than 10,000 employees and 2,000 physicians. Pattie explained that "Often leaders think about transparency at a corporate level. They see openness as sharing facts with team members, customers, shareholders, the media, and the general public. Usually, the information disclosed involves operations, corporate decision-making, and financial matters. Given the role healthcare has played during the pandemic, transparency has been essential not just organizationally but on a personal level as well. People needed to hear from leaders who were willing to share facts in the context of real human emotions. They looked to individuals who weren't afraid to speak from their humanity. Like always, people wanted accurate and readily available information, but they also needed that information to be related by leaders who didn't put up emotional facades. That authentic and emotionally present communication sounds easy, but it is far more challenging to practice because it renders leaders vulnerable." During the pandemic, team members were experiencing a host of vulnerabilities including family members contracting COVID-19, uncertainties about school reopenings, and many other hardships. They wanted to know their leaders understood and weren't immune to the same challenges. While employees looked to their leaders to share facts, they also needed them to express authentic human emotion.

The wants and needs of team members during COVID-19 converged with more than two decades of research on leadership vulnerability conducted by professor Brené Brown and others. Brené has summarized her findings in a widely viewed TED Talk and books like *Dare to Lead*. Her work, and the findings of thought leader Patrick Lencioni, author of *The Five Dysfunctions of Team*, resoundingly show a tremendous upside to leadership vulnerability and authenticity. According to Brené and Patrick, individuals who receive high scores on vulnerability:

- Are perceived as more approachable
- Drive heightened levels of trust
- Foster psychological safety
- Form enduring connections
- Build strong teams
- Ignite creativity

In her book *Daring Greatly*, Brené Brown provides an eloquent synopsis on the inextricable link between vulnerability and leadership success. Brené noted, "Vulnerability is not weakness, and the uncertainty, risk, and emotional exposure we face every day are not optional. Our only choice is a question of engagement. Our willingness to own and engage with our vulnerability determines the depth of our courage and the clarity of our purpose; the level to which we protect ourselves from being vulnerable is a measure of our fear and disconnection."

Enough about the rationale behind leadership vulnerability, let's see how leaders chose to bring it to life during the pandemic.

PART NECESSITY AND PART CHOICE

Jennifer Prosek is the Managing Partner at Prosek Partners, an integrated communications and marketing solutions firm with a specialization in the professional and financial service sectors. From Jennifer's perspective, working from home during the pandemic gave leaders an ideal opportunity to show more of their humanity. According to Jennifer, "When you jump on a video call from a makeshift office in your bedroom or living room, you are instantly sharing more of yourself. If leaders weren't willing to turn on their cameras or be seen more casually and naturally, they missed a special opportunity to connect. Choosing to be real in the moment communicated that we are all in this together." Jennifer observed, "Not everyone is comfortable conducting business in a relaxed and informal way, but it is something leaders can work on and train themselves to do. For the past five years, we've had a program here at Prosek Partners that we call 'Up the Humanity.' Every week we've challenged ourselves to share more of our humanity with one another and with those we serve. By its nature, the pandemic was an extraordinary opportunity for leaders to up their humanity." Leaders I interviewed gave countless examples of how the pandemic prompted increased sharing and humanity across their teams. For example, they cited employees finding and distributing personal care items (e.g., toilet paper or hand sanitizer) to their colleagues. Leaders dropped off food baskets on the doorsteps of quarantined COVID-19 positive team members. They also engaged in recorded happy birthday messages for the children of those on their team. Informality, crisis, and humanity merged during the pandemic.

Stephanie Linnartz, Group President of Consumer Operations at Marriott International, echoed Jennifer's perspective concerning the connection between working from home and opportunities for leadership vulnerability. Stephanie noted, "I strive to be open with my supervisors and my team. However, during one meeting from home, I demonstrated more openness than I'd planned. It happened when I was in a video meeting with our CEO, Arne Sorenson; Bill Marriott, the Executive Chairman and Chairman of the Board of Marriott International; and a few other leaders. Midway through the call, my 13-year-old daughter burst into my room and began sharing a teenage crisis. I thought I had muted my microphone, but apparently I was wrong. Within moments a colleague texted me 'turn off your microphone.' Thanks to her, the meeting didn't turn into a broadcast of my daughter's drama." The entrance of Stephanie's daughter was an unintentional disclosure. However, when Stephanie chose to share the incident with her team, she willingly offered them a glimpse into her challenges and normalized the realities of being a working parent. Stephanie explained, "Afterward, I was eager to share my home and work life collision with my team. I hope I assured them that if their child, dog, or anything else comes running into a Zoom call, it will be okay. I survived. So will they." Often by sharing our humanity, we help others connect with us. We show that we experience thoughts and feelings in common. We also demonstrate that the challenges of today are usually forgotten or may make for the amusing stories of tomorrow.

REWARDED WITH CONNECTION

Jennifer Prosek was vulnerable with me by acknowledging that she has worked at bringing more of herself into her business. She explained, "Sharing my personal experiences in a work context hasn't been natural for me. I've really had to push myself to be more willing to share. Even before this crisis, I was experimenting with this. For example, when I posted something on LinkedIn that mixed humanity with business, viewership skyrocketed. I wrote an article about the contract we forged with our 12-year-old daughter as part of our decision to purchase an iPhone for her. I called it 'A Promise to Your Parents.' The message was both funny and serious. It shared our angst in deciding on her readiness for the phone. It also captured the promise our daughter made based on the responsibilities that came with that life-changing technology purchase."

Jennifer reported that at first, she wasn't going to publish the article, fearing that it was too personal or wasn't relevant to her business audience on LinkedIn. However, with some nudging, Jennifer explained, "I took a chance, and it didn't take long for views to eclipse 60,000. If the popularity of the article wasn't surprising enough, it also drove personal connections, and it had a lasting impact. Long after the article appeared on LinkedIn, I got weekend calls from executives at private equity firms. They would tell me how they remembered the piece and wondered if I could send it to them. They wanted to share it with their partner as they worked together to decide on a phone for their preteen. By taking the risk to share a personal dilemma, I connected with an amazing number of people who faced similar challenges. Being real pays in more ways than I could have imagined." A willingness to take down part of the firewall between work and home enables you to connect with people you have never met, let alone deepen relationships with those you already know. That level of authenticity can be the springboard for leads, customers, employee prospects, and even future employment.

John McManus gives a poignant example of how disclosure can be a win for your customer, a win for your team, and a win for you. John is the Vice President–Editorial Director at Hanley Wood Media. His company serves the construction industry, with business intelligence, marketing tools, and published content. Among his many duties, John creates and oversees digital and print content for *Builder* magazine. John noted, "My wife, an infectious disease physician, was in the thick of the battle with COVID-19 as I was writing for builders who actively contributed N95 masks to healthcare workers like her. That allowed me to show builders the positive impact they were having and also keep them appraised of ongoing needs. However, to do that I had to be willing to share my concerns and my wife's experiences." From John's perspective, the anticipated benefits of being vulnerable warranted a personal approach. Here's an excerpt from one of John's articles in *Builder*, posted in April 2020:

> "He's doing it again." Some of you may be thinking that, as I write about face masks, and new rules, and COVID-19, and my wife, who's a doctor specializing in infectious disease. I've been doing it pretty much non-stop . . . since March 4. That's 54 days and counting. I'll admit, it's hard for me to think of much else these days. . . .
>
> My wife, for instance, set out to work one morning this week in the COVID-19 wards of one of the Central New Jersey hospitals. Like all of us, she's been heartened of late, to see the number of new COVID admissions start to shrink, gradually, but steadily. This particular morning, however, she was glum. It would have been understandable if it were from exhaustion. Of the 54 days we talked about since March 4, she'd had four days off. . . . Why was she down that morning? She was down because the masks—the N95 "duckbill" style masks builders had given tens of thousands of in March—had run out.

In that article, John eloquently tied his N95 mask comments back to the building industry and the importance of keeping workers safe and reducing community spread.

When I asked John about the impact of providing a series of disclosive articles, he said. "It's been a pivotal time for me, my team, and the builder community. The response from both our readers and my team suggests people had an emotional connection to the content, and the articles sparked additional donations of PPE, food, and other acts of kindness toward healthcare workers. Those were hugely important wins. I also was given a gift to share healthcare realities with our builder community. The entire experience helped me grow and consider the complexities of healthcare, social policy, capital, stakeholders, customers in homes, and the business community. Yes, I shared at a personal level, but it is amazing just how much I received in return." As a leader in his organization, John could have played it safe and taken a detached tone in his writing. He chose vulnerability and, in the process, strongly connected for a shared good. How willing are you to engage at that level of transparency? If you aren't engaged personally, what gets in the way?

THE HARDEST DISCLOSURE OF ALL: ADMITTING AN ERROR

Many leaders are comfortable being emotionally present and vulnerable up to the point that they have to admit a misstep or shortcoming. Jeff Dailey is the CEO of Farmers Insurance—a US insurer that provides coverage for automobiles, homes, and small businesses, along with other insurance and financial services products. Farmers Insurance has approximately 21,000 employees and more than 48,000 independent and exclusive agents.

Having worked for Jeff in the past, I wasn't surprised when he openly shared an errant decision. Jeff noted, "I have to give my team a lot of credit. Early in the pandemic, they projected automobile claims would go down due to reduced automobile use. Given that scenario, they suggested we should return money to customers, by adjusting personal auto premiums downward. It was such a murky period, so I passed on that idea in favor of shoring up the company's finances for uncertainties ahead. Shortly after that, another insurance company announced they would be the first to make a premium reduction, and we were a fast follower. Not every company followed behind us, but most did over time. I wished I would have sided with my team more quickly. It was my mistake."

In addition to openly admitting errors, Jeff and his leadership team reached out to customers and team members formally and informally. He also regularly provided video messages. Results from team member pulse surveys suggest that Jeff's vulnerable and transparent leadership paid dividends. For example, Farmers calculated an eNPS quotient based on one of the questions asked on a team member pulse survey (on a scale of 0–10, how likely are you to recommend Farmers Insurance as a place to work?). Research has linked eNPS performance to team member retention, productivity, and loyalty.

During the pandemic, the Farmers Insurance eNPS score went up 27 points from 40 to 67. Team members didn't lose trust in a vulnerable and honest leader who took responsibility for his choices. Instead, their trust and confidence in leadership soared. Everyone makes errors. Most leaders make the best decisions possible, given the information available and the scope of those they need to serve. When you acknowledge an errant choice or misstep, and you swiftly remedy it, your vulnerability forges trust.

YOUR TEAM IS WATCHING AND LISTENING

Kyle Hudson shared her insights on how leadership vulnerability sets the tone for team morale and creativity. Kyle is the Director of Team Marketing and Business Operations at the National Basketball Association (NBA), North America's premier men's professional basketball league. Kyle noted, "We have a senior leadership team filled with intelligent, worldly people that are incredibly knowledgeable about our business. From the onset, they were honest about what they knew and what they didn't know. They communicated emotion and passion. They shared anxieties and asked for our assistance to move through the pandemic together. Their request sparked our entire organization. People offered countless ideas, shared best practices, became increasingly active on collaborative platforms, and volunteered to be on working groups. I have emulated the senior leadership approach with my team and am proud of our idea generation especially as it relates to helping NBA teams virtually engage with their largest supporters. We worked closely together, and fluidly got things done."

When leaders ask for assistance from their teams with passion, vulnerability, and urgency, team members usually respond with speed, innovation, and collaboration. They find creative ways to connect with customers even when their core offerings, like the NBA season, are paused. When you ask your team for help, it signals trust placed in them. It also communicates your awareness of your limitations. Those requests acknowledge a need for the gifts, talents, effort, and ingenuity of those around you.

ALL THINGS IN MODERATION

Since vulnerability and personal sharing have so many positive business outcomes, why don't leaders demonstrate these behaviors all of the time? David Christ believes there is more to that answer than merely fearing harm from disclosure. David is the Group Vice President and General Manager of Lexus North America. Lexus is the luxury vehicle division of Toyota, marketed in more than 70 territories and countries globally.

David observed that leaders frequently have a positive intention when they limit personal disclosure. David noted, "I've learned a lot about vulnerability during the pandemic. I typically didn't share much about myself or my family at work. I wasn't afraid of what others would do with the information, I just wanted to keep the focus on my team. Early in my work life, I had a boss who always talked about himself. I didn't want to be like him. However, early in the pandemic, I shared that my son has asthma and that I was worried about his welfare. In response, team members shared concerns for their mothers, fathers, sons, daughters, cousins, and even their own health. We talked about how we could ensure each person's comfort and safety."

When asked the lessons he learned from talking about his son with his team, David concluded, "There are times when you have to be vulnerable. You need to explain to the team who you are and what is important to you. When you do, they can understand you, but more importantly, they will be more willing to let you know them. My final lesson is that my concern for over-disclosure pushed me toward under disclosure. As a leader, I am committed to striking the right balance as I journey forward."

We are all on a journey as leaders. Vulnerable leaders are more interested in how they are progressing and less interested in acting as though they have already reached their destination. By balancing disclosure, admitting mistakes, and sharing our victories and challenges, we travel the journey together. In the words of Helen Keller, "Alone we can do so little, together we can do so much."

RESILIENCE RECAP

➤ In the history of leadership, collaborative and participative approaches are relatively new.

➤ Despite advances in research, training, and organizational structure, remnants of old-school thinking remain—such as a belief that leaders should limit personal transparency and not show vulnerability.

➤ Corporate transparency often refers to accurate information sharing (as covered in Chapter 7).

➤ Personal transparency reflects a willingness to "be yourself" at work.

➤ Leadership vulnerability is a risk/reward perspective.

➤ Vulnerability correlates with approachability, trust, psychological safety, and team effectiveness.

➤ Working from home during the pandemic gave leaders opportunities—and in some cases forced them—to show more of their humanity (authenticity).

➤ You can play it safe and detached or increase the chance of connecting with others by sharing what's important to you.

➤ When you acknowledge a mistake and swiftly fix it, your transparency builds trust.

➤ When you seek your team's assistance with passion, vulnerability, and urgency, they are likely to respond with speed, innovation, and collaboration.

➤ Personal disclosure, like so many other things in life, is best provided in moderation.

YOUR STRENGTH PLAN

1. How would the people you lead rate you when it comes to creating outcomes on the following list? On what basis do you make each rating?

    - Trust

    - Psychological safety

    - Lasting connections

    - Creative teams

2. How would they rate you on vulnerability? How do you think your vulnerability rating correlates with your ratings on the list in Question 1?

3. It might seem like a contradictory question, but what are your *strengths* when it comes to leadership *vulnerability* (e.g., admitting mistakes, balancing self-disclosure, asking for team support, demonstrating the courage to be yourself)?

4. What are your areas of opportunity when it comes to vulnerability?

5. Think of a nonpolitical leader who demonstrates authenticity and vulnerability. Why did you choose that person? How do you feel, and what do you think about him or her?

6. What is one mistake you've made as a leader for which you should have taken greater responsibility? Where have you accepted blame for an error in a way that built trust?

7. Where are you on the spectrum from too little disclosure to too much disclosure? How do you (or can you) take steps to practice moderation?

8. Would you consider an "Up the Humanity" (authenticity and team support) program each week at your work? How will you (or do you) nurture healthy transparency, authenticity, and mutual support for you and your team?

PART III

MOVE WITH PURPOSE

*Without a mission statement, you may get to
the top of the ladder and then realize it was
leaning against the wrong building!*

—Dave Ramsey,
financial literacy expert and
syndicated talk show host

The next four chapters examine ways to drive a compassion-ate, value-producing culture by:

- Activating your mission, vision, and values

- Focusing on value over profit

- Tempering decisions and behaviors with sensitivity

- Standing with your team

CHAPTER 10

Act Your Culture

Vision without action is merely a dream. . . .
Vision with action can change the world.
—Joel A. Barker,
futurist, author, and lecturer

AN INVISIBLE FORCE MEETS
AN EXTENDED CRISIS

Leaders are aware of the strong connection between a company's culture and employee engagement, customer loyalty, and long-term success. They also expect a robust culture will help a business thrive during and after a protracted crisis. However, COVID-19 placed a substantial strain on many company cultures. For example, morale was challenged by salary freezes, furloughs, and team members who no longer worked from a central location. The pandemic caused leaders to ask questions like "How can we strengthen our culture through this crisis?" and "How can we leverage the invisible force of culture to manage immediate challenges and sustain meaningful progress?"

Throughout this chapter, leaders provide examples of how their cultures propelled them to stay on purpose, make efficient decisions, and resist distractions. They share how precrisis investments in culture produced returns like broad inclusivity, team cohesion, rapid deployment, and substantial impact inside and outside the walls of the business.

Children's author Lewis Carroll observed, "If you don't know where you are going, any road will get you there." Carroll's quote is a helpful way to think about culture, particularly amid the confusion of the pandemic. It also resonates with the insights shared by those I interviewed. For example, in this chapter, leaders explain how their cultural tenets kept them focused on their destination. Some describe how culture helped them choose their best path in the fog of the pandemic. Finally, others share how culture enabled them to move inclusively or efficiently along their journey.

KNOWING YOUR DESTINATION

Karen Meleta, Vice President of Corporate Communications at Wakefern Food Corp., emphasized the importance of knowing both your purpose and guiding principles, particularly when navigating uncertain times. Wakefern Food Corporation is a 51-member cooperative of independently owned and operated retail supermarkets. The company has 354 markets under the ShopRite, Price Rite Marketplace, The Fresh Grocer, Dearborn Market, and Gourmet Garage banners. It is the largest retailer-owned cooperative in the United States. Karen noted, "We are a family-owned business that has served local communities since 1946. We have invested a lot of time and leadership resources to align around our purpose of caring deeply about people and helping them to eat well and be happy. Those investments, combined with an active commitment to values of integrity, innovation, and teamwork, enabled us to maintain stability when so many other parts of our business were shifting around us."

From a tactical perspective, Karen added, "Because leaders linked our communications and activities to the importance of caring deeply and helping people eat well, we maintained our essential operational effectiveness. Additionally, our purpose and values fueled momentum on an aggressive strategic plan that included investments in everything from prepared foods and food service, to store design and brand development. All in the context of the pandemic."

From Karen's perspective, well-defined and integrated cultural tenets (like mission, purpose, vision, and values) had both short- and long-term benefits. Those cultural elements helped leaders and team members stay on-task during the crisis and created energy for future success. In Karen's case, as Wakefern leaders focused crisis efforts on helping people eat well, they created the momentum needed to pursue the company's mission well into the future.

EFFICIENTLY CHOOSING YOUR PATH

Staying with Lewis Carroll's journey metaphor from earlier in the chapter, let's turn to his most well-known work, *Alice in Wonderland*. As you'll recall from the story, Alice loses her sense of bearings after following the White Rabbit down a hole into Wonderland. The White Rabbit, who is typically in a rush, mutters phrases like "the hurrier I go, the behinder I get."

For many of the leaders I spoke with, the pandemic was not unlike falling through a rabbit hole. As they descended, they found themselves in an alternative reality where the pace of change was as harried as the White Rabbit—exceeding their capacity to adapt. Steve Klingman believes his company's culture enabled him and his leadership team to slow down and focus on issues that mattered most. Steve is the President of Hayden Homes, a homebuilder in the Pacific Northwest. The company based in Redmond, Oregon, routinely receives awards for its team member experience, customer service, and philanthropy.

According to Steve, "A lot was coming at us at once, especially since new home construction had very different restrictions across the states where we operate. Given the speed of change, we had the natural tendency to be reactive. We corrected that by doubling down on our guiding principles. Before the pandemic, we developed cultural rituals like reciting our principles at the beginning of meetings, sharing stories to demonstrate how we put our mission and core values into action every day, and building strategies based on the mission. We just needed to trust our culture would show us the way through the pandemic."

Steve added, "We exist to give as we go, so together we can build community and lead fulfilled lives. That mission guided us down paths of generosity and fulfillment for our homeowners, team members, and communities. During the pandemic, we stayed true to what we trained people on and talked about it incessantly before the crisis. That helped us slow down and manage challenges more effectively. We were less reactive and more proactive. In the process, we focused on the importance of home building, especially our commitment to affordable housing in the United States, and we navigated through the fog and darkness to execute our strategy. I am pleased with how we performed during the pandemic, especially in areas like homeowner experience improvement and even positioning a 'buy now' button on our website. More importantly, I am proud of our people because they are our culture in action."

Like many other leaders, Steve made a connection between the culture and the people in his organization. In essence, the more clearly you define, communicate, and select talent based on your mission and values, the more aligned your organization will be. Steve also indicated that mission and core values shifted the crisis paradigm from operational reactivity to strategic proactivity. With that shift, Steve reported the volatility of the crisis became more manageable. By focusing on guiding principles, leaders can effectively choose paths that are most likely to get them to their desired destination.

AVOIDING DETOURS

For Amy Nichols, Vice President of The Humane Society of the United States, the breadth of animal welfare needs during the pandemic made it challenging not to wander into areas beyond the organization's mission and core competencies. The Humane Society of the United States is the country's largest animal protection organization. The organization's mission is to fight for all animals across America and around the world, including companion animals, farm animals, animals in research, and habitat protection. Amy noted, "In the middle of a crisis, it is easy to attempt more than you can execute. Our team added 30 percent to 50 percent more work compared to prepandemic times, and we had so much more we wanted to pursue. While I wished we had more time and resources to extend ourselves further, we used our mission to select the areas where we could make the greatest difference. As such, our team reached out by phone to over 700 shelters. We created toolkits, collaborated with other nonprofits dedicated to the human-animal bond, and innovated crisis solutions. We also looked for ways to apply our best solutions in the future. Our mission helped us say yes to the things we needed to do and say no to things that were best left to others."

Dontá Wilson reinforced the importance of choosing business opportunities in the context of mission, vision, and values. He also demonstrated how culture could unite former competitors. Dontá is the Chief Digital and Client Experience Officer at Truist Financial Corporation, a bank holding company that formed in December 2019 with the merger of BB&T and SunTrust Banks. That merger made Truist the sixth-largest bank in the United States.

Dontá noted, "Our purpose, mission, and values provides a compass—when those elements are clear, decisions become clear. The pandemic has been an opportunity to show how we live our purpose of building and inspiring better lives and communities." In Truist's case, leaders also helped team members come together under a new brand with a unifying mission. Dontá shared, "We were just a few months into the merger, and our response to COVID-19 accelerated integration of teams and has allowed our culture to thrive. I firmly believe the strongest bonds form during the most challenging times, and Truist teammates have been a true testament of that. As we realized clients' needs were rapidly changing due to the pandemic, thousands of teammates mobilized to help respond. Many did jobs outside of their normal responsibilities, and many more worked long hours, late into the night and on weekends. We saw teammates coming together in ways that might not have been possible had we not put into action our purpose of inspiring and building better lives and communities."

In Chapter 14, we explore how setting priorities helped leaders navigate COVID-19. For now, however, it's crucial to see how an organization's mission can bring people together and guide that prioritization. Unless leaders know why they exist and what they value, it is impossible to act in unison or determine if an attractive opportunity is a "must" or a "nice to have." Failing to use your mission to strengthen your team and choose your tactical path can lead to fragmented efforts or lead you down a rabbit hole.

BRINGING EVERYONE ALONG
THE JOURNEY AT A SWIFT PACE

Until the pandemic, I used to ascribe to the African proverb, "If you want to go fast, go alone. If you want to go far, go together." Given what I observed during COVID-19, I suggest the following revision, "Working together, we can go fast and far." Steven C. Preston speaks to the importance of activating an organization's mission and values to ensure everyone is part of your rapid and enduring journey. Steven is the President and CEO at Goodwill Industries International, Inc. Goodwill is an American nonprofit organization comprised of 157 autonomous, community-based groups in the United States and Canada with a presence in 12 other countries. To meet community needs, each local Goodwill offers tailored programs and services to help people find work close to where they live.

Steven shared, "The mission at Goodwill is to enhance the dignity and quality of life of individuals and families by strengthening communities, eliminating barriers to opportunity, and helping people in need reach their full potential through learning and the power of work. To do that we respectfully strive to include all of our team members to help us provide innovative solutions. We are convinced that time invested up front in soliciting ideas from the team helps us come up with better solutions, drives team engagement and unity, expedites action, and assures accountability. While it may seem that leaders can get off to a faster start without that input, progress slows and sometimes comes to a complete halt when that step is skipped. The importance of inclusive participation has been magnified for us during the pandemic, as furloughs reduced our team to a little over half. We needed everyone's ideas to create the extraordinary value we provided for our member organizations."

Katie Fitzgerald offered an outstanding example of how inclusive mission-focused decision-making leads to lightning-fast action. Katie is the Executive Vice President and Chief Operating Officer at Feeding America. As the nation's largest hunger-relief organization, Feeding America's pantries and food banks serve more than 40 million people, including 12 million children and 7 million seniors. The organization's mission is to feed America's hungry through its nationwide network and engage the country in the fight to end hunger.

Katie shared, "Jeff Bezos reached out to us wanting to gift $100 million to our member food banks if we could assure him that the money would feed communities within 41 days of receipt—half that time could be for planning and the rest for distribution. Accepting this generous gift and distributing the food was wholly aligned with our mission, but accepting it also meant we would need to work at an incredible pace. Significant disruptions in the food supply chain would make this task even more challenging. Before we said yes to the offer, our team reached out to our network leader's council, and they said, 'Let's get this done, and do it faster than expected.'" Katie concluded by noting, "Within eight days of receiving the gift, the funds were deployed to Feeding America member food banks. To make that possible, people worked day and night in support of our mission. They created a data-driven process that directed those resources to where the need was greatest. They developed an elaborate set of guidelines to help food banks use the resources in accord with the donor's wishes and their communities' needs." Generosity, inclusiveness, mission, and speed are a remarkable combination.

I doubt you will ever need to distribute $100 million responsibly in less than 41 days. However, I suspect you will have many opportunities to bring people together to take urgent action. Lessons from leaders like Steven and Katie suggest you should focus on mission, involve everyone in decision-making, and solicit agreement on aggressive deadlines. I wonder how far and fast aligned mission-centric action will take you?

WHEN THE PATH FINDS YOU

To this point in the chapter, we've explored how mission, vision, and values help leaders progress toward a purposeful destination, make tactical choices, resist distraction, foster inclusivity, and act swiftly. When leaders talk about and celebrate purpose and values, team members usually take mission-centric action on their own.

Lily Lin offered several examples of how team members initiated purpose-filled action. Lily Lin is Vice President of Global Communications at Google Inc., a multinational technology company providing extensive products and services such a search engine, cloud computing, online advertising, hardware, and software. Google's cultural guideposts, in part, are composed of a commitment to significantly improve the lives of as many people as possible by including all voices, protecting users, expanding opportunity, responding to crises, and advancing sustainability. Against that backdrop, Lily shared, "We make phones, Nest devices, speakers, and so on. Those are our products. However, people understand that we are really in the business of making people's lives better. As such, our people didn't wait for titled leaders to start forging partnerships and developing ideas to help us live our broader commitment. Specifically, they came together to develop and accelerate the production of N95 masks. In-house experts on modeling, fabrication, and 3D printing pulled together a group that produced 49,000 face shields that were then donated to a local hospital group here in the Bay Area." When leaders select mission-focused individuals, orient them to their company's purpose, and foster regular conversations about activating the mission, team members often look for solutions on their own. In those cases, the role of leadership is to help prioritize and support those initiatives.

A FINAL WORD ON THE CULTURE JOURNEY

During the pandemic, every leader struggled to chart a course that would position their teams and organizations for success. After reeling from initial disorientation, effective leaders leaned into their guiding principles and cultural infrastructure. In so doing, they helped team members rise above fear in pursuit of a shared purpose. As thought leader Ralph Buchanan observed, "When you walk in purpose, you collide with destiny."

RESILIENCE RECAP

➤ During the pandemic, leaders who focused on mission, vision, and purpose derived benefits that included:

- Stability
- Proactivity
- Ease in selecting tactics
- Inclusivity
- Rapid and effective action
- Team-initiated projects with purposeful outcomes

➤ When it comes to bringing mission, vision, and values to life, leaders should determine when they need to show the way, when they need to clear the way, and when it's best to get out of the way.

➤ When you need to bring about urgent, purpose-filled action, you should focus on mission, involve everyone in decision-making, and solicit agreement on aggressive deadlines.

YOUR STRENGTH PLAN

1. Without consulting any resource, write down your company's mission, vision, and values. Now go and check your writing for accuracy. Was there anything you missed? If so, you might want to work on committing those resources to memory—it's difficult to encourage others to take action on concepts that you have not internalized.

2. Ask your team to do the exercise listed above. Facilitate a discussion about gaps. Work with your team to develop a plan to commit the cultural tenets to memory by a specified date.

3. Take time to go from a word-level understanding of your mission, vision, and values and begin to think about behaviors that are in keeping with your culture and those behaviors that run afoul. Consider having a discussion about this topic with your team.

4. How do you assess the health of your company's culture? Similarly, how do you assess your effectiveness at spotlighting mission, vision, and values?

5. Based on your direct experiences or what you've observed about other businesses, how has company culture made work easier or harder?

CHAPTER 11

Be a Value Leader

Strive not to be a success, but rather to be of value.
—ALBERT EINSTEIN,
Nobel Prize–winning physicist

VALUES, VALUE, VALUE LEADER, LEAD VALUE

What a difference a single letter can make. In this case, it is the letter "s." Chapter 10 centered on mission and *values*, and this chapter is all about stakeholder *value*.

Let's look at how the *Business Dictionary* defines the sizable difference between these two words. First, the plural—*values*:

Important and lasting beliefs or ideals shared by the members of a culture about what is good or bad and desirable or undesirable. Values have major influence on a person's behavior and attitude and serve as broad guidelines in all situations.

Contrast that with the singular word—*value*:

The extent to which a good or service is perceived by its customer to meet his or her needs or wants, measured by customer's willingness to pay for it.

I think you get the picture. I've labeled this chapter "Be a Value Leader" to challenge you to lead value creation across your organization.

Enough about words, let's first look at the simple connection between value and business. From there, we will preview the complexities of value delivery (including micro-human interactions and evolving needs).

SIMPLY COMPLEX

At its core, business is simple. Success involves six components of value creation and exchange:

1. **Explore value:** Understand the wants and needs of your consumers.

2. **Create value:** Craft solutions to address your consumers' needs.

3. **Market value:** Communicate the benefits of your solutions to your consumers.

4. **Sell value:** Help consumers find sufficient value in your offering so they will provide something of value to you in return (e.g., make a purchase).

5. **Deliver value:** Ensure your consumers receive the value you promised.

6. **Prosper through value efficiency:** Deliver value economically so you can sustain and grow your ability to provide it.

It looks so easy on paper, but even under normal circumstances, value creation and value exchange are difficult to achieve consistently. When you add the volatility of a crisis, that difficulty level increases inordinately.

This chapter focuses on how leaders addressed value exchanges at the business to customer level during the pandemic. However, it's good to note that value exchanges occur in every business and individual human interaction. As such, the model above applies to relationships with your team members and families. For example, you can replace the words *customer/consumer/prospect* with the word *employees* in the six components above and the value creation/value exchange model still applies.

When we are looking at the value your business provides for customers; you need to consider changing perceptions of value over time and in the context of crisis. For example, economists Jim Gilmore and Joe Pine wrote a groundbreaking book in 1999 (and updated it in 2019) called *The Experience Economy*, where they catalog shifts in perceived consumer value. For example, Gilmore and Pine say that for a period in history, the most significant economic value came from extracting materials from the Earth. That value shifted to product creation and then to service value. Most recently, from their perspective, value shifted again from service delivery to staging experiences—thus their book's title *The Experience Economy*.

I caught up with Joe Pine, Cofounder of Strategic Horizons LLP, as I was writing this book to discuss how the pandemic further altered perceived value and what leaders should do to deliver it. Joe noted, "Undeniably experience stagers like theaters, shopping malls, events, and types of tourism were hit hard, but digital experience stagers like entertainment, gaming, and video-conference platforms boomed. Experience creation remained and will remain a central driver of perceived customer value. While health conditions dictate available experience delivery platforms, there is no denying that customers want to do business with those who stage experiences for them."

Joe added, "Throughout the pandemic and beyond, value involves refreshing the places where you deliver experiences, redesigning offerings, and renewing capabilities. Leaders that effectively staged experiences during the pandemic, did so by building value that was robust, cohesive, personal, dramatic, and transformative. Those leaders also renewed their capabilities to succeed in a new environment."

Throughout this chapter, we will show what it means to refresh, redesign, and renew customer value. You will read about leaders who slightly modified existing core offerings and those who substantially redesigned service experiences to address emergent and urgent needs. All insights are shared to highlight how you can effectively lead customer value in and out of a crisis.

KNOW YOUR STRENGTHS AND DIRECT THEM TO NEEDS

In full disclosure, I have known and worked with Amir Dan Rubin intermittently for more than a decade. As part of that relationship, I wrote a book, *Prescription for Excellence*, about UCLA Health in 2011 when Amir was that company's COO. He and I reconnected in the context of his current position as Chair and CEO of One Medical. As a consultant for One Medical, I have watched Amir and his team create value before and during the pandemic. One Medical is a membership-based primary care platform providing seamless digital health and in-person medical care in 12 major US markets and growing. In addition to its direct-to-consumer enrollment of members, roughly 7,000 companies offer One Medical membership to their employees and dependents to improve employee health, engagement, and productivity, while reducing benefits costs.

When I asked Amir how he adjusted value drivers in response to the pandemic, he noted, "We continued to focus on delivering the highest quality care, providing accessibility, and delivering service affordably. Being based in San Francisco and having a robust technology team, we sped up our cycle times on human-centered design and technologies that make the lives of our providers, members, and company clients easier. We also moved heavily toward our existing and highly popular virtual care platform. Virtual services were of increased importance to provide 24/7 patient access when face-to-face care became limited."

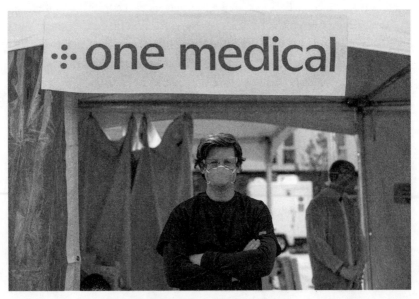

One Medical on the Front Line

Concerning new or redesigned value delivery, Amir noted, "We ran toward needs that our members and employers expressed, and that we were well-suited to fill through our human-centered and technology-powered model. For example, we launched online COVID-19 screenings, virtual assessments, and testing services in all our markets. We also looked to serve our broader communities by offering our digital health membership and testing services for free to the public for the summer, in partnership with the mayors of New York City and San Francisco. We quickly rolled out these COVID-19 services to all our markets with software modifications, numerous drive-through testing locations, home-based testing solutions, and in-person treatment services.

"We also had our providers in full PPE volunteer in hospitals and emergency departments in New York City, as the call for help was put out. We also rolled up our sleeves and created value for many of our major employers by developing worksite reentry programs, with daily screenings of employees integrated in our technology, arrangement of testing, and seamless follow-up from our virtual providers on any employee medical needs. We felt energized by playing a role in serving key employers such as Airbnb, NASDAQ, Google, and Instacart. Also during this time we extended our virtual behavioral health and pediatric services to better address the well-being needs of our members and their families." From Amir's perspective, value delivery involved discerning when to amplify current offerings and when to launch your competencies in the direction of emerging needs. Value creation and delivery also involved the awareness that sometimes you have to fill a need first and discuss economics later.

Barbara Humpton, President and CEO of Siemens USA, shared that the company refreshed value delivery through the lens of core competencies supplementing value streams through creativity and urgent action. Siemens employs roughly 50,000 people in the United States and provides digitalization, electrification, and automation solutions.

From a core offerings perspective, Barbara said, "Early in the COVID-19 crisis, our focus at Siemens has been on addressing the country's immediate needs head-on. That included making sure people stay connected to vital services and keeping critical infrastructures like healthcare, power, and transportation up and running." Barbara also noted that her team proactively looked for ways to add value in emerging areas of need, "Whether it involved building a temporary hospital for COVID-19 patients or 3D printing face shields from a home basement, our employees took action. Sometimes they did this on a moment's notice, and they brought solutions to the table. Our people pinpointed needs in local communities and built networks outside of organizational silos and hierarchies to make a difference. It's shown how powerful, even in the most unpredictable of times, our ingenuity and creative problem-solving can be."

Barbara's comments are a crash course on value creation. First, maintain value delivery in your core areas of excellence. Second, "pinpoint" emerging needs toward which you can stretch your people and your solutions. Third, network people outside of organizational silos. Finally, unleash collaboration, ingenuity, and creative problem-solving.

FIND COLLABORATIVE VALUE

A key element in Barbara's value creation steps included building "networks outside of organizational silos." J. Scott Omelianuk, Editor-in-Chief at *Inc.* magazine, not only broke down silos, he helped his team move out of traditional roles and redesign offerings. *Inc.* is an online solutions provider dedicated exclusively to managers and owners growing private companies. *Inc.*'s total monthly audience reaches more than 25,000,000.

Scott shared a radical value-producing transformation involving elevated service levels and re-created work roles, "We serve the entrepreneurial and small business community in the United States. When the country locked down and our advertising dollars dried up, our audience needed us the most. Our value comes in helping our audience succeed, so we had to find ways to keep communicating with them and not just traditionally but in amplified ways. Our staff ramped up our communication. That meant our titles no longer applied. We weren't editors, photo editors, or video producers; instead, we were all supporters of small business in the United States. Overnight we transformed our website into a 24/7 news operation because our audience trusted us and needed news that could help them."

Scott noted that *Inc.* team members aggressively sought to add value through alliances outside of the company, "We created partnerships with people who were competitors because together we could provide information more readily. Our first big event of the year is South by Southwest, and when it canceled, we found ways to take our events business and re-create value through virtual offerings like a series called 'Real Talk,' which featured leaders and thought leaders like Mark Cuban and Seth Godin. We also gave back where we could, such as providing a million dollars of advertising to struggling small business owners."

Scott was similar to many other leaders who, out of necessity during the pandemic, redesigned, reinvented, and created new working relationships inside and outside their companies. They did so to both maintain value and increase the value for customers who needed them most. Often these partnerships served their customers while strengthening each collaborator.

Kathryn Pace, the Senior Human Resources Director at Kendra Scott, understands the rapid redesign of value streams and the shared value of partnerships. Fashion designer and philanthropist Kendra Scott founded and oversees the business that bears her name. Now valued at $1 billion-plus, Kendra Scott is known for fine jewelry, fashion jewelry, beauty products, and home accessories.

Since Kendra Scott's portfolio included retail stores that closed for a portion of the pandemic, leaders rapidly needed to transition to online sales. In the process of making that transition, leaders re-evaluated their business. According to Kathryn, "We'd been super-high growth for many years, but we were starting to hit a place in our maturity curve where things were taking longer, and bureaucracy was creeping in. We used the pandemic as a way to speed up value delivery and reengage an entrepreneurial perspective. That shift got us moving faster than we could have imagined. For example, we had online ordering and store pickup slated on a technology road map for about a year out. We were able to make that a reality in six weeks."

Despite the turmoil of closing stores and pivoting to online commerce, leaders at Kendra Scott didn't falter when it came to creating value in partnership with customers. According to Kathryn, "We have a philanthropic community–driven business model, so we quickly identified a product suite where 50 percent of the sales would go to Feeding America. We supplemented that shared giving by converting excess bandanas into face coverings. The sale of those items resulted in our customer community partnership contributing 2 million meals to Feeding America."

Kendra Scott was forced by health regulations to change its retail operation radically. Rather than resigning themselves to a narrow tactical response, leaders took a more entrepreneurial perspective on customer value. That perspective, in turn, refreshed organizational urgency and fostered rapid change. Through it all, their business maintained a partnership with its customer community to create impactful social value.

A Breath of Insight

True leaders will come out of the pandemic having reviewed "what they have always done" and replaced legacy habits with new learnings and a refreshed commitment to relevance, value, and growth.

—**Bobby Pang,** Founder and Chief Visionary, Ten Stars Network Inc. (South Korea)

THE VALUE OF BRINGING PEOPLE TOGETHER

Sterling Shea's response to a question about collaborative value creation cast a new light on the subject. Sterling is the Global Head of Wealth Management at *Barron's*, a leading financial investment newspaper, website, and magazine published by Dow Jones & Company. *Barron's* provides comprehensive research about US investments and finance.

From Sterling's perspective, business leaders like himself are collaborating more in the context of crisis value creation, while also facilitating collaboration. Sterling shared, "We are in the business of partnering with those we serve to help them with business solutions, so partnership outreach kicked into high gear during the pandemic. We also offer value by connecting people. While I've always been a connector, that behavior increased in response to COVID-19. For example, I talked to two asset managers individually and found that they'd benefit from a strategic discussion. I facilitated their meeting, and they developed a business relationship that will likely produce long-term benefits. I strive to be of value by first trying to solve problems, and if I can't bring a solution, I try to help by finding someone who can assist. There may not be a direct business benefit from helping people connect, but over time I receive value fivefold."

The lesson learned from Sterling is the importance of driving value by connecting people who can help one another. In keeping with that idea, I propose we modify an adage. The one I'm thinking of goes "It's not what you know; it's who you know." Why don't we extend it to "It's also what you know about who you know"? Okay, my version is a mind-bender, so here's the point. To add value as a connector, we need to learn what people in our network are wanting, needing, and achieving. Through that knowledge, we can create value by bringing people together.

TRUST RECIPROCAL VALUE

Bracken Darrell has an innate ability to produce value and a fundamental belief in the law of reciprocity. Bracken is the CEO at Logitech, a Swiss manufacturer of software and computer peripherals headquartered in both Lausanne, Switzerland, and Newark, California. In addition to the Logitech brand, the company also produces products with brands like ASTRO Gaming, Ultimate Ears, Jaybird, Blue Microphones, and Streamlabs.

When asked how he led value during the pandemic, Bracken noted, "I'm proud of what we do for a living. The experiences that we've brought to people, whether cameras, pointing devices, microphones, etc., have delivered such value during the pandemic. Our solutions enabled doctors to treat patients, teachers to educate students, and so much more. Our focus throughout the pandemic has been to get value to the people as quickly as possible. If hospitals reached out to me for a product, I shipped it to them. Often there were no invoices." "How can you make money that way?" I asked Bracken. He responded, "We have both humanity and reciprocity on our side. You just need to create value, and profits follow."

For Bracken, value delivery is an extension of trust. He operates on the premise that people are drawn to value creators and will support them over time. He focuses first on meeting a need, knowing that need fulfillment ultimately pays. Not every act of goodwill will result in a future customer purchase. However, you shouldn't provide value only when payment is guaranteed.

VALUE CREATION IS A LEADERSHIP MINDSET

Mark Miller, Chief Strategy Officer at Team One and coauthor of the book *Legacy in the Making*, summed up value creation by placing it in the context of a leadership mindset. His perspective encompasses much of the behavior exemplified throughout this chapter. Mark suggested that a value creation mindset involves "contribution preceding extraction." According to him, leaders with this perspective ask, "What meaningful difference can I achieve versus how much money can I make?" They also invite outsiders into their business. They don't build walls around their companies or industries. They open their doors a bit wider, knowing the collective "we" produce more value than the individual "me."

What meaningful difference can you achieve during challenging times? That's a question that can launch a competitive advantage over leaders who seek profit before customer value. It also sets the stage for our next chapter concerning compassionate leadership.

For now, I'll let the late sales trainer Zig Ziglar have the final word on what it means to be a value leader. Zig noted, "You can have everything in life you want, if you will just help other people get what they want."

RESILIENCE RECAP

➤ Value is the extent to which a good or service is perceived by its customer to meet his or her needs or wants.

➤ The six steps of value are (1) explore, (2) create, (3) market, (4) sell, (5) deliver, and (6) prosper through efficiency.

➤ According to Gilmore and Pine, during the most recent economic shift, customer value moved from service delivery to staged experiences.

➤ In the context of a crisis, Pine recommends refreshing the places where you deliver experiences, redesigning offerings, and renewing capabilities.

➤ All of Pine's recommendations should lead you to "stage" a robust, cohesive, personal, dramatic, and transformative experience.

➤ Four steps to consider in value creation are:

1. Maintain value delivery in your core areas of excellence.

2. Pinpoint emerging needs so you can stretch your people and solutions to meet them.

3. Network people outside of organizational silos.

4. Unleash collaboration, ingenuity, and creative problem-solving.

➤ In times of crisis, value creation is more likely to involve redesign, reinvention, and the creation of new working relationships inside and outside your company.

➤ Successful value-creating collaborations address customer needs and strengthen the contributors.

➤ Partnerships with customers can produce considerable social value and impact.

➤ Connecting people who can help one another is a value add.

➤ Leaders with a value creation mindset believe contribution precedes extraction and that the first question in value exchange should be, "What meaningful difference can I achieve?"

YOUR STRENGTH PLAN

1. What brands bring value to your life? How would you describe the value those brands or their products deliver?

2. What brands or products have you stopped using? How is it that their value no longer justifies the cost?

3. Think about the products and/or services you provide. Averaging across all your offerings, evaluate each component below. For example, do your products generally reflect an understanding of the wants and needs of your customers?

   • **Explore value:** Understand the wants and needs of your consumers.

   • **Create value:** Craft solutions to address your consumers' needs.

- **Market value:** Communicate the benefits of your solutions to your consumers.

- **Sell value:** Help consumers find sufficient value in your offering so they will provide something of value to you (e.g., make a purchase).

- **Deliver value:** Ensure your consumers receive the value you promised.

- **Prosper through value efficiency:** Deliver value economically so you can sustain and grow your ability to provide it.

4. In what ways have you refreshed (or should you refresh) the virtual or physical places where you deliver experiences?

5. Where have you redesigned (or can you redesign) your offerings to drive cohesive, personal, dramatic, and transformative experiences?

6. What processes do you have in place to pinpoint the emerging needs of each of your stakeholder groups (team members, customers, etc.)?

7. What have you or your organization done to break through silos? How effective have those efforts been? To the degree that they aren't entirely effective, what gets in the way of silo elimination?

8. In what ways do you partner with customers to create a broad social impact? What are the benefits to companies, customers, and social causes in these situations?

9. How might you create value by introducing some of your clients to one another? What do you know about those clients who suggest they might benefit from an introduction?

10. Think of each stakeholder group and possibly even segments within each group. For each group or segment, ask yourself, "What meaningful difference can I achieve on their behalf?"

CHAPTER 12

Convey Compassion

*Our human compassion binds us the one to
the other—not in pity or patronizingly, but as
human beings who have learnt how to turn our
common suffering into hope for the future.*
—NELSON MANDELA,
former president of South Africa

HOW WILL THIS TIME BE REMEMBERED?

Over our lifetimes, tragic and triumphant moments become seared into our memory. While we forget most of the details that occur on an average day, emotion-filled events are stored and readily recalled. Some refer to our most emotion-laden memories as "Where were you?" moments. If you lived in the United States for the past 60 years, those moments likely include:

- Assassinations of John F. Kennedy and Martin Luther King

- Neil Armstrong's first steps on the moon

- The terrorist attacks on 9/11/2001

I suspect for many leaders and the people they serve, the global pandemic will be more than a moment. It will be a "Where were you?" era.

So, what will you remember about the pandemic? Some of us will recall how technology was our lifeline. It's hard to imagine how we would have operated any business if this type of pandemic had occurred in the late 1970s without the benefits of the World Wide Web. Many of us undoubtedly will remember the value of cloud computing, online commerce, home delivery, and videoconferencing. But what else will we recall?

Universally, the people I interviewed indicated they hoped compassion would define the COVID-19 crisis and their leadership going forward. Before I get into a definition of compassion, and how compassion relates to empathy, let me provide a representative example of how contributors challenged themselves and others to be compassionate leaders during the pandemic.

This example comes from John Timmerman, PhD, a leader I've worked with for more than a decade, starting when he was the Vice President of Quality and Program Management at The Ritz-Carlton Hotel Company. Knowing that John had conveyed a compassionate leadership message to his team, I expressly asked him to forward that message so I could use it here.

John is currently the Vice President of Operations at Mercy Hospital Saint Louis, a US health system that serves millions of patients across 900 physician practices and outpatient facilities, and more than 40 specialty hospitals. In his letter, John looked at leadership priorities for the crisis, "Things like managing supplies, margins, and policy are all very important, but they didn't make it to the top of my list. Compassion strongly resonated with me, to do the right things and, more importantly, do them in the right way." Reflecting on the Survival, Evasion, Resistance, and Escape (SERE) training he received as a Force Recon Marine, John added, "Prior to that POW training, I would have thought less of people that broke under pressure and didn't have a John Wayne persona. A lot of people will experience some type of a breaking point during this pandemic, and the teams with compassionate leadership will get through it together."

Concerning the specific challenges of healthcare, John noted, "Compassionate leadership is both encouraging people to show up each day on the front line while preserving the dignity of others that struggle with serving on the front line." John concluded his letter with self-reflection and a challenge that sets the stage for the pages ahead.

John shared:

> I've always felt like an effective leader but frankly not a compassionate one in the way we need it now. I'm committed to doing better and asking myself every day what I did to break away from a comfortable routine because things are not comfortable for many people. Did I challenge myself and others to give more than they thought possible because others are finding themselves

in an impossible situation? Am I pausing to get a pulse on how someone is feeling, seizing every opportunity to recognize people for going the extra mile and encouraging those that don't feel they can run another mile? This pandemic is causing a lot of suffering and hopeful it will change us all for the better.

Each of John's questions warrants consideration so that we can all change for the better. To make progress on those improvements, let's explore compassion and compassionate behavior in relation to empathy.

EMPATHIC LISTENING PLUS COMPASSIONATE ACTION

In Chapter 6, we discussed empathy and listening to the feelings of those we serve. While some people use the word *compassion* as a synonym for *empathy*, the words communicate subtle yet significant differences. I'll lay out those differences as strikingly as possible. As mentioned in Chapter 6, empathy involves relating to the feelings of another person. By contrast, compassion reflects an emotional connection specifically to another person's "pain or suffering" *and* a desire to act (or actually take action) to alleviate that pain.

Let's use a couple of examples to highlight these differences. I can empathize with you when you celebrate a personal victory, but I can't show compassion since you aren't suffering. Similarly, if someone falls in front of me, I can experience empathy but continue walking. To show compassion, I'd need to stop and offer help. One last quick distinction (and it's implied in the excerpt of John's letter), compassion shouldn't be confused with sympathy. Sympathy is the acknowledgment of another person's sorrow. Compassion is seeking to alleviate the underlying pain or suffering. In a business context, I think of sympathy as being courteous and compassion as being actively involved in the emotional well-being of those you serve.

"RADAR ON AND ANTENNA UP"

In 2007, I took note of a phrase used by a Ritz-Carlton Leadership Training Center leader. She advised, "When you serve others—customers or team members—always have your radar on and antenna up." In the context of compassion, I interpreted that to mean—be vigilant to the pain and suffer-ing that may be on the horizon. By my interpretation, Dr. WandaJean Jones is a practitioner of vigilance and a compassionate leader. WandaJean is a Global Learning Administrator at GE Healthcare. With 50,000 employees globally, GE Healthcare innovates digital solutions and medical technol-ogy to enable rapid and informed clinical decision-making.

WandaJean reflected on the very early days of the pandemic noting, "Uncertainty was affecting people in obvious and less than obvious ways. One subtle, almost unspoken manifestation of fear was the need to prove you were relevant. It was as if team members feared layoffs and felt like they had to do everything possible to create job security, even if it meant depleting all their emotional and physical resources in the process. Inad-vertently, this underlying fear could cause employees, teams, or leaders to subtly compete with one another to show their jobs or departments were essential. To get ahead of this, I made it clear that I cared more for each in-dividual's well-being than I did for unrealistic performance. I also watched out for those individuals on my team who needed help disconnecting from work. I tracked when my people connected to our network. If someone worked until one o'clock in the morning and then logged back on for a seven o'clock meeting, I'd reach out to talk to them about what was driving them to sit at their computer for 16 hours straight. Together we found ways to ensure they didn't burn out."

WandaJean had her radar on and picked up a shift in team member behavior. Rather than ignoring that behavior and reaping short-term pro-ductivity benefits for her department, she looked for ways to help em-ployees find a healthy balance. Her ability to sense pain and take action to alleviate it, by its very definition, is compassionate leadership.

Keith Grossman, President of *TIME*, and the company's Editor-in-Chief and CEO Edward Felsenthal, credit their ability to navigate the early phase of the pandemic with anticipating team member needs and taking proactive measures. *TIME* is a media organization with an estimated reach of nearly 100 million people globally. The company's website, magazine, and social feeds cover topics such as politics, science, health, technology, and entertainment.

According to both Keith and Edward, "We publicly announced a 90-day no-layoff policy at the end of March to address the safety, stability, and security needs of our team. We knew we couldn't evolve unless we removed uncertainties about employment. Once that fear and anxiety were off the table, we could lean in and address other practical and emotional needs around us. As we looked around, we saw the frustration of parents and educators. Their worlds had turned upside down, and they were looking for age-appropriate content to help children. We took action and modified a print-only product, launching *TIME for Kids* online. Our team did amazing work to share that content in all 50 states and global markets. We've also steadily made *TIME for Kids* available in more and more languages. In the process, we have grown a network and community of parents, educators, and children." When your "radar is on, and your antennas are up," you can anticipate emotional pain, anxiety, and uncertainty. When you act on signals early, before they surge, you can tamp down anxiety, avert emotional distraction, and refocus your team to innovate solutions for customer needs. The art of leadership is finding the compassion and balance needed to address the pain of all stakeholders.

A Breath of Insight

Humanity matters most. Leaders need to show empathy more than ever and put themselves into the shoes of their teammates. What I've witnessed is that in times like these we come together, cast aside personal and professional agendas, and focus on what's most important— taking care of ourselves, our loved ones, and taking the time to help others. Each day the sun comes up is a day closer to us having this awful situation behind us. It will come and when it does we'll all be a little stronger and also more appreciative of all that we have.

—Geoff Cottrill, SVP—Strategic Marketing, The Coca-Cola Company

---

BALANCING CUSTOMER AND TEAM MEMBER COMPASSION

The scale and importance of customer needs at Matt Renner's organization require intense focus. Matt is the President of Enterprise Commercial at Microsoft, a multinational technology company that creates, builds, licenses, sells, and services computer hardware, software, and related services. Microsoft is one of the most highly valued publicly traded companies in the world.

Matt and his team support the technology infrastructure for telemedicine, collaboration tools for those working on a vaccine, and the needs of major clients who assure public safety, transportation, communication, and other critical elements of daily life. Given Microsoft's integral role in support of these clients, Matt and his team prioritized the rapid resolution of customer pain points. Matt believes his team must treat clients with empathy, compassion, and urgency. He also noted that throughout the pandemic, "Microsoft needed to be a company that showed up prepared. We also needed to show our competence and compassion by being consistent, responsive, and reliable."

To make those critical customer experiences possible, Microsoft leaders like Matt also had to convey compassion for the emotional needs and pressures experienced by their employees. According to Matt, "Our inbound customer calls jumped roughly three times that of prepandemic levels. When you mix that high demand with a host of other concerns like health risks and work from home adjustments, we had to find ways to help our employees close their laptops, get away from their screens, and take some time for themselves. We needed to show employees that Microsoft would still be here for them." By providing work flexibility tools and having discussions with team members, leaders at Microsoft navigated the challenges of critical customer needs and the emotional capacity of their team.

To this point in the chapter, leaders like WandaJean and Matt have highlighted compassionate acts directed toward helping team members reduce or take breaks. This is reminiscent of insights shared in Chapter 2. However, in that chapter, the target of the recommended action was you—the leader. You were encouraged to challenge the notion that self-care is selfish, to create self-care rituals, and to resist the urge to lose yourself in the importance of your work. Some psychologists and wellness professionals refer to self-care as self-compassion. The more leaders learn to spot and take care of their fears, anxiety, and work-life imbalances, the better equipped they are to help others. Moreover, the more your people see you logged in at all hours of the day and night, the more they think that is what you expect from them. Sometimes the first act of compassion needs to be directed inward so you can sustain your efforts to convey compassion toward your stakeholders.

MORE THAN ONE PATH TO COMPASSION

Thus far, most of the examples of compassionate behavior involve a leader doing something for another person or a group of people. WandaJean at GE Healthcare watched for, reached out to, and problem-solved with team members who were working excessively. Edward and Keith at *TIME* took action by guaranteeing 90 days of no furloughs.

Since leaders tend to be doers, it's important to mention that compassion doesn't always require a leader to fix a problem. For example, sometimes, a problem simply can't be fixed. In those cases, often the most compassionate thing you can do is sit quietly with someone in their time of need. Other times, it might be more compassionate to encourage someone to take action to fix a problem for themselves, rather than jumping in to fix it for them. Chris Recinos, CEO of the Nurse Leader Network and Chief Nurse Executive for a healthcare system in Los Angeles, described an experience that has elements of both the "being with" and "encourage others" approaches to compassion.

Chris shared, "Many of my nurses lacked experience caring for a patient that faced death alone. Before COVID-19, family members would usually be in the room at the time of a patient's death. It is a humbling responsibility and honor to stand in for family members or to help them connect remotely. I had a nurse who was using an iPad, so a patient's family could see their loved one take their final breaths. The nurse was crying and shaking so hard she could barely hold the iPad. As a leader, I wanted to run in and protect my staff member, but the best thing I could do was to be there for that nurse when she needed to grieve. I could also help her develop resiliency. I brought in therapists, chaplains, and similar resources so our team could learn how to best work through their suffering."

In Chris's example, her team member demonstrated compassion by taking direct action so the patient wouldn't die alone. When nurses needed to grieve, leaders like Chris conveyed compassion by sitting with them, even in the absence of words. When nurses needed to internalize a coping response, leaders helped them find ways to drive resilience.

Throughout the pandemic, Steven J. Anderson similarly focused on helping members of his organization access the tools they needed to cope with their emotional challenges. Steve is the Founder of the Crown Council and Total Patient Institute, an organization that helps raise the standards of dental care and service in the United States. Steve noted, "We needed to get tools in the hands of our members so they could take care of their emotions first. Our dentists' practices came to a screeching halt almost overnight in much of the country as health regulations dictated.

"We had to give them useful and memorable tools to help them address the things they could control and help them manage the maze of different regulatory bodies weighing in or not weighing in about the practice of dentistry. Where we could, we developed new competencies like securing PPE for our members, but the bulk of our work involved giving our members the tools they needed to manage their own challenges. It seemed like the most helpful and compassionate thing we could do." Helping others find ways to manage their emotional distress builds efficacy and resiliency. Both of those aptitudes are likely to have greater lasting value than most direct acts of assistance.

POWERFUL TOOL TO BE USED WISELY

David Hudson, Commissioner and National Commander of The Salvation Army, shared his insights on instilling an often overlooked yet powerfully compassionate resource. With more than 1.5 million members across 130-plus countries, the Salvation Army has provided services like disaster relief, homeless shelters, and job relief since 1865.

David noted, "The most compassionate thing we can do as leaders is to offer hope. In times like these, hope can be hard to come by, so I help people on the front line see how we are making a difference—so they will continue to help us create a better tomorrow. Some time ago, I read that a man can live about 40 days without food. He can live about three days without water and about eight minutes without air. But he can't live one second without hope. I suspect that is an oversimplification, but hope is an intangible that leaders must be able to convey. Our teams and communities at large look to leaders who can offer a realistic sense of hope. We've provided emotional and spiritual care to more than 780,000 people since the start of this pandemic. Some people reached out just because they needed someone to talk to and to help them see a possibility where tomorrow could be better than today. I am working to be a compassionate beacon of hope to our front line, my team, and all I serve."

I am struck by how David frames hope for his team. He offers it as an act of compassion anchored to the impact they had today. For him, hope is the possibility that the next moment, hour, or year can be better through collective faith and effort. Maybe that is why Napoleon Bonaparte said, "A leader is a dealer in hope."

There are many ways to demonstrate care and compassion for those we serve, including doing things for them, helping them do things for themselves, being with them, and nurturing hope. In keeping with lessons from previous chapters on the importance of telling the truth and being honest, all acts of compassions must be genuine. They will miss the mark when founded on false promises, fantasy, or intentions that lack follow-through.

I am convinced leaders are becoming stronger and more compassionate through adversity.

RESILIENCE RECAP

➤ Emotion-filled events are more likely to be remembered when compared to routine activities.

➤ Compassion reflects an emotional connection to another person's "pain or suffering" *and* a desire to act to alleviate that pain.

➤ Sympathy is the acknowledgment of another person's sorrow.

➤ When you serve others—customers or team members—always have your "radar on and antenna up." In other words, be vigilant to pain and suffering that may be on the horizon.

➤ When your "radar is on, and your antenna is up," you can anticipate emotional pain, anxiety, and uncertainty. If you act on signals early, before they begin to surge, you can tamp down anxiety, avert emotional distraction, and refocus team members to innovate solutions to meet customer needs.

➤ The art of leadership is finding a way to resolve the pain of all stakeholders compassionately.

➤ Compassion doesn't always require a leader to fix a problem.

➤ In addition to taking direct action for someone, alternative forms of compassionate behavior can include being with someone, helping others fix a problem for themselves, or inspiring hope.

➤ All caring actions should reflect authenticity, truth, and the true spirit of compassion.

➤ Be a purveyor of realistic hope!

YOUR STRENGTH PLAN

1. List five "Where were you?" moments. What do you remember about each one? What feelings do you associate with each event?

2. In the distant future, when you look back on the pandemic, what do you think will stand out in your memory? What feelings do you think you will associate with the pandemic era?

3. Think of a situation where you have been empathic but not compassionate. How did you relate to another person's emotion without feeling a desire to take action?

4. How do you stay vigilant (antenna up/radar on) about the emotional needs of those you serve? When have you accurately gauged underlying emotional issues?

5. What is your preferred way to demonstrate compassion (do for, enable others to do for themselves, be with, offer hope)? What is your least utilized? When would an approach, other than your preferred option, be the most useful?

6. What is the difference between instilling constructive hope and dealing in false hope?

7. Have you seen an increase in compassionate leadership? Has your level of compassion changed? If so, in what ways?

CHAPTER 13

Shift Front,
Middle, Back

*The art of life lies in a constant
readjustment to our surroundings.*
—Okakura Kakuzo,
Japanese author and scholar

WHAT'S YOUR POSITION?

In nature, animals shift leadership roles and the position of the leader depending upon the circumstances they face.

In her book, *Leadership Beyond Measure*, speaker and Horse Assisted Educator Jude Jennison writes about the leadership behavior of horse herds, "The alpha mare is the most dominant . . . if dogs are close by, she will set off at a gallop. If they are further away, she will set off at a walk . . . the majority of the horses in a herd lead from the side, and this is the least dominant position you can take."

Jude further observes that the alpha stallion leads from the rear, and his primary role "is to exert pressure from behind to move forward. The alpha stallion works closely with the alpha mare to ensure the team follows her lead and moves forward in the direction and pace set by her."

Each leader in a horse herd is a specialist. The alpha mare offers direction and pace. The alpha stallion drives momentum, and leaders in the middle of the heard foster team cohesion. By contrast, business leaders are generalists. We must guide our teams by providing direction, setting the pace, fueling momentum, and building teamwork. As generalists, our effectiveness depends upon the position we take relative to our teams and how we shift positions to match business conditions.

In this chapter, you will see what it means to lead from the front, the middle, or the back of a team. Leaders will also share how the pandemic required different positioning approaches. In some situations, these leaders moved up front to set direction and pace. At other times, they moved to the middle to serve alongside their teams or shifted to the back in supportive and encouraging roles.

The model provided in this chapter is consistent with the adage, "There is a time and place for everything." In crisis or calm, leaders need to be aware of how circumstances shape whether they should be leading from the front, middle, or back.

LOOK AND MOVE FORWARD

Let's assume your task is to help a group get from point A to point B. Let's also assume, no one in your group has ever made this journey before and you don't have a compass or a map, but there is an elevated platform that helps you see the possible paths you could choose. That scenario is an apt description of leading during a global pandemic or other uncertain times.

When faced with challenges resulting from the global COVID-19 pandemic, leaders like Bradley H. Feldmann, Chairman, President, and CEO of Cubic Corporation, stepped up on their platforms, assessed options, communicated widely, and led from the front. Cubic is a market-leading provider of innovative, mission-critical solutions that increase operational effectiveness and readiness by enabling superior situational understanding for transportation and defense customers all over the world.

Having consulted for Brad (a US Air Force Academy graduate) before and during COVID-19, I watched him establish a lookout position (in keeping with officer training) at the front of his organization. Brad noted, "I needed to be visible and lead from the front, especially early on or when there was an adjustment in our course. This has been an unprecedented time of uncertainty and rapid change that has touched all parts of the globe. People were—and still are—looking for clear and action-oriented leadership. They wanted the ability to see your face and have the opportunity to ask hard questions—to express their fears and concerns. Dealing with the unknown and constant changing dynamics of COVID-19 meant we had to be agile, flexible, and responsive. I was broadcasting virtual town hall meetings every other week to thousands of our team members around the world and across time zones; I supplemented that with regularly scheduled and ad hoc written communication. My goal was to share what changes my team and I were seeing in the midst of the pandemic and what we, as an enterprise, were doing to respond to these changes while prioritizing the safety and security of our people. In those town halls, my leadership team and I sought to deliver clear communication on a few mission-essential items or policy decisions and made sure to dedicate time to answering any and all questions from our team members."

Since circumstances and regulations varied widely across the many countries where Cubic team members worked, Brad's highly visible leadership approach required a considerable investment of time. The virtual biweekly town halls were open to all employees and held in two sessions to accommodate global time zones. Where able, Brad and other key leaders made an effort to visit site-essential personnel in person. For example, the Vice President of Cubic Global Manufacturing & Procurement spent an entire afternoon hosting eight separate sessions at a single manufacturing plant in Mexico so team members could take turns safely assembling in the plant's cafeteria.

While many other leaders also increased their visibility during the pandemic, Brad stepped forward in an unusual and self-impacting way. Brad noted, "We attacked this with fiscal responsibility so we could continue to invest in the future. We didn't want to reduce staff salaries or make sweeping layoffs. We were looking for a more human option that considered our Cubic family members' sense of security during this uncertain time. We elected to freeze retirement and pension contributions for the remainder of the year and froze wages for the following year. So leadership could help personally absorb some of the financial impact, I asked the board to cut my salary and to reduce their compensation as well. They agreed."

It's one thing to increase visibility through virtual meetings and quite another to do eight separate live meetings for a single operating unit. Effectively leading from the front requires more than motivational speeches, internal communication campaigns, or arranged photo opportunities.

Leaders must be willing to do what it takes to clear the way and create stability in a time of unknowable change. They must communicate a vision and strategy that promotes their team's best interest. When they effectively lead from the front, people follow. By choosing to protect staff salaries while reducing their compensation, Brad and the Cubic Board of Directors showed team members they could be trusted to prioritize team welfare while stewarding Cubic on its mission-critical journey.

MEETING IN THE MIDDLE

Let's go back to the scenario I posed earlier in the chapter, the one where you are leading a group from one location to another. Let's assume you've been leading from the front, and the group is progressing swiftly on a well-defined path. Let's also assume there is restlessness and possible division within the group. In that situation, you should consider placing yourself in the middle of your team. That repositioning will enable you to coach, assist, or otherwise contribute to team unity.

Lawrence Weathers, Chief of Police for Lexington, Kentucky, is an excellent example of leading from the middle. Lawrence shared, "It is vital for a leader, especially in this field, to be physically present alongside his or her officers. I owe that to my people. So, I came into the department on all my scheduled days throughout the pandemic. Some days it was just me and a Staff Commander in the building. In addition to being with my team, I also needed to communicate support for those working from home. I didn't want our department divided by where people chose to work. I was impressed with my officers for staying together and not complaining or passing judgment when people chose to stay home. If anything, our department took care of one another in inspiring ways, including volunteering to switch shifts as needed."

When individuals like Lawrence lead from the middle, they erase the gap between titled leaders and frontline staff. Leading from the middle also models servant leadership. It sets a behavioral standard for community behavior—Lawrence's acceptance of differing work choices mitigated potential team division and fostered team support. When you lead from the middle, you are essentially saying, "I am one of you," *not* "I am better than you."

Angus Jameson MD, MPH, Medical Director Pinellas County, Florida's Emergency Medical Services, demonstrates how leading from the middle establishes credibility, trust, and cohesion. Angus noted, "I was talking about a COVID-19 field protocol during a live online update when a medic posted a comment that said, 'Easy for him to say from behind his desk.' Within seconds several other medics jumped into the message stream with responses like, 'You must be kidding, he is working in the hospital seeing patients and on the scene with us regularly.' Nothing I could have said in my defense would have sounded credible. That spontaneous support established my credibility."

While Angus suggests that his credibility came from the support of others, I believe the support of others came from his credibility. Angus added, "People who are willing to take additional risks to serve others don't want to be led by people who aren't willing to take those same risks. In other words, people want to know that you will do what you ask them to do. The easiest way to prove that is to stop talking about what they need to do and start doing it with them."

Credibility and trust don't occur by accident. People believe leaders who produce results, fulfill promises, and lead from the middle. In times of crisis, when fear and mistrust prevail, people look to leaders for coaching, mentorship, and a willingness to serve alongside them.

Years ago, then CEO of Starbucks Howard Schultz told me, "Leaders have a responsibility to make regular deposits in their team's reservoir of trust." He shared that with me as he was heading to work alongside Starbucks partners doing a community service project. Leading from the middle is one of the most robust ways to make deposits in your team's reservoir of trust. Often leadership can seem complicated, if not impossible. Other times it is as simple as an insight shared by ancient Chinese philosopher and author Lao Tzu: "To lead people, walk beside them."

GETTING AHEAD BY MOVING BACK

Let's make one last twist on the scenario presented previously. This time let's assume the group is on the right path, moving at a brisk pace, and working effectively as a team. At this point in the journey, where is the best place for you to be?

As teams advanced successfully during the pandemic, leaders often told me they intentionally stepped back. By moving to the back, these leaders encouraged the groups' autonomy, supported their momentum, and celebrated their victories. Robert Greenleaf, founder of the servant leadership philosophy, put it this way, "The best test as a leader is: Do those served grow as persons; do they become healthier, wiser, freer, more autonomous, more likely themselves to become leaders?"

Ann Ayers JD, Dean of Colorado Women's College at the University of Denver, learned the value of leading from the back when she was a child. Ann noted, "I grew up in the mountains hiking with my father. When we'd set off for a hike, he encouraged me to go ahead of him. I didn't like being in front, and it didn't make sense to me. He was taller, more experienced, and could follow the trail better. One morning we started hiking before daylight, and he wore a headlamp. As he walked behind me, he shined the light on our path."

Ann explained how that experience shaped her leadership, "My job is to hire people who have talent and put them in positions where they can grow. To be effective, I need to stand behind them, shine a light so they can see their path, and help them work around obstacles. During the pandemic, I had to adjust the beam of my metaphoric headlamp based on my team's stress level. Some days it needed to shine just a few steps ahead of them, and on other days I needed to point it toward a bright horizon."

As evidenced by Ann's headlamp metaphor, leading from the back is not a passive activity. It shouldn't be confused with abdicating responsibility or delegating projects and failing to assure accountability. If anything, leading from the back requires a leader to continue to shine the light on the optimal destination, help team members sustain momentum, and foster growth opportunities as the team ventures forward.

Leading from the back means your team will arrive at the destination before you. As such, the accomplishment is not "yours." It is "ours." By stepping back to a supportive and encouraging position, you can best see leadership talent emerge and give space for others to wrestle with problems and craft their solutions. All those benefits occur as you continue to nudge, prod, and keep your light shining on the destination. The ultimate success for leading from the back is how it ignites collective wisdom and shared decision-making. Put simply by leadership guru Ken Blanchard, "None of us are as smart as all of us."

YOUR FEET

So far, I've only spotlighted leaders in either the front, middle, or back of their teams. In reality, all leaders featured in this chapter have expertly made positional shifts based on the situational needs of their organizations. For the sake of illustration, we will explore how Marcia Harnden moved fluidly from the front, middle, and back leadership positions.

Marcia was selected Chief of Police for the City of Albany, Oregon, shortly before COVID-19 gained momentum. Since she had transferred from another city, Marcia had to establish herself as a leader in Albany. Accordingly, she led from the front by being visible, sharing her vision, aligning critical messages with other public safety leaders like the Fire Chief, and communicating consistently. Marcia also had to develop strategies that maintained public safety and reduced the risk of COVID-19 for her team and the jail population.

Marcia led from the middle by connecting with and serving alongside her team. She noted, "I've started work at 9:30 in the morning and went home at 10 in the evening so that I could do ride alongs with every shift." Marcia also led from behind by supporting and serving her team members, "I'm a strong subscriber to servant leadership. I exist to serve our people. Leadership is not about me; it's about them. I distributed decision-making, encouraged new ideas, and celebrated accomplishments. For example, a senior staff member came up with the idea of cooking breakfast and doing barbecues for the night shift. It was an honor to take part in those meals. I did so not as a leadership checkbox, but because it allowed me to be of service to the officers I am privileged to lead."

Marcia's example demonstrates how quickly leaders can and must shift their position. For instance, I can imagine Marcia presenting her organizational vision at 10 a.m. (leading from the front), conducting ride alongs at 4 p.m. (leading from the middle), and preparing a barbecue for the night shift at 10 p.m. (leading from the back).

Leadership positioning is a useful construct to ensure you are moving to the needs of those you serve rather than staying in your comfort zone. For example, if you thrive in the background, it can be challenging to lead from the front when you need to share a compelling vision. The art of leadership positioning is to accurately assess whether you should be in the front, middle, or back and shift with dexterity and fluidity, as circumstances require.

A DIFFERENT TYPE OF FLUIDITY

We've looked at how leaders shift their leadership positions (front, middle, back) within a given role, but for some leaders, that shift must occur from one leadership setting to the next. Suzy Whaley is the Professional Golfers' Association (PGA) Director of Instruction for the Country Club at Mirasol in Palm Beach Gardens, Florida. She is also the first woman elected to serve as an officer of the PGA of America and holds the title of PGA President.

To be effective in each role, Suzy has to shift her leadership position nimbly. Suzy noted, "In my role as PGA President, I'm happy to be out front communicating a vision for a reset to our business model. That includes advances in areas like inclusion, technology, and virtual options that will allow us to connect more directly to consumers. Regarding efforts to navigate the pandemic, I've been fortunate to work with others to identify strategies and approaches to help address the needs of 29,000 members and 15,000 courses across the US."

Suzy's role as PGA President shines a spotlight on her, demands a well-articulated vision, and pulls for leadership from the front. Conversely, her role as the director of instruction at a PGA club pulls for leadership from the middle. Suzy noted, "In my director role, I am a member of the organization for which I am President. I am a leader, and I am also an employee. I don't need to be out front in that capacity. I need to work alongside my team. So, I do. I put on my face mask to serve team members and the wonderful people who want to improve and enjoy the game of golf."

Whether you are functioning in a single role or jumping across roles, leadership is about adapting to help pull, partner with, or push the team from an appropriate position. As you practice situational awareness and shift your leadership in the context of this paradigm, you might consider the wisdom of Nelson Mandela, "It is better to lead from behind and to put others in front, especially when you celebrate victory when nice things occur. You take the front line when there is danger. Then people will appreciate your leadership."

RESILIENCE RECAP

➤ In a horse herd, the alpha mare is the most dominant. That mare is responsible for direction and pace. The alpha stallion leads from behind, ensures the team follows the lead of the alpha mare, and moves forward in the direction and pace she sets.

➤ Most of the behavior of a herd is shaped by horses that lead from the side.

➤ Unlike the naturally occurring leadership of horse herds, the effectiveness of human leaders depends upon where we position ourselves with our teams, and how we shift positions to match business conditions.

➤ Leading from the front involves stepping on your leadership platform, assessing options, and communicating a vision or strategy that promotes your team's best interest.

➤ Leading from the middle will enable you to coach, assist, or otherwise contribute to team unity.

➤ When you lead from the middle, you erase the gap between you and frontline team members. You also model servant leadership and set a behavioral standard for community behavior.

➤ Leading from the middle is one of the most robust ways to make deposits in your team's reservoir of trust.

➤ By moving to the back, you encourage your team's autonomy, support their momentum, and celebrate their victories.

➤ Leadership involves selecting talented people and putting them in positions that help them develop their talent. It also requires a willingness to stand behind those people, shining a light on their path and helping them work around obstacles.

➤ By leading from the back, you support and encourage your team, see leadership talent emerge, and give space for others to wrestle with problems and craft their solutions.

➤ The ultimate success for leading from the back is how it ignites collective wisdom and shared decision-making.

➤ Leadership positioning is a useful construct to make sure you are moving toward the needs of those you serve rather than staying in a comfort zone.

➤ Whether you are functioning in a single role or moving across roles, leadership is about shifting your position (front, center, or back) to meet the needs of the moment.

YOUR STRENGTH PLAN

1. What does the adage "There is a time and place for everything" mean to you? How does it relate to the situations you encounter in leadership?

2. Think of a time you effectively led from the front. What did you do? What was it about the situation that warranted that positioning?

3. On a scale from 1–10 (with 1 being extremely ineffective and 10 being extremely effective), how would you rate your ability to lead from the front? What was the basis for your rating? How might you further develop your skills in this area?

4. Think of a time you effectively led from the middle. What did you do? What was it about the situation that warranted that positioning?

5. On a scale from 1–10 (with 1 being extremely ineffective and 10 being extremely effective), how would you rate your ability to lead from the middle? What was the basis for this rating? How can you further develop your skills in this area?

6. Think of a time you effectively led from the back. What did you do? What was it about the situation that caused you to lead from this position?

7. On a scale from 1–10 (with 1 being extremely ineffective and 10 being extremely effective), how would you rate your ability to lead from the back? Why did you give yourself this rating? How can you improve your skills in this area?

8. Rank order (1, 2, 3) your comfort level for leading from the:

   _____ Front

   _____ Middle

   _____ Back

9. In your role, please segment the circle below, indicating the *optimal* amount of time you need in each position. For example, if the optimal division is 33 percent for the front, middle, and back, you would divide the circle into thirds and write "front," "middle," or "back" in each segment.

10. Repeat the activity from the previous question, but this time consider how much time you *actually* spend in each position.

11. Compare the circles. Reflect on your rationale for each segmentation activity and think about how you can bring the actual division in line with the optimal.

PART IV

HARNESS CHANGE

It's not enough to be busy, so are the ants.
The question is, what are we busy about?
—HENRY DAVID THOREAU,
essayist, poet, and philosopher

The next four chapters explore how to maximize operational effectiveness in times of continual change by:

- Ranking and simplifying
- Taking swift action
- Being decisive
- Increasing team functionality

CHAPTER 14

Streamline Productivity

Great leaders are almost always great simplifiers,
who can cut through argument, debate, and doubt to
offer a solution everybody can understand.
—COLIN POWELL,
retired four-star general and
US security advisor

BUSY DOES NOT MEAN PRODUCTIVE

You know that kind of day—the one where you race around frantically, running from meeting to phone call to email. As you look back on what you accomplished, there's little to show for your efforts. You were busy, mind-numbingly busy. Yet, you were unproductive, confoundingly unproductive.

For many leaders and frontline staff, the demands of the pandemic produced runaway busyness at the expense of demonstrable productivity. Leaders were checking in more and communicating at an increased cadence. Team members were balancing the demands of work with the needs of virtual education for their children. Everyone waded through an onslaught of news stories about the virus. Crisis response meetings supplemented regularly scheduled team huddles. People were developing or receiving training on topics like how to work from home or operational changes required in response to rapidly changing government health guidelines. How could anyone filter the necessary from the clutter?

The leaders featured in this chapter share how they maximized performance amid a backdrop of uncertainty and disruption.

They offer insights on setting priorities, emphasizing optimal outcomes, removing barriers, and placing limits on nonprioritized activity.

Since this is a chapter about productivity, let me take a moment to make sure we have a shared understanding of the concept. Productivity is a combination of efficiency and effectiveness. Efficiency reflects a company's outputs (goods and services) over their inputs (human and material resources). The higher the outputs relative to inputs, the greater the efficiency of a business. Effectiveness, by contrast, is an external measure of meeting stakeholder needs. A manufacturer could run a very efficient operation (high volume output with low costs for production) and achieve minimal effectiveness (the items produced don't satisfy the needs of the consumer). The reverse can also be true. The manufacturer could effectively meet customer demands but be inefficient. Management consultant Peter Drucker noted, "Efficiency is doing things right; effectiveness is doing the right things." Since productivity combines efficiency and effectiveness, I've modified Drucker's perspective to read, *productivity is both doing things right and doing the right things*. Let's look at leadership lessons offered to help you streamline productivity.

CRISIS AS AN OPPORTUNITY
FOR INCREASED PRODUCTIVITY

Prolonged crises can wreak havoc on productivity. About four months into the pandemic, the Institute of Corporate Productivity conducted a survey that found a substantial impact on efficiency and effectiveness reported by 96 percent of the 518 respondents (global, multinational, and US-based human resource leaders of variable-sized companies). Forty-one percent assessed that impact to be in the "high" to "very high" range.

During the pandemic, many leaders sought to limit the crisis's adverse impact on productivity. Joe Duran set out to have the pandemic *increase* his company's output. Joe is the CEO and Founder of Goldman Sachs Personal Financial Management, a US wealth management firm with more than 100 offices and 240 financial advisors located across 30 states. Joe explained, "If you are a strong company, a crisis can drive constructive change by accelerating movement into areas of opportunity. In a crisis, there is less resistance to innovation. As the pandemic unsettled my team,

I focused on resettling us in the direction of growth. I know that most people don't share my view. However, being raised in a violent home in war-ravaged Zimbabwe, I'm very comfortable running into chaos and driving productivity by focusing on three C's—communication, care, and clarity. Specific to clarity, your people need to know your priorities and how they can innovate to address them productively."

To turn disruption into productive change, leaders need to channel the emotional energy of the crisis (fear, uncertainty, discomfort) toward critical objectives. In the absence of clear priorities, team members can expend energy aimlessly. By setting clear, prioritized targets, your teams can plan and use their resources wisely. Let's imagine your prime objective was to have a tree cut down in the next five minutes. If given that clear priority, Abraham Lincoln said he would use his time and effort by spending "the first three minutes sharpening the axe." For teams to engage in effective planning and productive action, they need a manageable list of priorities.

RESTORING ORDER IN CHAOS

All crises have three common elements—surprise, threat, and minimal time to respond to the threat. Some crises are acute like a tornado, and others are protracted like a pandemic. By definition, crises provoke chaos (disorder and confusion). That disorder, as stated by Joe Duran, has the potential for both harmful and beneficial impact on your business. In their book *Effective Crisis Communication*, Robert Ulmer and Timothy Sellnow define crises in the context of potential organizational impact:

> An organizational crisis is a specific, unexpected, and non-routine event or series of events that create high levels of uncertainty and simultaneously present an organization both opportunities for and threats to its high-priority goals.

Since high-priority goals are both vulnerable to threats and ripe for opportunities in a crisis, Cathy Lanning emphasized her company's priorities. Cathy is the Senior Vice President for Property and Casualty Marketing at Nationwide, a Fortune 100 company founded in 1926. Nationwide is one of the largest insurance and financial services companies globally.

Cathy shared, "We stayed committed to delivering solutions designed for simplicity and ease of use. As opportunities emerged, we quickly envisioned permanent consumer shifts and pivoted to meet those new needs. Going into the pandemic, Nationwide had invested well in tools to help make things easier and less complicated internally and for our agents and consumers. During the crisis, we accelerated the development of digital tools and capabilities, which enabled us to provide more seamless and frictionless experiences."

Cathy's emphasis on simple design is congruent with a priority the late Steve Jobs maintained at Apple. Steve Jobs once noted, "That's been one of my mantras—focus and simplicity. Simple can be harder than complex; you have to work hard to get your thinking clean to make it simple. But you can move mountains." From my perspective, you can also streamline productivity.

During the pandemic, Ashok Kartham, the CEO of Mize, pursued simplicity by championing a single overarching priority. He positioned his team to deliver solutions so Mize's clients could serve their customers with ease and choice. Mize is a customer experience platform designed to help end users register products, access warranties, and receive service.

Ashok added, "I was careful to keep my single priority consistent and clear. To succeed beyond the pandemic, we had to help our customers grow. That required us to enable them to provide options and ease to their consumers. Where possible, a consumer should be able to choose between a service technician coming out to their home or receiving remote assistance to troubleshoot an issue. With that as an optimal end state, our teams innovated solutions. In the process, we also helped our customers be more efficient and more effective for those they served."

Since Cathy and Ashok both mentioned technology as an enabler of their priorities (stakeholder ease of use and simplicity), you shouldn't jump to the conclusion that technology *is* the priority. Bill Gates once put it this way, "The first rule of any technology used in a business is that automation applied to an efficient operation will magnify the efficiency. The second is that automation applied to an inefficient operation will magnify the inefficiency." Technology is a tool that can expedite productivity *if* there is clarity around prioritized outcomes.

CLARIFYING PRIORITIES AND RESULTS

Wouldn't it be terrific if you could call a meeting, state your priorities, and check in intermittently to track your team's progress toward those objectives? In reality, the formulation and communication of clear objectives represent the beginning steps on a journey toward productivity. The process also requires dialogue with team members. Bryan Langford emphasized the role of conversation in priority clarification—particularly in a rapidly changing environment. Bryan is the Vice President, Commercial Operations at Roche Diagnostics, a global company that creates and delivers medicine and diagnostic tests to millions of patients globally.

Bryan observed, "You can't assume that your priorities are clear or that they translate to action. You have to check in with your teams, listen to how they understand the priorities, clarify any misalignment through dialogue, and assess how your team will approach objectives. You also have to ask about any concerns they have when it comes to meeting those priorities. Your team has to know that you will advocate for needed resources and remove obstacles that stand between them and the goal."

When it comes to ensuring that a company's key objectives are understood, especially given the emotionality and volatility of crisis, leaders need to engage in discussions with their teams and offer clarity. To Bryan's point, an understanding of mission-critical priorities comes from dialogue, not through a bullet-point presentation. Once there is a clear understanding of objectives, the leader must shift into a streamlining mode. That shift involves removing barriers, availing resources, and limiting nonessential activities.

A Breath of Insight

Ultimately you must select leaders that you have a great amount of certainty embody these time-honored character traits: trust, honesty, respect, integrity, and commitment.

—Roberto van Geenen, General Manager,
The Ritz-Carlton Bacara, Santa Barbara

LEADER AS STREAMLINER

Not only is Ben Salzmann the President and CEO at Acuity Insurance, but he is also an expert at enabling organizational productivity. Acuity provides insurance products to individuals, families, and businesses with innovative solutions backed by world-class customer service. With more than $5 billion in assets, Acuity is routinely one of the best places to work in the United States, according to *Forbes* magazine.

Ben noted, "To streamline performance during a crisis, it helps to have invested in people and technology beforehand. Assuming you have selected talented people and provided them with cutting-edge tools, it's just a matter of modifying those tools in response to the crisis. In our case, we were able to adapt technologies so our employees could focus on our agents and customers without being disrupted. Instantly, 98 percent of our employees stopped working at headquarters and began working in their bedrooms or at client sites. It happened flawlessly. They were handling large, complicated commercial and individual policies, and executing smoothly. We looked at our business much like building an Olympic marathon team. We selected the best talent and provided them world-class training and technology tools to focus on the goal of extraordinary care for one another, our agents, and customers. That approach served us well before the pandemic and may have even served us better throughout it."

Ben's Olympic marathon team analogy is especially illustrative. Designing streamlined productivity begins with talent selection. It then moves through enculturation, tactical prioritization, training, and tool enablement. Ben's perspective concerning a leader's role in developing people and providing enabling tools is consistent with remarks made years ago by Apple CEO Tim Cook when he noted, "The most important thing we can do is raise people up—that is, either by giving them the ability to do things they could not otherwise do or allowing them to create things they couldn't otherwise create. It's about giving them tools; it is about empowering people." At Apple, Acuity, or your business, streamlining productivity is a function of driving human-powered, technology-aided experiences.

PEOPLE PLUS TOOLS MINUS BUREAUCRACY

Rob Rosenberg underscored how restrictive policies curb the productivity of well-equipped and talented teams. Rob is the Global Head of Human Resources at DHL Supply Chain, the global leading contract logistics provider. DHL operates 1,400 warehouses and offices, with more than 146,000 supply chain employees.

Rob noted, "As the Head of HR, I am always looking at how I can better enable our people. During the pandemic, that enablement involved lessening reporting requirements or approvals and supporting local decision-making. From our board down, we yielded more autonomy to our local teams. For example, in Singapore, our roughly 1,000 employees run vital life science operations, which ensure the distribution of pharmaceutical supplies. Nearly half of that team lives in neighboring Malaysia. During the pandemic, the borders locked down between the two countries. Rather than trying to address that problem remotely, we empowered our local team to take action."

Rob added, "Within 24 hours of the closure, that team found a way to work collaboratively with governmental agencies, third-party housing partners, and border control authorities. Our Malaysian employees were allowed to reside in Singapore for an extended period. The local team assured safe living and working conditions for our Malaysian employees and operated our life sciences and healthcare distribution without interruption." Rob's example demonstrates the need for leaders to challenge policies and procedures that disempower team members or slow business operations. We should see ourselves as enablers, poised to drive needed decision-making to the front line while removing barriers to effectiveness.

SAYING NO TO NONPRIORITIES

When I conduct strategic planning sessions with leaders, I pause after we've explored the current state, optimal future state, and likely tactics needed to achieve their vision. Following that pause, I ask the question, "What will you have to stop or avoid doing to get you where you want to be?" Chinese inventor and philosopher Lin Yutang expressed the rationale behind my question this way: "Besides the noble art of getting things done, there is the noble art of leaving things undone. The wisdom of life consists in the elimination of nonessentials."

Mark Mader is continually looking for ways to make resource decisions that reduce or eliminate nonessentials. Mark is the CEO at Smartsheet, Inc., a software-as-a-service collaboration and work management solution. More than 75 percent of Fortune 500 companies use Smartsheet tools to assign tasks, track projects, manage calendars, and share documents.

According to Mark, "We stack rank our priorities. That helped us make resource decisions with confidence during the pandemic. Before COVID-19, we had the capital to fund tremendous opportunities for the upcoming fiscal year. However, with changing economic conditions and the need to focus on our core functions, we said 'no' to a range of possibilities. For example, we prioritize existing team members, so we had to be willing to delay hiring. We decided to push back expenditures for ancillary projects. We declined things like hiring a subject matter expert for an area that was a nonessential business function. These are examples of investment decisions at a senior level. But we have all leaders engaged in resource allocation that drives productivity and excellence. That typically involves balancing resources across priorities and being willing to say no to things that fall outside of the mix."

"No" is a powerful business tool. Its power is most notable when "yes" would decrease efficiency by squandering precious human, material, or financial resources. In a crisis, the desire to reach for stability can lead to urgent expenditures or projects that drain resources. Rank your overarching priorities and critical initiatives. Then evaluate every new opportunity or resource expenditure against that ranking. Ask, "What will I need to give up or displace if I pursue this new initiative?"

BIGGER ISN'T ALWAYS BETTER—
BETTER IS BETTER

Often companies become less efficient because they grow without removing clutter. Increasing size can have advantages but also liabilities. For example, a cruise ship is more stable than a speedboat but less maneuverable. Don Oakley is a proponent of rightsizing a business to maximize productivity. Don is the President at VSP, a world-class provider of eye care products and services to employers, their employees, and eye care professionals.

Founded in 1955, VSP serves roughly 88 million members worldwide. Don noted, "Throughout my career, I've asked myself, 'If I had this decision or that decision to do over again, would I have made the same choices?' Guess what, with the pandemic, we had the chance to do a lot of things all over again." According to Don, "The dramatic impact of the lockdown allowed us to hit the pause button and think about what we should stop doing. What were the less valuable aspects that became legacy elements of our businesses? Through that evaluation, we decided to build ourselves to two-thirds the size we were going into the pandemic. That was in the face of opportunities where we could have come out larger. For us, efficiency meant getting lighter on our feet to seize opportunities that we hadn't been able to run down in our prior structure. For example, we launched a new antibacterial coating for our lenses." Whether you decide to get bigger, get smaller, or stay the same size, that decision should be guided by what it will take to drive relevance, impact, and productivity.

Streamlining productivity is a matter of establishing priorities, discussing those priorities with your team, removing barriers, modifying policies, resisting nonpriority items, and being willing to let go of elements that weigh your business down. As overwhelming as that may seem, philosopher and philanthropist Paul Meyer wrapped it up well when he observed, "Productivity is never an accident. It is always the result of a commitment to excellence, intelligent planning, and focused effort."

RESILIENCE RECAP

➤ Busyness shouldn't be confused with productivity.

➤ Productivity is a combination of efficiency and effectiveness.

➤ Efficiency is an internal measure of business outputs (e.g., products and services) relative to inputs (e.g., material and human resources).

➤ Effectiveness is an external measure of stakeholder need fulfillment.

➤ Companies can be efficient and not effective, and vice versa.

➤ Crises have three common elements—surprise, threat, and minimal time to respond to the threat.

➤ Some crises are acute like a tornado, and others are protracted like a pandemic.

➤ During the pandemic, 96 percent of HR leaders surveyed by the Institute of Corporate Productivity reported impacts on productivity.

➤ Of those respondents, 41 percent reported impact in the "high" to "very high" range.

➤ To turn disruption into productive change, leaders need to channel the emotional energy of the crisis (fear, uncertainty, discomfort) toward critical objectives.

➤ The formulation and communication of clear objectives represent the beginning steps on a journey for productivity.

➤ The process of priority setting also requires leaders to engage in clarifying conversations with team members.

➤ Once priorities are clear, you must shift into a streamlining mode by removing barriers, availing resources, and limiting nonessential activities.

➤ Streamlining productivity is like building an Olympic marathon team. You have to select the best talent, provide world-class training and technology tools, and focus the team on high-priority objectives.

➤ Leaders should be poised to drive needed decision-making to the front line and challenge productivity-limiting policies and procedures.

➤ Rank your overarching priorities and critical initiatives. Evaluate every new opportunity or resource expenditure against that ranking. Be willing to say "no."

➤ As you grow your business, you should declutter, so company size is an asset and not a liability to productivity.

YOUR STRENGTH PLAN

1. In the context of your company's mission, list your top three priorities or objectives. How confident are you that your answer is correct? What is the basis for your level of confidence?

2. What percentage of your team would have the correct answer concerning the top three priorities or objectives? Ask them and engage in a dialogue that builds accuracy and alignment.

3. What are the efficiency and effectiveness metrics in your business? How are you performing on each? Are you balanced across those scorecards, or are you performing better in one of the two areas?

4. What tools or technologies have had the most impact on your productivity? How did they help? Have you ever had a technology decrease productivity? What happened in that situation?

5. When has saying "yes" to a new initiative or project adversely affected productivity on a higher priority objective? Think about how that lesser priority encroached.

6. Make a list of activities or initiatives that might add weight and not muscle to your business. What would it take to remove any of those items from your list?

7. How well do you remove clutter *before* you add new initiatives or priorities (in your professional and personal lives)? Give an example of success and missteps in these areas.

CHAPTER 15

Pivot with Urgency

*An organization's ability to learn, and
translate that learning into action rapidly,
is the ultimate competitive advantage.*
—JACK WELCH,
former CEO of General Electric

AGILE NAVIGATION

In the preceding chapter, I made a comparison between a cruise ship and a speedboat to illustrate how building a larger business doesn't necessarily translate into making it better, especially when it comes to productivity. That chapter also shows how, at times, leaders need to assess and remove counterproductive parts of their organizations to make room for growth and efficiency. In this chapter, let's look at how during a crisis, even cruise ships (stable, orderly, legacy companies) have to find ways to maneuver like speedboats (fluid, nimble, start-ups).

During the early days of COVID-19, we saw how leaders guided their teams to make tactical shifts at astonishing speeds. In this chapter, leaders share how they suspended traditional business processes, reduced fear of failure, focused on the urgent as opposed to the important, and seized naturally occurring opportunities. As you read their stories, you'll see how these leaders guided adaptability and flexibility in all aspects of their businesses.

Entrepreneur and author Sir Richard Branson once observed that "Every success story is a tale of constant adaption, revision, and change." For those who have led successfully throughout the pandemic, it was also a tale of pivoting with urgency.

SUSPEND "NORMAL"

It's hard to give up habits or tools that have brought success in the past. That tendency to cling to the familiar is named the Law of the Hammer or Maslow's Hammer. Psychologist Abraham Maslow did considerable work on this fixation on the familiar and observed, "I suppose it is tempting, if the only tool you have is a hammer, to treat everything as if it were a nail." During the pandemic, a slow swing of a leader's hammer (traditional and systematic planning processes) could render a company incapable of making a constructive impact (innovating solutions to respond at the speed of change). Instead, COVID-19 required leaders to assess quickly, act with urgency, and willingly let go of familiar tools and processes that were not well-suited for tumultuous and rapidly changing times.

Brian Gallagher acknowledged the "Law of the Hammer" and the need to resist "business as usual" when faced with unusual times. Brian is the President and Chief Executive Officer at United Way Worldwide. The United Way creates community-based and community-led solutions in nearly 1,800 communities across more than 40 countries and territories worldwide. Their primary areas of focus are education, financial stability, and health.

Brian shared, "Normal is a powerful, powerful force. Often people and organizations adjust only at the margins and resist fundamental change. What is different about the pandemic is how it is affecting virtually everyone on a scale unlike anything since World War II."

Concerning his team, Brian noted, "We had to resist the power of the normal and acknowledge a wake-up call. We needed to find new ways to raise money—anyway we could. When we did succeed virtually, we had to allocate and distribute to our network more than $750 million donated early in the pandemic. We realized this is a new world, and old approaches wouldn't apply. We couldn't conduct detailed planning exercises or take an overly bureaucratic approach to the assessment of community needs. We had to act urgently and scuttle processes designed for normal times. So we took our approach down to the essentials. We focused on basic needs and got the resources out swiftly. If food was needed, we expedited food. Because of our altered thinking and approach, I am proud of how quickly and effectively we distributed resources to 600 funds around the world."

Brian recognized that normal is a powerful and sometimes limiting force. It can tempt leaders to cling to so-called normal methods (hammers) in abnormal times. However, to succeed in a crisis, you have to challenge your organization to suspend the normal in pursuit of the needed.

REMOVING THE FEAR TO ACT

To act urgently, people have to believe the risk of doing nothing is greater than the risk of doing something. According to Maria Ortega, leaders must create an environment of responsible risk-taking.

Maria is a Regional Vice President at Quest Diagnostics Incorporated, a multinational Fortune 500 diagnostic information company that services one in three American adults every year. During the pandemic, Quest developed both COVID-19 diagnostic and antibody tests. At points throughout the pandemic, Quest was processing approximately 50 percent of all COVID-19 diagnostic testing.

Maria said, "Responding to the virus required leaders and companies to stay fluid and accept miscalculations. You could make a decision based on the best available information, and the guidance and the data you relied upon could change the next day. That meant leaders and team members had to be able to say, 'Okay, that didn't work, let's try something different.' It was essential to sidestep judgment, determine lessons learned, and forge on." Maria added, "In environments where there is no fault-finding, people thrive. We had individuals from all specialties step out of their comfort zones and take a risk to make a huge impact. People walked up to their directors and said, 'I know you're expanding testing, and I want to volunteer for that team.' I hate to think that a pandemic can be a force for good, but I believe it helped create an environment where people could feel more comfortable stepping forward."

I have written that anyone can make a mouse. Provide seeds, grain, nesting material, and *poof* a mouse appears. Similarly, leaders can either create environments that foster innovation and urgent action, or they can create settings where team members lockdown in fear of judgment. It's all about the context we establish.

RESPOND TO BUSINESS CRITICAL

Kevin Clayton is a leader I've worked with closely, who not only fosters an environment of innovation but also directs that innovation to critical business needs. Kevin is the CEO of Clayton Homes, a Berkshire Hathaway company with 18,000 team members providing a range of affordable housing solutions. Clayton ranks as the United States' eleventh largest site-builder, according to *Builder* magazine, and is the country's largest builder of manufactured and modular homes.

Kevin noted, "We had a lot to deal with from the onset of the pandemic. For example, we dealt with added safety concerns in our manufacturing plants and an early positive case in our corporate office. On top of that, business slowed 50 percent with lockdowns. It was like juggling a bunch of balls and finding out each time one dropped, they would explode. Much of what we had to cope with was out of our control, so we started by focusing on things we could either control or at least substantially influence. From there, we identified our most essential strategic need. For us, we had to turn the tide on declining mortgage applications. To get that done, we made sure everybody in our organization knew the importance of dedicating their creativity to the task. Our teams then did their research, mined data, and gathered customer insights. Those inputs informed options, which quickly led to an innovative and hugely successful touchless solution that turned that mortgage application decline around. I feel so blessed to work with such talented people."

While Kevin is the last person to take credit for the success of his organization or team, effective leaders help others sort the urgent from the important. To use Kevin's analogy, they help identify which balls can drop (causing only minor damage) and which ones must stay in the air (to ensure both the short- and longer-term viability of the business).

VEER TOWARD PRESSING CUSTOMER NEEDS

In addition to vital business operations, many leaders reported they redirected teams to meet emergent customer needs

For Jeff Jones, that redirection involved launching an online tool with bewildering speed. Jeff is the President and CEO of H&R Block, a US-based global tax preparation, financial services, and small business solutions company founded in 1955. H&R Block is disrupting the industry by offering consumers price transparency and developing solutions that blend digital capability with human expertise and care. Since its inception, H&R Block has prepared in excess of 800 million tax returns through its digital services and network of 11,000 company-owned and franchise locations.

Jeff explained, "We are in business to provide help and inspire confidence in our clients and communities everywhere. To do that, we expanded our urgent response beyond our core business offerings. As an example, people needed assistance with elements of the government's economic relief package, referred to as the CARES Act. So, within 48 hours of announcing the stimulus payment program, we had a stimulus check calculator available online. That way, people could determine eligibility and estimate their payment amount. Throughout the pandemic, we made similar adjustments to help people navigate the complexities and opportunities available to them. Many of those activities were in areas that we don't do every day, but they were needed to help individuals confidently move through tumultuous times."

In a precrisis world, most companies would be reluctant to stand up a service offering outside core business operations. Moreover, they would have beta tested and subjected that offering to multiple levels of reviews and approvals. Seldom would an online tool be created and deployed for widespread use within 48 hours. However, COVID-19 produced tight opportunity windows, and companies that couldn't pivot quickly found themselves solving problems that were in their rearview mirror, not those emerging on the road ahead.

TURN INTO OPPORTUNITY

While urgent or emergent needs drove many course adjustment decisions, leaders also turned tactically toward less critical opportunities. Edward Felsenthal, Editor-in-Chief and CEO at *TIME* magazine and Keith Grossman, the President of *TIME*, noted, "We launched a lot of products in 10 weeks by looking for ways to accelerate our digital transformation. For example, we'd started doing live events about a year and a half before the pandemic, and we were having success in that business. Unfortunately, with the impact of the pandemic on live events, we expected we would need to postpone our April TIME 100 Summit and Gala. That event features speakers and leaders from past and present TIME 100 lists. In the days between the originally planned live event and the rescheduled date, we had an opportunity to use the convening power of our brand to engage and communicate content from leaders of government, science, business, health, and entertainment. Our team seized that opportunity to deliver a new online product called TIME 100 Talks, which helped people find hope and ways to cope in the crisis. That series included talks with individuals like Sir Elton John, Dr. Anthony Fauci, Spike Lee, and Deepak Chopra."

As evidenced by Edward and Keith's example, not every quick pivot needs to be in reaction to urgent or emergent needs. Many of the best course corrections bend toward naturally occurring opportunities. All adjustments, however, have one thing in common. They all require a commitment to move projects forward with an emphasis on speed.

KEEP MOVING

Minister and civil rights activist Martin Luther King Jr. advised, "If you can't fly, then run. If you can't run, then walk. If you can't walk, then crawl, but whatever you do, you have to keep moving forward." Leaders like Randy Pritchard echoed Reverend King's brilliance regarding the criticality of leading with urgency for action. Randy is the Senior Vice President of US Marketing for Roche Diagnostic. During the pandemic, Roche launched both COVID-19 rapid detection and antibody tests.

Randy noted, "Long before the pandemic emerged, Roche had spent a lot of time working to be more agile. This global health crisis highlighted the value of that work at individual, team, and company levels. The critical nature of our mission also gave us no choice but to keep moving forward rapidly. For us, that meant accelerating a mindset shift to get comfortable with advancing products that met standards of minimal viability. That was a transition for leaders, even though we knew that our products would be continually improved one iteration at a time. We had to get comfortable with not slowing down to make sure the fonts in presentation decks matched perfectly. We needed to keep stepping forward with a commitment to quality, urgency, and evolution."

Listening to leaders like Randy, I marvel at the adaptability of the human spirit. Despite longstanding tendencies, individual leaders and organizations recast their business approaches to meet the rapidly changing needs of those they served. This adaptability is especially crucial in organizations that impact life, death, health, and wellness.

IT'S NOT AN EITHER/OR

Lest you think pivoting with urgency involves always moving forward toward only one destination, let's hear from Mindy Grossman. Mindy is the

President and CEO of WW (formerly Weight Watchers)—the world's leading commercial weight management program and a robust global wellness company. Mindy is a veteran leader who took a prior company public in the middle of the 2008 recession. Given her experience, Mindy talked about how urgent pivots can and must occur across multiple dimensions of business simultaneously during a crisis. Mindy noted, "Success is about moving quickly and empowering people to do their work. Companies that will come out of a crisis stronger are the ones who use it as an opportunity to innovate broadly. From an operational level, we pivoted from 30,000 physical workshops to virtual workshops and trained thousands of coaches in six days. We launched the virtual workshops simultaneously across the globe and our member base readily participated."

From the perspective of imminent customer need, Mindy continued, "People increased their health awareness during the pandemic and wanted more wellness support so they could make it through the stress of the crisis. We acted with urgency to amplify our content platforms and help people take control of behavior that would contribute to positive health outcomes." Finally, from a noncrisis opportunity perspective, Mindy assembled a cross-functional team "from all levels of the company to think in a very different way. We met with no-holds-barred to look for opportunities where we could advance confidently for the future."

Whenever I hear the word *advance* used in combination with the word *confidently*, I am reminded of an observation from essayist and philosopher Henry David Thoreau. Thoreau noted, "If one advances confidently in the direction of his dreams and endeavors to live the life that he has imagined, he will meet with a success unexpected in common hours." Leaders like Mindy have a track record of pivoting with urgency, which has helped their companies enjoy uncommon levels of success.

Mindy's example demonstrates that necessary business adjustments aren't an either/or proposition. It is not a matter of pivoting toward customer needs versus business needs. Instead, leading in times of uncertainty requires customer-focused, business-focused, *and* opportunity-focused pursuits. Successful leaders modulate across these domains and track progress on all fronts.

SPOTLIGHT ORGANIZATION FLEXIBILITY

In Chapter 4, I mentioned how corporate communication firm SJR tracks the way CEOs were perceived internationally. Near the top of that list during the pandemic was Brian Cornell, the CEO of Target. Target is a US-based merchandise retailer with more than 350,000 employees and roughly 1,900 stores. Seventy-five percent of the US population lives within 10 miles of one of those stores.

Brian's popularity among Target team members and consumers is the result of many leadership strengths, including humility and his ability to drive flexibility and rapid adaptation. Consistent with his humility, Brian answered my question about Target's successful pivots by highlighting teams across his organization. Specifically, Brian shared, "Our team has demonstrated throughout this crisis their ability to be flexible, adapt to rapid change, and continue delivering outstanding service for our guests. Our frontline team members, in particular, showed incredible resiliency as they quickly adapted routines and processes to guests' rapidly changing shopping habits. Our merchandise and sourcing teams worked through tremendous volatility to ensure we had the essential items our guests needed most. The stress on our supply chains is unprecedented, and those teams moved quickly to build capacity and keep the pipeline flowing. Target has been making strategic investments over time that positioned us well coming into this environment. The adoption of our same-day services is at levels we were expecting to reach three years in the future, and our operations and our teams have been able to flex and meet the demand."

Brian credits some of his company's adaptability to not having to worry about financial stability, "It's at times like these we also see the benefit of our strong balance sheet and fundamentally sound business model. The financial strength gives us the flexibility to focus on what matters most, our guests and our team, and confidence that we'll emerge from this crisis as a stronger, more relevant retailer with an even higher level of affinity and trust among our guests."

When leaders effectively activate all levels of their organization urgently toward critical business needs, emergent customer concerns, and opportunities, they are stronger, are more relevant, and gain increased affinity and trust from those they serve. Ironically, companies that maneuver like speedboats often emerge with the stability of cruise ships.

RESILIENCE RECAP

➤ The Law of the Hammer describes a cognitive bias where people overly rely on a familiar tool or process.

➤ Leaders often cling to normal or traditional methods in abnormal times.

➤ Leaders can either create environments that foster innovation and urgent action, or they can create settings where team members lockdown in fear of judgment.

➤ Effective leaders help others sort the urgent from the important.

➤ Leaders must direct their inventive resources aggressively toward the necessities of those they serve.

➤ Not every quick pivot needs to be in reaction to urgent or emergent needs.

➤ Many of the best course corrections bend toward naturally occurring opportunities.

➤ All course corrections require a commitment to move projects forward with an emphasis on speed.

➤ Despite longstanding tendencies, individual leaders and organizations can and do recast their business approaches to meet the rapidly changing needs of those they serve.

➤ Necessary business adjustments aren't an either/or proposition. They aren't a choice between pivoting toward customer needs versus business needs. Instead, leading in times of uncertainty requires customer-focused, business-focused, *and* opportunity-focused pursuits.

➤ When leaders effectively activate all levels of their organization urgently toward critical business needs, emergent customer concerns, and opportunities, they are stronger, are more relevant, and gain increased affinity and trust.

YOUR STRENGTH PLAN

1. When it comes to speed and maneuverability, is your company more like a speedboat or a cruise ship? What is the basis of your conclusion? Do you have teams within your organization that act differently? If so, which ones and how?

2. Is your industry and competitive landscape made up predominantly of speedboats or cruise ships? Who are your fastest and most agile competitors?

3. How have you seen the Law of the Hammer in action in your professional life or your personal life? What are the benefits and risks associated with having a bias toward a particular tool or process?

4. How and when has your organization or team pivoted urgently to meet a critical business need? What was the nature of the need? What did you do to rally behind that situation?

5. How and when did your organization or team pivot urgently to meet an emerging customer or stakeholder need? What was the nature of that need? What did you do to address that situation quickly?

6. Where have you moved swiftly as an organization to seize a nonurgent opportunity?

7. Identify one area where your business should pivot with urgency. Is that area being addressed? If so, what will increase the probability that you will make that adjustment successfully? If that area isn't receiving attention, how can you raise awareness of the importance of that concern?

8. How safe is it to take reasonable risks in your organization? What are you doing as a leader to minimize fault-finding and blaming within your team?

CHAPTER 16

Decide with Moral Courage

Courage is not simply one of the virtues, but the form of every virtue at the testing point.
—C. S. LEWIS,
author and theologian

NOT FOR THE FAINT OF HEART

The word *courage* derives from the Latin word for *heart*, and heart-filled behavior comes in many forms. Physical courage is the willingness to put yourself in a position to endure pain or even risk survival. It manifests in those who risk injury or death in battle. By contrast, moral courage reflects thoughtful consideration of right and wrong before taking decisive action. That thoughtfulness involves contemplation of your values, the well-being of others, and the best course of action. While each demonstrated physical bravery, leaders like Nelson Mandela, Mother Teresa, Martin Luther King Jr., and Mahatma Gandhi are celebrated for their moral courage.

Before COVID-19, leaders rarely faced physical harm in the course of their business lives. However, they did routinely encounter opportunities to demonstrate moral courage. If anything, the pandemic increased the importance of moral decision-making in the face of uncertainty. In previous chapters, you have seen examples of morally courageous leadership behaviors. They include:

- Being willing to ask for help

- Acknowledging when you don't know an answer

- Admitting mistakes

- Demonstrating vulnerability and transparency

- Honestly sharing information, even when it may be difficult for others to hear

- Creating value without the guarantee of return

- Showing compassion

- Acting based on values

This chapter focuses on a specific form of moral courage: decision-making. Leaders provide examples of the challenging decisions that surfaced during the pandemic. They offer insights into their decision-making process, how they communicated the rationale for controversial choices, and how they faced positive and negative fallout. You will also read about two leadership teams that made vastly different decisions when addressing a similar dilemma. Finally, you will see the unrelenting decision-making required during the pandemic and how moral courage cascades through an organization.

The actor and writer Christopher Reeve observed, "Either you decide to stay in the shallow end of the pool, or you go out in the ocean." In a crisis, there is no shallow end to the pool, and the ocean is choppy. Let's look at how leaders made it through those rough waters by taking bold and decisive action.

PUSHING THROUGH

Carly Fiorina is the Chairman and Founder of Fiorina Enterprises and Unlocking Potential. Previously she served as CEO of Hewlett-Packard and ran for President of the United States. Of late, Carly provides leadership training and helps leaders navigate challenging situations. Her insights underscore the role courage plays in leadership. According to Carly, "One of the most important qualities of any leader is courage. I remind the people I work with that courage is not the absence of fear. Courage is the ability to get over fear. We all fear things as we go through our lives. As leaders share and face their fears, they make it easier for others to do the same. For example, I work with wounded warriors. These men and women might have demonstrated an absence of fear as they ran running through a hell-fire of bullets to save a buddy, but they might fear being pitied. Leading with courage starts with acknowledging your fear, labeling it, and saying it out loud. Those steps take away some of the fear's power and give you the chance to take a breath, gather your thoughts, and make the decisions needed to move through it."

Carly pummels the myth that leaders should be unemotional and fearless. From her perspective, fear mastery starts with acknowledging and labeling emotions so you can move through them. With fear heightened by crisis, her words are especially relevant to leading through the pandemic. They also align with the perspective of Nelson Mandela, when he described courage as the ability to triumph over fear, noting, "The brave man is not he who does not feel afraid, but he who conquers that fear." When it comes to making decisions in times of substantial uncertainty, leaders must conquer many anxieties. For example, they have to overcome the fear that their choices will put others in harm's way, that others will resist their chosen path, and that they aren't making the right choice.

IS THERE A "RIGHT" CHOICE?

Leadership choices seldom have a "right" answer. They are not mathematical functions like addition or subtraction. Instead, business decisions are usually complex, multivariate calculations. To come to a solution, leaders must blend inputs such as data, business intelligence tools, assumptions, past experiences, and stakeholder input. Depending upon the quality of information, some decisions turn out more prudent than others. To demonstrate the fallacy of searching for a "right" answer, let's consider two very different choices made in response to a similar dilemma during the pandemic.

The two leadership teams were Airbnb and StubHub. Both businesses operate online marketplaces. Airbnb primarily connects hosts with guests for short-term property rentals. StubHub primarily connects ticket sellers with ticket purchasers for sporting and entertainment events.

When the pandemic surged, most guests who had booked travel on the Airbnb platform canceled their reservations. Those guests wanted their money refunded. Similarly, live event cancelations left those who purchased tickets on StubHub also seeking refunds. Caught in the middle between buyers and sellers, each leadership team carefully analyzed options.

Both teams needed to make the best (albeit not perfect) decision for their diverse set of stakeholders. Let's learn more about each business and the different choices made by their leaders.

I will start with Airbnb, a brand very familiar to me as I released a book about the company titled *The Airbnb Way* in 2019. In that book, I outlined leadership principles that led to the company's meteoric rise and disruptive impact on the hotel and travel industry. Airbnb's online marketplace lists more than 7 million accommodations and 50,000 local activities. The platform has brokered more than three-quarters of a billion guest arrivals across 220-plus countries and regions.

As for their dilemma, Christopher Lehane, Airbnb's Vice President Global Policy and Communications, noted, "When the World Health Organization officially decreed the global pandemic, we became one of the first online marketplaces to provide a full refund to our guests. That decision immediately created some challenges and tensions with our hosts, as they depended on that prospective income. The 'North Star' for that refund was the priority we placed on public health. We didn't want guests in a position of having to make travel decisions where they needed to choose between their health and their money. We then took a series of steps to offset the impact our decision would have on hosts, including distributing $250 million from our company funds directly to them."

Airbnb's leaders needed to have the moral courage to make refund decisions based on public health considerations, the financial impact on hosts and guests, and also the impact on the company's employees and Airbnb's overall financial future. Every decision had the potential to affect one stakeholder at the expense of another. For example, in the context of refunds, Airbnb leaders were working to raise $2 billion in capital while laying off 25 percent of their workforce. They faced every gut-wrenching decision in the context of declining revenues, increased debt, and the impact of the decision on Airbnb's employees. Leaders also filtered their decisions through the company's values. Christopher added, "We led with a desire to be a trusted platform, a trusted partner, and to show an emotional awareness of just how hard this was for everyone. We applied our values to this and to every decision we faced."

Despite all that careful consideration, Christopher indicated that even after Airbnb made the refund decision, they looked for improvement opportunities. Christopher added, "In retrospect, I wish we would have communicated in more detail with hosts as we made our refund decision. That way, they could have better understood how we made that difficult choice."

While Airbnb offered refunds to the buyers (guests) who booked on their platform, StubHub's leadership sought to offset buyer losses differently. Sukhinder Singh Cassidy is the former President of StubHub that led the company through its refund decisions. StubHub is the world's largest ticket marketplace. The company has enabled buyers to access 10 million live sports, theatre, and music events in more than 40 countries.

According to Sukhinder, "We had a tough choice. Buyers paid for tickets for countless events that were being postponed or canceled. Sellers had already received the money for those tickets. We sought to recoup funds from the sellers, but that wasn't happening quickly. We issued full refunds in states where that was required. Otherwise, we had to take decisive action and change our refund policy."

That policy change, posted on the company's website, read:

> We are providing customers of canceled events a coupon valued at 120% of their original order. The coupon will be available in a customer's account immediately after StubHub's announcement of the cancellation. . . . Customers can apply this coupon to one or multiple StubHub orders in the same currency within the next 12 months.

Like Airbnb, StubHub also completed a round of layoffs to absorb the economic impact of COVID-19. In that context, Sukhinder added, "This was not an easy choice for us, but we had to maintain the health of our marketplace in alignment with our values. Despite the necessity of our decision, it was not popular, and I received a lot of Twitter hatred."

Airbnb made full customer refunds and sought to mitigate the impact on hosts. StubHub attempted to recoup funds from sellers and changed its refund policy to offer 120 percent credits to buyers. There was no "right" choice for this dilemma. Every option had impacts on buyers, sellers, employees, and the future of Airbnb and StubHub. Leaders at both companies had to wade through multiple scenarios and understand the intended and unintended consequences of each possible option. They then needed to step forward with the courage of their convictions to make the best decision. The willingness to render a choice in the absence of a clear right answer is at the heart of moral courage. By contrast, a failure to decide represents the abdication of leadership responsibility and results in the ultimate "wrong" answer.

A Breath of Insight

Well-researched and thoughtful consideration of ideas during a crisis has to be a priority, and leaders have to get better at looking at first, second, and third order implications of decisions.

—**Diane S. Hopkins,** Certified Experience Economy Expert; author of *Unleashing the Chief Moment Officers*; coauthor of *Wake Up and Smell the Innovation* and *Advice from a Patient*; CEO, ExPeers

---

IT'S NOT JUST WHAT YOU CHOOSE

As suggested by the examples of Airbnb and StubHub, the pandemic (and conflicting guidance from different levels of government) put leaders in situations where they faced many potentially polarizing decisions. These choices affected team members, customers, and other stakeholders. For example, many leaders wrestled with issues like, should we require all customers to wear masks? Should we shut down our office if a team member tests positive for COVID-19? Do we check the temperature of everyone who enters our building?

Against that backdrop, Kurt Kuebler suggested leaders needed to ready themselves for discord. Kurt is a Partner at Kopplin Kuebler & Wallace (KK&W), a premier consulting and recruiting firm in the private club and assisted living sectors. KK&W also conducts workshops, training seminars, consulting services, and audits for private clubs.

According to Kurt, "I've had countless conversations with managers and board members in the club industry. These are strong leaders who make very methodical, big-picture decisions. They run through scenarios and contingency plans. Conscientiously, they weigh the likely impact of their decisions on all stakeholders and make hard calls. If, for example, they decided to close their golf course voluntarily, they might have half of their membership opposed and half praising their decision."

Kurt added, "Emotions ran high at various points during the pandemic. In one month, I had more people ask for help managing anger and bad member behavior than I had in the prior 15 years. Often my guidance not only covered ways to manage pushback but also how to effectively communicate the rationale for their decisions in the first place. For many leaders, the way they made and communicated their decisions will likely shape their personal leadership brands for years to come."

In regular times, and to an increased degree in crisis, leaders must both think carefully about their decisions and the respectful, honest, and nondefensive manner by which they share them. A well-crafted explanation, especially for a controversial choice, can generate support for that decision. Even when people disagree with the course taken, a cogent explanation can show a leader has weighed the dissenters' interests. As Kurt suggests, people will likely forget the specific decisions a leader makes. Conversely, they will probably remember leaders who respectfully demonstrate thoughtfulness in the way they explain their decision-making process.

NO DECISION HOLIDAY

The pandemic not only forced leaders to face a multitude of potentially polarizing decisions, but it also presented waves of decision-making. Michelle Gass offered perspective on the harrowing scope of her team's crisis quandaries. Michelle is the CEO of Kohl's, a department store featuring clothing, shoes, home decor, appliances, electronics, and toys. With more than 1,100 stores in 49 states, Kohl's is one of the largest US retailers.

Michelle shared, "The pandemic required us to face evolving challenges with clarity and decisiveness. At first, we focused our energies on making decisions to protect the health and safety of our associates and our customers. That shifted into making choices to preserve the company's financial viability. The next phase was decision-making for the safe reopening of our stores." As for the challenges in the initial stage of store closings, Michelle advised, "We faced a cascade of decisions to guide our company down a path Kohl's had never gone. We had to decide how to close all of our stores at once."

From a financial decision-making perspective, Michelle explained, "With our stores closed, we needed to manage a 75 percent pause in our $20 billion of sales revenue. So suddenly, our daily routine was looking at a cash flow statement, considering multiple daunting forecasts, and making very swift and clear decisions. My team spent an incredible amount of time looking at how to preserve our financial viability. That required a focus on cash outflows to ensure that we could get more money on the balance sheet. We made tough decisions to cut expenses dramatically. Normally we wouldn't touch our marketing budget, but all options were on the table, and marketing got cut. We worked with vendors to pause payments, not just on merchandise, but across the board. Through those aggressive efforts and grueling decisions, we reduced our capital budget significantly by $500 million. We also accessed $600 million in unsecured bonds and maintained our status as an investment-grade company. That got us to another wave of decisions concerning safe store reopenings."

Michelle paints a picture of unrelenting and courageous decision-making. In a crisis, it's not unusual for leaders to make painful choices that simply get them to the place where they can make a different set of challenging decisions. Had Michelle and her team failed to navigate Kohl's financial challenges, they wouldn't have been able to face the complexities of store reopenings. Leadership is not for the faint of heart. It is for those willing to decide with moral courage.

EVEN THE MOST CONFIDENT LEADERS ANGUISH

To close this chapter on decisive moral courage, I'll turn to a longstanding mentor—Horst Schulze. Horst is the founder of the modern-day Ritz-Carlton Hotel Company (the hotel brand I highlighted in my book *The New Gold Standard*). It was under Horst's leadership that The Ritz-Carlton Hotel Company became the first service-based business to receive the prestigious Malcolm Baldrige National Quality Award—not once, but twice.

Horst has been in the hospitality sector for 65 years, starting as a server's assistant in a resort town in Germany and has written the book *Excellence Wins*. Horst noted, "Watch the decisions of leaders, and you will see a company's real purpose. Don't listen to a leader's words; judge them on the totality of their decisions. The best leaders I have seen across my long career all agonized about decisions. They chose based on what they believed would serve the highest good for employees, customers, shareholders, and society as a whole. I have spent more than my share of time crying in private as I've needed to make decisions about issues like furloughs, but those are exactly the type of decisions that leaders are obligated to make."

For Horst, leadership is synonymous with making hard decisions, and excellence demands a willingness to stand up to difficult choices. It also involves striving to balance the needs of employees, customers, shareholders, and society. Without moral courage, organizations grind to a halt or render their fate to external forces. To be effective, especially during periods of crisis, leaders must understand available options, consider the impact on all stakeholders, calculate the most viable choice, and then move forward decisively. When leaders practice moral courage, they enable their people to take constructive action and make course corrections. When leaders avoid morally courageous decisions, they surrender themselves, their teams, and their businesses to fear and rampant uncertainty.

RESILIENCE RECAP

➤ The word *courage* derives from the Latin word for *heart*.

➤ Physical courage is the willingness to put yourself in a position to endure pain or even death.

➤ Moral courage reflects thoughtful consideration of right and wrong before taking decisive action.

➤ Courage is not the absence of fear. It is the ability to triumph over it.

➤ Mastering fear starts with acknowledging and labeling emotions so you can move through them.

➤ Business decisions are usually complex, multivariate calculations that rely on data, business intelligence tools, assumptions, past experiences, and stakeholder input.

➤ While many leadership choices don't have a "right" answer, there is typically a consistent "wrong" choice—not deciding at all.

➤ In regular times, and to an increased degree in crisis, leaders must think carefully about their decisions and about the respectful, honest, and nondefensive manner by which they share them.

➤ Effectively explaining the rationale behind a decision can increase support for your choice while demonstrating respect for dissenters.

➤ People are likely to forget individual choices we make and are more likely to remember how respectful we were when we explained our decision-making process.

➤ Crisis often forces leaders to face evolving challenges with clarity and decisiveness.

➤ It's common for leaders to make painful choices that simply get them to the place where they can make a different set of challenging decisions.

➤ Leadership is synonymous with making hard decisions.

➤ Excellence in decision-making requires a commitment to balance the needs of employees, customers, shareholders, and society.

YOUR STRENGTH PLAN

1. Where have you seen leaders make decisions that demonstrated moral courage? What specifically did they do?

2. Think of a situation where you made a personal or professional decision that reflected moral courage. What was it about that choice that brought it top of mind?

3. When, if ever, have you made a business decision with absolute certainty that you were right? When, if ever, have you made a business decision knowing there was no "right" answer?

4. Have you ever had an experience where someone failed to have the courage to make a needed decision? What were the circumstances and consequences of neglecting the decision?

5. When have you seen a leader deliver a controversial decision in a nondefensive and respectful way and, in the process, demonstrated their thoughtfulness? What did they do? How did their communication style affect the way the message was received?

6. How would you have handled the Airbnb/StubHub dilemma? How did each brand balance (or not balance) the needs of their employees, customers (host/guest or buyer/seller), and other stakeholders? Are their lessons to be learned from their experience for your company? If so, what are those lessons?

CHAPTER 17

Foster Collaboration

Alone we can do so little;
together we can do so much.
—HELEN KELLER,
author and political activist

MAKING WORKING TOGETHER WORK

Collaboration is like physical fitness, everyone wants it, but not everyone is disciplined enough to make it a reality. In his book *Collaboration*, University of California, Berkeley management professor Morten Hansen warned that poorly executed collaboration is worse than no collaboration at all. Given the time, money, and resources invested in bringing teams together, collaboration can only be justified if it improves innovation, sales, service, or operations.

If collaboration wasn't tricky enough in traditional work environments, the pandemic produced a seismic shift in how teams worked together. Instead of rushing from one overbooked conference room to the next, many work groups turned to technology. They juggled overlapping video conferences and rapidly increased their use of virtual collaboration and project management tools like Microsoft Teams, Google Drive, Slack, and Trello.

Of course, collaboration tools were just that—tools. Even with training, there were no guarantees that teams could produce results with entire companies working virtually. Faced with this unwanted and unplanned challenge, leaders needed to find ways to achieve the significant benefits of collaboration, while mitigating potential counterproductivity.

In this chapter, leaders share how they sparked robust collaboration as their teams worked from home or physically distanced in an office setting. Specifically, leaders show how they encouraged team communication, brainstorming, innovation, and growth. You will also see how these leaders challenged their teams to care for one another, attack business deficiencies, reach beyond their defined roles, and adopt an entrepreneurial mindset.

COVID-19 dramatically altered the way teams traditionally work. It also exposed the importance of becoming more inclusive and leveraging technology to accomplish mission-critical goals. To be effective during and beyond the pandemic, leaders needed to adjust the way they led remote work groups, maximized team member input, and challenged their teams to look out for one another.

LEAD DON'T MANAGE

For Joe Haury the first step in fostering collaboration involved evaluating his role as the team leader. Joe is a graduate of the US Military Academy at West Point and the Vice President of Global Logistics at Panasonic North America, one of the largest Japanese multinational consumer electronics corporations. Panasonic's five core business areas are smart mobility, sustainable energy, immersive experiences, integrated supply chains, and consumer lifestyle.

To cultivate meaningful team outcomes, Joe suggested leaders needed to strike a balance between "command and control" and "team empowerment." Joe likened the command and control element to military operational communication and alignment strategy. Specifically, he noted, "In normal operating mode, especially in the corporate world, you might have weekly team meetings because your mission has a reasonably long lead time. In crisis mode and many military situations, your time horizon is that day. You have to ask, 'What must get done today to meet the mission?' So, when we first went into the pandemic, we immediately launched twice-a-day crisis meetings." Joe compared these calls to a military premission operations meeting, and a postmission debrief. At Panasonic, the morning call would align leaders on the daily mission and ensure they could communicate the daily mission to their teams. The evening call assessed progress toward the daily mission and previewed the next day's mission.

Concerning team empowerment, Joe noted, "Crises are often under-led and overmanaged. So as the senior leader of my team, I had to make strategic decisions and support my team as they worked together to innovate solutions and tactics to achieve our goals. For example, we produce batteries for Tesla in the US. Shutdowns of manufacturing lines created huge oversupplies of raw material with more on the way. Although it's not something our team had encountered before, we needed to find storage for 200-plus shipping containers arriving at different ports. The team's collaboration was inspiring. They worked with stakeholders and procurement teams at the manufacturing site and different logistics locations to secure new partnerships at warehouses. Within 24 hours, as freighters were in route, the team had accomplished their extraordinary storage solution."

From Joe's perspective, effective team collaboration begins with leaders making strategic decisions and conducting premission meetings with their teams. It continues by empowering teams to innovate solutions and develop tactics to meet the mission. It also requires regular debriefing sessions to assess progress and reset goals. The frequency of pre- and postmission meetings depends on the urgency of mission execution. Since we already addressed ways to prioritize and communicate critical objectives in Chapter 14, let's look at how leaders encourage ideation and innovation within their teams.

FUELING BRAINSTORMING
AND IDEA SHARING

Karyn Twaronite offered practical tools for helping leaders include all team members in collaborative idea-sharing. Karyn is the Global Diversity and Inclusiveness Officer at Ernst & Young (EY). EY provides tax, audit, and human capital services worldwide. The company, one of the Big Four accounting firms, operates in more than 150 countries and employs over 300,000 people.

Karyn shared, "We grow through our commitment to diversity and inclusion. By acting on that commitment, we live our purpose of building a better working world. Throughout the pandemic, we focused on strengthening inclusive leadership. To do that, we put tools in the hands of all leaders to make sure they were involving and looking out for all people. We offer resources and processes for expanding thinking patterns, listening to every voice, and resisting the tendency to hunker down with your team to the exclusion of others. We also emphasized the importance of checking in individually with every team member on how they were doing both personally and professionally."

According to Karyn, effective team idea-sharing starts with "authentically valuing the input of others and not just humoring people by asking them to weigh in. Since we work on global teams, we demonstrate that authentic interest by respecting cultural and language differences as well as time zones. One best practice for leaders of international teams is letting people know in advance that you will be looking for their input on a specific subject. That way, they will have the chance to think about the topic. Additionally, they will have time to think about how they will share their input in what may be a second, third, or fourth language to them." More broadly, Karyn recommends, "using something we picked up from Adam Grant when he talks about 'the hippo speaks last.' That means the leader should withhold opinion or input until everyone else has spoken. We also encourage leaders to simply slow down to make sure there is space for everyone to participate. We have seen outstanding performance when leaders apply these best practices, and team surveys indicate that people feel their input is valued."

Individuals process information and offer input in different ways. Some team members are comfortable jumping directly into a conversation when a new topic surfaces. Others need time to mull over an idea before they provide input. To give everyone a chance to speak, leaders should provide advance notice on topics (whenever possible), speak last, and slow down the conversation. As leaders take these actions, they model desired behavior for discussions that will occur in their absence.

In healthy collaborative environments, teams establish ground rules for communication and coach one another when behavior falls outside of those rules (e.g., limit interruptions, respect divergent ideas, limit overtalk, have full input before devising solutions). These types of rules can be especially helpful with lags and choppy interactions that occur during video conferences.

HELP CONSOLIDATE LESSONS LEARNED

Richard C. Shadyac focused his insights on helping teams learn together. Rick is the President and CEO of American Lebanese Syrian Associated Charities (ALSAC). ALSAC is the fundraising and awareness organization for St. Jude Children's Research Hospital. Supported by the work of ALSAC, St. Jude Children's Research Hospital is leading the way the world understands, treats, and defeats childhood cancer and other life-threatening diseases. Families never receive a bill from St. Jude for treatment, travel, housing, or food because in the words of its mission: all a family should worry about is helping their child live.

According to Rick, "It's important to take time to learn, iterate, and grow. For example, we had some prior experience in virtual fundraising, but we certainly weren't doing it predominantly. During COVID-19, we pivoted to innovate virtually and engage with our supporters. We had victories while also making our share of mistakes. In every new experience, we were learning. So, I encouraged my team to take the last month of the fiscal year to do nothing but learn, synthesize best practices, and identify how we could start our new fiscal year smarter and better equipped for success. Besides becoming more effective, we got the chance to share stories that inspired us. We heard about supporters who gave us their stimulus checks. We learned of people who found virtual ways to celebrate their child finishing chemotherapy and so much more." Rick added, "By taking time together for reflection, we saw how interdependent we all are. It showed us that when we work together, nothing's impossible."

Amid crises, leaders can overlook the importance of taking time to synthesize learnings. Rick reminds us that those periods of group reflection help our teams learn together and appreciate interdependence. It just takes awareness and effort to provide these learning sessions. As first lady Abigail Adams observed, "Learning is not attained by chance, it must be sought for with ardor and diligence."

CHALLENGE THE TEAM TO
TAKE CARE OF ONE ANOTHER

Aria Finger believes ardor and discipline should also apply to helping team members take care of one another. Aria is the CEO at DoSomething.org, the largest not-for-profit organization dedicated to young people and social change. DoSomething's millions of members represent 131 countries and every US area code. Using their digital platform, DoSomething members engage in social change as well as volunteer and civic campaigns.

Aria noted, "This may sound odd, but during the pandemic, we focused less on the quantity of contribution each person made and more on equity. Given circumstances, not everyone on our team was able to shoulder the same amount of burden. Some people were dealing with work from home, and it was harder for them. Several people on our executive team had young kids and no childcare help. So, we asked everyone to do what they could and to work with one another to take care of one another's needs. As leaders, we also worked to channel output in the context of the competing demands on team members. Our message was that to perform as a team, we needed to fill in gaps for each other, and invariably, we would all have a time when we needed others to do the same." Aria's wisdom is in keeping with a sports analogy of a star player having an off night and needing their team to "carry them." Collaboration occurs not only in performance outcomes but in the dynamics of filling in the gaps for one another.

Brent Eichar expands on this team support concept. Brent is the Senior Executive Vice President of Certified Angus Beef (CAB)—a nonprofit organization owned by the American Angus Association with roughly 30,000 rancher members. The Certified Angus Beef brand helps build demand for high-quality Angus beef. CAB distributes its products through a network of nearly 17,000 grocery stores and restaurants globally.

Brent shared, "We communicated a message to our team members that 'we have your back and be sure to do the same for one another.' If the crisis meant a person was able to do only 10 percent of their job, we needed to support them through that collaboratively. As a result, we saw incredible innovation and partnership at the team level. As an example, we have five chefs on staff. When events canceled, we assured them their jobs were safe. They, in turn, found ways to collaborate on training videos. One chef and his son made an iPhone video on how to make beef jerky. We had other chefs teaching segments on how to cut steaks for people who had to become impromptu weekend butchers given that meat shops were closed. It was a case of us helping the team and the team helping each other."

Research on employee engagement shows that once you provide adequate compensation, teams focus on mastery, autonomy, and purpose. Team members find fulfillment by stretching themselves, exerting control in their work, and connecting with something larger than themselves. Brent shows that when you extend trust to your team and encourage them to find ways to help one another in times of need, they innovate and add value. Eighteenth-century Scottish philosopher David Hume captured the essence of collaborative support by noting, "Your corn is ripe today; mine will be so tomorrow. 'Tis profitable for us both, that I should labour with you today, and that you should aid me tomorrow."

CONNECT TEAM FUNCTION TO IMPACT

While leaders like Aria and Brent focused on collaboration for team support, Charlie Acevedo emphasized collaboration for impact. Charlie is the Senior Vice President of Sales and Merchandising at Costa Farms, LLC, the largest house and garden plant grower and distributor in the world. Costa Farms provides plants to garden centers, home improvement stores, and other retailers.

Charlie noted, "We fostered collaboration by helping teams see how their efforts had transformative power. We positioned team performance as a driver of our brand's future. For example, we asked our eCommerce team to not only help us address the moment but also help us shape Costa Farms' destiny and our customer relationships. We linked collaborative tasks to something larger and more lasting."

Tony Hsieh connects collaboration to personal and entrepreneurial impact. Tony is the CEO at Zappos—an online retailer purchased by Amazon. My book *The Zappos Experience* is a deep dive into the company's unique culture, legendary customer service, and business development division, Zappos Insights.

Tony noted, "We moved away from a hierarchical organizational structure toward a team-based, purpose-driven approach. Our teams, referred to as circles, operate as micro-businesses. These circles look for opportunities that supplement Zappos' core online retail offerings. As an example, Zappos Insights is a group that helps outside companies develop culture and differentiation. Their offerings reach far beyond online retail."

Tony added, "Each circle is a self-governing collaborative unit that is free to venture into areas that meet their passions, drive value for others, and likely will generate additional revenue. These circles evaluate opportunities through our triangle of accountability. A new offering, internally or externally, must check three boxes. It needs to be in line with our values and culture. It needs to be brand congruent and differentiate through customer service or customer experience. Finally, it needs to make financial sense and drive value, either in the form of profits or in terms of savings to the company."

From a performance perspective, Tony noted, "We track each circle on our CFO tool to ensure they are operating in the black, but otherwise, they self-manage and self-organize. This approach has produced remarkable results for us before and through the pandemic. Our benefits include diversified revenue streams, energizing entrepreneurial spirit, and complete collaboration. My goal is for all employees to work together to engage their passions and strengths, in pursuit of innovative value for Zappos and those we serve."

Self-governing, fully autonomous, revenue-producing work groups are at the outer edges of comfort for many leaders. However, Charlie and Tony help us understand how collaborative success connects to personal and organizational impact.

DEVELOPING LEADERS FOR THE FUTURE

Brian Schaeffer expanded the discussion of impact in the context of resilience and succession planning. Brian, the Fire Chief for the Spokane, Washington, Fire Department, noted, "COVID-19 helped me appreciate how vulnerable every organization is when it comes to succession planning and bench strength. We collaborate to fight long event wildland fires and perform all team-related public safety functions. However, our organization hadn't developed enough leadership depth to address a situation where the virus would have sickened a sizable number of our command staff. As such, our collaboration challenge focused on building teams of leaders. Instead of focusing on succession planning to fill a key position, we asked our leaders and teams to work together to maximize resilience. What were the skill sets we could help one another develop, so anyone could step up if and when called? We had a lot of people ready with the right behaviors, temperament, and vision to ensure we could continue operations. We just needed to make sure we consciously collaborated to position the department well past this crisis."

Collaboration is fostered by leaders who encourage team members to care for one another, meet challenges that cause them to stretch, and drive organizational resilience. Effective leaders also nurture collective input, emphasize measurable output, help team members use their strengths and talents to fill gaps, and focus on collective learning. Throughout COVID-19, leaders fought against the potential negative impacts of physical separation. They also stewarded teams to produce rapid and tangible results. Skilled leaders improvised, inspired, and aligned their teams to overcome fragmentation and instead produce results well beyond expectations.

RESILIENCE RECAP

➤ Given the time, money, and resources invested in bringing teams together, bad collaboration can be worse than no collaboration at all.

➤ To justify collaborative investments, leaders should track returns in areas such as innovation, sales, service, or operations.

➤ Effective team collaboration often begins with leaders making strategic decisions and conducting premission meetings with their teams.

➤ Successful collaboration requires regular debriefing sessions to assess progress and reset goals.

➤ The frequency of pre- and postmission meetings depends on the urgency of mission execution.

➤ To afford everyone a chance to speak, leaders should give advance notice on topics (whenever possible), speak last, and slow down the conversation.

➤ In healthy collaborative environments, teams establish ground rules for communication and coach one another when behavior falls outside of those rules (e.g., limit interruptions, respect divergent ideas, limit overtalk, and have full input before devising solutions).

➤ Taking time to synthesize learnings helps teams grow and appreciate their interdependence.

➤ Once you provide adequate compensation, teams focus on mastery, autonomy, and purpose.

➤ Teams find fulfillment by stretching themselves, exerting control in their work, and connecting with something larger than themselves.

➤ Collaboration is fostered by leaders who encourage team members to care for one another and meet challenges that cause them to stretch and drive organizational resilience.

YOUR STRENGTH PLAN

1. Think of teams for which you have been a member (in your personal or professional life). Which ones were the most collaborative? Which ones were the least collaborative? What factors contributed to that collaboration?

2. Have you ever participated in a group where the output didn't warrant bringing people together? If so, why didn't the collective wisdom and effort of the group deliver results?

3. For the next week, practice giving team members advance notice of topics (where possible), speak last, and slow down discussions. Observe how your behaviors affect discussions and brainstorming.

4. What rules do you have in place for team communication? Are they formalized? Have all team members agreed to those rules? How often are they reviewed? Does the team honor them?

5. How frequently do you set aside time for teams to debrief, assess progress, share best practices, and realign their work? List three or four lessons learned from recent debriefing sessions.

6. How do you link team success beyond tactical victories (e.g., connecting outcomes to mastery or purpose)?

7. How might collaboration help you develop deeper "bench strength" to assure your organization prevails?

PART V

FORGE THE FUTURE

The most reliable way to
predict the future is to create it.
—ABRAHAM LINCOLN,
sixteenth president of the United States

The next four chapters explore ways to thrive beyond crises by:

- Demonstrating consistent recognition
- Addressing individual needs and preferences
- Running toward tomorrow
- Focusing on what will last

CHAPTER 18

Reenergize with Gratitude

Gratitude unlocks the fullness of life. It turns what we have into enough, and more. It turns denial into acceptance, chaos to order, confusion to clarity.
—MELODY BEATTIE,
self-help author

ON LOW POWER

You've likely had it happen. It's that anxious feeling that surfaces when you realize your cell phone battery is about to die. If you are lucky, you have access to your power cord and an outlet. If not, you sense an imminent disconnection from the broader world.

Much like a cell phone getting ready to power off, many people ran on low power and stamina throughout the pandemic. They were in perpetual firefighting mode with brief or nonexistent recovery periods. Mental and emotional exhaustion set in, and amid that fatigue leaders risked losing three of their most effective reenergizing tools: recognition, gratitude, and levity.

From the standpoint of team members, leaders often struggle to provide consistent recognition in the best of times, and the pandemic was far from the best of times. In a prepandemic Gallup study, only a third of employees said they had received recognition for good work in the past seven days. A 2019 survey conducted by the employee success platform *Achievers* found "lack of recognition" was the third most common reason for employees to leave a company (after compensation issues and career advancement challenges).

In their book *Appreciate*, authors David Sturt, Todd Nordstrom, Kevin Ames, and Gary Beckstrand observed, "For some reason, the workplace hasn't followed suit with our global culture of celebrating greatness. . . . Why aren't more celebrations happening at work? . . . Why are employees expected to perform monumental tasks without praise?"

Employees indeed performed monumental tasks during the pandemic, but were they receiving praise? What about those who were enabling other businesses to function during the crisis (healthcare workers, truck drivers, delivery teams, supermarket employees, etc.)? How much recognition did they receive and from whom? Other than the 7 p.m. cheer that frontline workers received from a grateful public, were leaders recognizing the extra effort of their team members? For that matter, were companies recognizing the sacrifices of customers and seeking to create positive or uplifting experiences for them?

In this chapter, leaders share how they recognized, thanked, and sought to reenergize team members, customers, and others in their respective communities. They offer insights on the power of a thank you, gestures of appreciation, and even playfulness during times of fatigue, anxiety, and crisis. The poet William James once wrote, "The deepest principle in human nature is the craving to be appreciated." Let's look at how leaders addressed that craving through acknowledgment and gratitude.

RECHARGING THE HELPERS

COVID-19 disrupted my own business travel plans in route to the GODIVA 2020 Leadership Conference and plant tour. Founded in 1926, GODIVA Chocolatier is a premium chocolate manufacturer and retailer. It has distribution in more than 100 countries across the globe, including through their iconic chocolate boutiques, GODIVA Cafés, and GODIVA .com; at many fine retailers; and in the chocolate aisle.

Having consulted and presented for GODIVA, my disrupted travel involved research for a planned book. Rightfully, leadership at GODIVA was laser-focused on the health and well-being of its team members as well as maintaining its global operations. In addition to those pressing priorities, leaders at GODIVA continued an emphasis on positive social impact. Evidenced in social media posts like the following:

Is there anything better for stress relief than chocolate? Our thanks to GODIVA to sending sweet treats to HCA Healthcare facilities across the country, including Tulane Medical Center.

GODIVA Acknowledged in Social Media Posts

This commitment to social impact also appears in articles from industry publications like *Confectionery News*, which mentioned GODIVA "partnered with the Tenet Healthcare Corporation in the United States to donate over 600,000 pieces of chocolate to hospital networks across the country." Similar contributions occurred in countries like China, Belgium, the United Arab Emirates (UAE), the United Kingdom, Saudi Arabia, and Turkey.

When asked why leaders at GODIVA chose to think about healthcare workers in the midst of managing their own operational challenges, the CEO of GODIVA, Annie Young-Scrivner, noted, "At our core GODIVA brings comfort. We wanted to recognize heroes fighting for us and give them moments of enjoyment within the chaos. People share our chocolates with those they care about and purchase them to nurture themselves. We also wanted to share GODIVA with those who were tirelessly caring about us all. In posted photos and self-made videos of masked healthcare workers holding their gift of GODIVA, you can see the smiles through their eyes."

Leaders at GODIVA were certainly not alone in their efforts to demonstrate appreciation and have a positive social impact. Thomas Tighe, President and CEO of the global nonprofit Direct Relief (the agency receiving a portion of the proceeds from this book), observed, "Individuals and companies went to bat for one another. Frontline workers and others stepped up to enable the rest of us to live our lives, and in return, many people matched that response by providing funds for PPE, food, and other supplies for those on the front line or in need. It's heartening to see both sides of shared social responsibility and to watch so many leaders and organizations reflect their gratitude through social giving."

Thomas shared his perspective on Direct Relief's intermediary role, noting, "We let donation recipients know supplies or food were not coming from Direct Relief, that instead, those donations were acts of support and appreciation from countless leaders, organizations, and individuals. It was equally important for us to thank those who gave their time, attention, and resources to help the front line and those in need. I didn't want the critical nature of our work to be an excuse for not saying thank you. For me, giving and receiving during the pandemic was a continuous flow of gratitude and appreciation for service to one another." Thomas's perspective reminded me of the words of Scottish philosopher James Allen who noted, "No duty is more urgent than that of returning thanks."

Before we turn to acts of acknowledgment directed toward team members, let's look at a company that demonstrated both formal corporate giving (to nonprofit relief agencies) and direct gestures of gratitude. It is a brand I know well having written *The Starbucks Experience* and *Leading the Starbucks Way*. Starbucks is the world's largest coffee house chain with roughly 31,000 stores and 350,000 employees serving across 80 countries and territories.

John Kelly, the Executive Vice President of Public Affairs and Social Impact at Starbucks, credits the brand's focus on appreciation and gratitude to the combined efforts of leaders and employees (referred to as partners). John noted, "We've learned that during a crisis, social impact matters more than ever. As we were trying to keep our partners safe, keep our doors open, or recover our business, leaders maintained social giving as a priority. As usual, our partners guided paths we should take to have the most significant impact. They asked, 'How can we help frontline responders?' Immediately we decided the least we could do was provide first responders a free cup of coffee to acknowledge, welcome, and tell them that we are here for them." In just one month in the United States and Canada alone, Starbucks had served more than a million cups of free coffee to first responders.

Starbucks leaders and partners joined with organizations like Operation Gratitude and Feeding America to volunteer service and make financial contributions. Operation Gratitude is a Los Angeles–based nonprofit that sends care packages and handwritten letters globally to first responders, healthcare workers, and military personnel. Starbucks partners participated in an online letter-writing campaign for Operation Gratitude, and a donation from The Starbucks Foundation helped the organization deliver roughly 50,000 care packages.

Concerning Feeding America, John noted, "Our nearly four-year relationship with that organization helped us understand that Feeding America's first two challenges would be fewer volunteers at food shelters and a disruption of their food supply. As such, our partners mobilized as volunteers. We donated food and made donations for roughly an additional 20 million meals."

Diligently leaders at companies like Starbucks demonstrate gratitude and support for people that directly or indirectly supported them. They partnered with their team members to identify opportunities to say thank you and to apply volunteer hours and financial resources to energize the lives of others. Primatologist Jane Goodall once said, "You cannot get through a single day without having an impact on the world around you. What you do makes a difference, and you have to decide what kind of difference you want to make." For many leaders, the pandemic was an opportunity to make a difference beyond operational excellence. It was a chance to recognize, acknowledge, and serve their communities and team members.

FUELING THE TEAM

Many leaders such as Michelle Gass, CEO at Kohl's, underscored the importance of personally recognizing individual and team accomplishments. Michelle noted that during the pandemic, "One of my top priorities was to consistently express my tremendous gratitude and thanks to our 100,000 associates. In every message, I was intentional about saying thank you. Sometimes it was in recognition for people who are on the front lines in our e-commerce fulfillment centers. Other times gratitude would be expressed for those who made curbside pickup possible."

In addition to broad messages of praise, Michelle suggested it was essential to interact with the front line personally. She noted, "My leadership team and I knew we had to get out and thank our people. For example, as soon as our stores started opening, I was visiting teams to thank them and hear their incredible stories." Michelle shared that often when she would say thank you, she heard thank you in return. One store manager suggested that his most significant event in a long career at Kohl's was the day he reopened his store after the shutdown. Michelle noted, "He was so grateful for the chance for his team to be of service to his community. How can you not recognize people like that?"

Whether it was through team "shout-outs," one-on-one praise, or investing extra effort to engage employees on a personal level, many leaders increased team member recognition in the context of crisis. They understood the need to replenish energy through one of the simplest, least costly, and most readily available means—warranted praise and recognitions.

A Breath of Insight

I am learning that store franchisees that take action are able to achieve sales while feeding their communities and safely employing their teams. More importantly, I marvel at my wife, who has been so supportive while teaching a third-grade class by video, from our garage!

—**Anthony Fontana,** VP Company Operations, Marco's Pizza

A LIGHT IN THE DARKNESS

Customers and team members alike encountered many moments of anxiety and gloom during the pandemic. Inescapable updates on infections, hospitalizations, and death rates drained emotional energy, as did lifestyle disruptions and increased time pressures. In response, leaders like Troy Bader positioned their goods and services to reenergize those they served. Troy is the President and CEO of International Dairy Queen (IDQ). A subsidiary of Berkshire Hathaway, IDQ began in 1940 and now operates a food and treat restaurant concept in roughly 30 countries.

As Troy noted, "The pandemic has been tragic for some and, at minimum, a highly stressful time for everyone else. As leaders, we wanted to communicate with a tone that was consistent with the crisis; however, we also wanted to be a place where guests could escape the negative. We encouraged franchisees to think about their opportunities to surprise and delight Dairy Queen fans. Maybe that meant putting a little something extra in the bags of a guest or focusing more on smiles or saying thank you. We didn't want to let the fear of COVID-19 interfere with our ability to bring joy into the lives of the people who came through our drive-thrus or dined in with us. It's not always easy to strike the right balance between respecting human pain and delivering delight, but we weren't willing to let the virus define or drain us of our positive energy."

Ben Salzmann, President and CEO at Acuity Insurance, concurred with Troy regarding the importance of maintaining positivity and light-heartedness in crisis. Ben applied those valuable emotional tools to interactions with employees and his community.

Given Acuity's playful culture, Ben noted, "We couldn't let the crisis affect who we are, and we needed to maintain our connection even though we were working remotely. So to maintain our playfulness and keep our teams energized to serve our agents and customers, we did things like send bunny slippers to all employees. That way, our people could work in style from their bedrooms or wherever they felt most comfortable. We also worked on win/win surprises like giving employees a $100 gift card to local restaurants. Employees got a convenient meal and a break from cooking. In the process, we supported local businesses." While a pair of bunny slippers or a gift card may seem like small gestures, Ben and other leaders like him reported those types of actions prompted an outpouring of laughter, tears, and gratitude from team members. In Ben's case, it also provided a catalyst for business growth during the pandemic.

Public safety leaders like Frank Donchez also reported the importance of counterbalancing the seriousness of a crisis. Frank, the Police Chief at the Overland Park, Kansas, Police Department, noted, "In addition to managing all the somber elements of our work, we wanted to be a source of joy in our community. Since birthdays were affected by COVID-19, we set out to make them better. As such, we let our community know that they could schedule a birthday drive-by during a couple of hours of the day. Once scheduled, we'd send an officer by with lights on, and they would announce the birthday over their P.A. I'm not sure who enjoyed those drive-bys more—the person having the birthday, those that arranged it, or our officers." His department also hosted virtual tours of precincts and had a resource officer read children's books from her cruiser via livestream.

In my early career as a clinical psychologist, I researched the health benefits of laughter and wrote about a stress management concept I referred to as one's "amuse system" (the aptitude to find the naturally occurring humor of reality). As leaders, we should help our team members develop their "amuse system" and identify the play and humor around them while also being respectful of those suffering during a crisis.

PUTTING IT ALL TOGETHER

To get a sense of how leaders extend gratitude and playfulness to all stakeholder groups, let's look at the approach taken by James Yarmuth, President and CEO of Sonny's BBQ, and his leadership team. James noted, "Our mission is to spread the spirit of barbeque. That spirit welcomes people, brings them together, and is both kind and playful. The pandemic posed challenges for us, especially when the dining areas of our restaurants were closed, but the spirit of barbeque needed to stay strong for our franchise team, our franchisees, our guests, and the communities we serve."

At the franchise team level, James noted, "We expressed gratitude with one another through phone calls, emails, and shout-outs at daily meetings. We maintained our connections and playfulness by playing trivia or 'get to know you' games through video calls multiple times a week. Some of those activities involved sending in baby pictures and guessing the team member or 'this or that' games (e.g., would you rather stay at a hotel or an Airbnb?). We sent gift cards to everyone's home so we could virtually eat breakfast from the same restaurant together. We also had spirit weeks where team members dressed in accord with a theme like 'mullet Monday' or 'Sonny's swag Wednesday.'"

As it relates to franchisees, James indicated, "We partnered together with our franchisees to spread the spirit of barbecue to first responders and others in need in their local communities. These acts of appreciation included everything from delivering meals to hospital staff and other essential workers to sponsoring and providing food for blood drives. In essence, we 'Q'd kindness' (a pillar of our brand) by recognizing and acknowledging those helping in the fight against COVID-19."

At the guest level, James shared, "We held virtual family trivia nights with hundreds of people on each call and had our Pitmaster provide live cooking tips. We developed educational tools for kids and randomly surprised guests with complimentary food items and personal notes in their takeout bags. We also took the time to call and thank members of our loyalty program who had recently purchased from us. We had team members dedicated to making those calls, and I participated as well."

Sonny's BBQ Spreading Gratitude and Kindness

James gave a flavor for those calls by suggesting some guests were suspicious, "I think they wondered if there was more to the call than a simple thank you. One person even asked, 'Why are you calling me? I'm nobody.' In the spirit of BBQ, we said, 'You are somebody—you are part of Sonny's family—thank you.' They cried, talked about feeling alone, and let us how much the call meant to them."

The law of reciprocity suggests that what you put into the world you receive in return. Based on that law, it is little wonder that Sonny's sales during the pandemic were in the top tier of casual dining restaurants in the United States.

Undeniably, it's challenging to step away from a crisis long enough to say thank you to your team, colleagues, or customers. It is equally difficult during a crisis to justify expenditures designed to "give back" to your community or to invest in what might seem like team frivolity. In truth, playfulness and gratitude are far from frivolous. They are especially necessary to reenergize and sustain effort.

RESILIENCE RECAP

➤ In the best of times, leaders struggle to provide consistent employee recognition.

➤ Research shows that a lack of recognition is the third most common reason for employees to leave a company (after compensation issues and career advancement challenges).

➤ The urgency of your work should not be an excuse for failing to say thank you.

➤ During a crisis, social impact initiatives matter more than ever.

➤ Crises offer an opportunity to make a difference beyond operational excellence. They provide ample chances to recognize, acknowledge, and serve your communities and team members.

➤ Be intentional about saying thank you.

➤ Whether it is through team shout-outs, one-on-one praise, or investing extra effort to engage employees on a personal level, many leaders increase team member recognition in the context of a crisis.

➤ It's not always easy to strike the right balance between respecting human pain and delivering delight. However, leaders shouldn't be willing to let a crisis define or drain the positive energy from their organization.

➤ As leaders, we should help our team members derive benefits of play and positive emotional experiences while being respectful of those suffering during a crisis.

➤ The law of reciprocity suggests that what you put into the world you receive in return. When it comes to gratitude and playfulness, reciprocity applies.

YOUR STRENGTH PLAN

1. Has someone recognized your quality work in the past seven days? Whose work have you praised in that period? Commit to finding something worthy of praise daily and offering that recognition for the next month.

2. To offer praise well, you have to provide it immediately and with specificity. Using those criteria, how well do you provide recognition? What creates delays in delivering your feedback? How do you ensure you are not offering vague praise like "you did a great job"?

3. In what ways do you demonstrate your appreciation beyond saying thank you (e.g., gestures, volunteering time, donations)?

4. To what degree and how do you demonstrate appreciation for the following—employees, peers, customers, supervisors, and members of the community?

5. How would you rate the playfulness of your culture (high, medium, low)? What is the basis of that rating?

6. How does a crisis affect the playfulness and humor of your team?

7. How should playfulness and humor change in the context of crisis? What should decrease, stay the same, or increase?

8. What team building do you do (in or out of a crisis)?

CHAPTER 19

Make It Personal

*We must establish a personal connection
with each other. Connection before content.
Without relatedness, no work can occur.*
—PETER BLOCK,
author and consultant

TAKING BUSINESS TO THE INDIVIDUAL LEVEL

Leadership action, in and out of a crisis, can be viewed as either general-ized, customized, or personalized. The basic level, generalized action, is a "one-size-fits-all" approach. For example, from the previous chapter, Ben Salzmann and his leadership team at Acuity demonstrated general-ized (albeit playful) behavior when they shipped bunny slippers to *all* team members.

The middle-level customized action addresses the wants, needs, or de-sires of a segment of stakeholders. Annie Young-Scrivner and her team at GODIVA took customized action by donating chocolate to a *segment* of the population—healthcare workers.

Personalized leadership behavior targets *individual* needs and pref-erences. When an Overland Park Police officer did a drive-by birthday celebration, he exhibited personalized care.

During the crisis, leaders reported they increased their personalized leadership behavior as much as possible. The key words in that sentence are obviously "as much as possible." Personalization takes extra effort, and in some circumstances, it isn't necessary or helpful. For example, a gen-eralized action taken by *TIME* magazine's leaders to guarantee 90 days of work to all employees was broadly beneficial. Such was the action by Jeff Dailey and the team at Farmers Insurance to provide insurance discounts to personal auto policy owners.

Ultimately, I believe all business is and should be personal. Moreover, personalization is increasingly important during times of crisis. Let's look at why and how leaders enhanced personal care during the pandemic. Additionally, let's examine the impact personalization has on team members, customers, and other stakeholders.

WHO ARE THEY?

Kurt Kuebler, Partner at Kopplin Kuebler & Wallace, reported that during the pandemic, he and his team invested time to get to know colleagues on a more personal level. Kurt noted, "Things didn't slow down for us in our work with clients in the club industry, but we used our time differently. We, like so many other people, conducted more video conferences in six weeks than we had during years of business. We saw our twice-weekly team meetings not only as a time for communication and alignment but also as a chance to get to know industry partners more personally. My partners and I have developed many personal relationships with colleagues over the years, but our 15 other staff members haven't had the same opportunity. So we invited an industry partner to each of our team meetings. It was a time for our team to get to know that partner, understand their business top-to-bottom, and to enable our partner to make a personal connection with our team." Videoconferencing enabled Kurt's team to strengthen personal connections with industry partners, but it took the insight of Kurt and his leadership group to recognize and facilitate this personal opportunity.

FEAR IS PERSONAL

Jonathan Sachs seized a critical opportunity to understand how his team members experienced an intensely personal emotion—fear. Jonathan is the Vice President of Patient Experience and Foundation at Adventist HealthCare, a faith-based, not-for-profit network of healthcare providers including hospitals, mental health centers, rehab facilities, and home health care. Adventist HealthCare is based in Gaithersburg, Maryland.

Jonathan noted, "Before COVID-19 was getting much attention in the US, I talked to an acquaintance that imports and exports goods from

China. He reported being anxious and alarmed by the likely impact the virus would have in the United States. Others I spoke to had minimal to no fear as the pandemic was accelerating in our country. I was particularly vigilant about COVID-19 because my wife and I are expecting our first child. All of these different responses to the crisis meant I needed to listen carefully to understand what people were feeling and not make assumptions. As healthcare leaders, we needed to customize preparation plans to a range of hypothetical situations. However, the people we serve play out their own hypotheticals. Those scenarios produce different fear responses for them, ranging from denial to panic. It became clear that I frequently needed to ask each person I served about their specific fears and their overall fear level."

Nido Qubein frames the importance of understanding the fears of individuals in the context of an overarching communication principle. Nido is the President of High Point University, a private liberal arts institution offering both graduate and undergraduate degrees. High Point's 430-acre campus is located in North Carolina and serves students from all 50 US states and more than 37 other countries. Nido suggested that during a crisis, leaders need to "remember the law of identification: When something becomes personal, it then becomes important. Self-interest, yes, but more so it is about enlightened self-interest. Ask this question: How must this person feel first so they can do what we need them to do to achieve personal and organizational success? To communicate, you merely need to master the skills of speaking, listening, observing, and writing. But to connect, one must speak from the mind and the heart. To be reason-based and emotion-sensitive. To connect, you always start where the other person is. Their goals. Their fears. Their aspirations. Their needs."

Jonathan's and Nido's perspectives are rich with actionable takeaways. The more personal something is, the more important it becomes. Fear, by its nature, is profoundly and personally experienced. Understanding how people experience fear helps leaders connect with individuals by going "where the other person is." This connection provides leaders the opportunity to help team members or customers manage fear and achieve their goals and aspirations. Before we get to those aspirations, let's look at how leaders took personalized action during the pandemic based on the fears and needs of their stakeholders.

FROM UNDERSTANDING TO
PERSONALIZED ACTION

Abigail Kies acted personally to address the fears and needs of both her students and her peers. Abigail is the Assistant Dean of Career Development at the Yale School of Management, a world-renowned business school offering a portfolio of advanced degree programs as well as Executive Education, located in New Haven, Connecticut.

Abigail noted, "Every student and colleague had very individualized needs during the pandemic, and it was important to understand them and address them where possible. For one student, it could mean allaying anxiety by arranging a virtual mock interview so they could prepare for postgraduation jobs. For another, it might mean reducing their concerns by working closely with faculty to find a meaningful summer project. For someone else, their fears might involve changes in their financial situation, which required creative approaches for funding. There was a lot of listening, reaching out to faculty, and coming up with individualized solutions. Where possible, we scaled those solutions to meet and anticipate the needs of other students."

From the perspective of personalization with colleagues, Abigail noted, "Before we could effectively collaborate, we needed to understand each team member's unique circumstances and build flexibility around their situation. I started by asking everyone, 'What work schedule is best for you?' We followed that up with open dialogue. For example, a divorced mom on my team splits custody of her son during the week with his father. Both parents spend two and a half days with their child. On days when her son was not with her, she wanted to be able to work extra hours so she could focus on his care during the days he was at her home. As a team, we agreed to support her schedule. She's thriving, and the team has adjusted well."

Ann Ayers, Dean of the Colorado Women's College at the University of Denver, also demonstrated the power of peer-to-peer personalization. Ann noted, "We have something we call a team 'hug' meeting twice a week during which we answer a question that helps us get to know and serve one another in more personal ways. That question is posed in advance of the meeting, so we have time to think about our response. For example, one team member asked everyone to talk about their favorite nonprofit organization. After that call, she sent an email to each participant noting she made a $20 donation in our honor to every organization mentioned. At a time of economic uncertainty, her act of personalized generosity was hugely inspiring."

By taking the time to connect with and address personal needs and values of colleagues, Abigail and Ann report their teams are inspired and thriving. It would be easy to conclude that Ann's team "hugs" are unnecessary or that Abigail's team should adhere to a strict schedule, but based on their results, both leaders know the powerful impact of their personalized approaches.

> ### A Breath of Insight
>
> Have a plan, confront the short-term brutal facts,
> but spend time daily visualizing the future.
> Paint that vision in a vivid way so that the *why* behind
> your team's efforts makes the journey worthwhile.
> **—Ivan Tornos,** Group President, Zimmer Biomet

IT'S ASPIRATIONAL

During the pandemic, Rainey Foster reported that clients needed and asked for more personalization. Rainey is a Partner and Executive Vice President at Leading Authorities Inc., a premier speakers bureau, video communications, and live events production company based in Washington, DC. Rainey noted, "The live events industry has taken a massive hit during this crisis. Event planners have been scrambling to postpone, reassess, and work through the challenges of planned in-person meetings. At Leading Authorities, we've always seen ourselves as putting our clients' needs first, but our consultative role has broadened during the pandemic. While we've always taken the time to understand our clients' objectives and help them find the perfect speaker for their event, we've been asked to assist clients cope with many new challenges. Meeting planners, for example, are reaching out for help with hotel cancellation policies or whether to pivot to a virtual event. Organization clients are looking for ways to deliver value to their memberships and to have entire virtual events produced. I find myself asking clients a lot more questions about what's keeping them and their members up at night. Each question produces an answer that's unique and personal to them. Those answers require equally unique, personal, and creative solutions."

Vic Keller builds on Rainey's observation concerning increased client interest in personalized crisis solutions. In Vic's experience, clients are looking for partners to create individualized solutions that will enable them to have a future competitive advantage. Vic is the CEO and Chairman of multiple companies, including Optym and KLV Capital. Optym is a multinational technology solutions provider with offices in the United States, Armenia, India, and Australia. Optym specializes in transportation and logistics software that serve the airline, trucking, railroad, and mining industries.

Vic noted, "Many companies that I work with are in reinvention mode. They are looking for partners who can understand their unique needs, challenges, and aspirations. Fulfillment partners are a commodity. It is not about customizing a solution to their project specifications. The crisis has clients looking for companies who understand them and can assist them in meeting their reinvention goals. I think we've known the importance of this level of customer intimacy, but the crisis has amplified the critical nature of deep customer understanding and personalized solutions."

Rainey and Vic identified a surge in customer expectations regarding personalization. Increasingly clients are not content with "off-the-shelf" or slightly modified solutions. Instead, they are searching for personalized solutions to help them survive or reinvent themselves. To achieve that level of personalization, leaders can't rely exclusively on formalized listening strategies like surveys (discussed in Chapter 6). They must take time to reach out to clients and immerse themselves in their clients' strengths, weaknesses, opportunities, and threats. Steve Jobs put it this way: "Get closer than ever to your customers. So close that you tell them what they need well before they realize it themselves." Where Steve Jobs used the words "get close to," I use the words "get personal with." When we get personal with our customers, we understand, anticipate, and tailor solutions that help them address short- and long-term needs. Of course, we also have to be willing to take bold actions on their behalf.

PUTTING YOURSELF WAY OUT THERE

In classic Zappos style, Tony Hsieh, the company's CEO, and his team took bold and personal action at scale. About a month into the pandemic, Zappos announced its "Customer Service for Anything" program—a targeted personalization offering. Tony explained, "We hire extremely talented people who intrinsically understand how to create personal emotional connections, or PECs, with our customers. We also train them to develop that talent. So, it made sense to find a way to have our people help anyone who contacted us to navigate the pandemic." Tony announced the Customer Service for Anything Hotline on the Zappos website by saying, "Like many of you, most of our employees have been working from home for over a month now, and there's definitely a lot of new challenges in our new environment. Our history has been about trying to provide the very best customer service and customer experience for selling shoes online, clothing, and so on. But we want to do more than that. We want to help everyone navigate this new world. So we launched customer service for anything. It can be anything from just needing someone to talk to, finding out if certain restaurants offer delivery, or helping with research. We really want to be of service to anyone and everyone that wants to call in. So, give us a call at the number below. We're here, and we'll do our very best."

The "very best" personal care provided through the Zappos Customer Service for Anything line was the source for stories in publications like the *New York Times* and *Forbes* and on CBS News. Moreover, Zappos captured some of the most impactful stories on their site. One of which was a call from a doctor whose health system was running out of pulse oximeters with no stock available from his suppliers. His call to the hotline asked if Zappos could locate a large number of pulse oximeters for him. Zappos procured 300 devices, noting on their website, "The 300 pulse oximeters didn't wholly solve [their] problem as they were looking for nearer a thousand. Still, the ones that Zappos were able to find are helping . . . provide crucial remote monitoring to 300 discharged patients that have suspected positive diagnoses of COVID-19." There you have it, a seeming contradiction—widespread yet personalized care. In other words, personalization for everyone.

Unlike Tony and his team at Zappos, Amir Rubin seeks for his organization's team members to collectively engage in designing and managing robust processes to support highly reliable and scalable performance levels. Amir, the Chair and CEO of One Medical, noted, "We leverage process improvement and innovation approaches—which collectively we call TOPS or The One Medical Performance system—which utilize, Lean, Design Thinking, Agile, and Behavior Design approaches to support a common performance management framework across the organization. By having a common management system with reliable processes, our talented team members can focus their efforts on caring for our members rather than using heroic efforts just to complete day-to-day activities.

"As an example, I recently received a letter from the adult daughter of two older members of ours from Scottsdale, Arizona. The daughter, who lived in another state, explained that we had established a primary care relationship with her parents roughly two weeks before her father began showing COVID-19 symptoms. Given the severity of the father's symptoms, our team was able to directly arrange for him to be hospitalized and later treated with a confirmed case of COVID-19. Our team was concerned about the spouse's health as well, and thus arranged for her to get tested in one of our drive-through locations. When she showed active symptoms and then also tested positive with lab results returned directly in our technology platform, we arranged to get her hospitalized through our digital and clinical integration with the hospital. Additionally, our team then worked with the ambulance company to make sure we got her admitted into the same hospital with her husband, so they might have the opportunity to be closer to each other. The story ends well for the couple, as both were ultimately treated and released. By having robust workflows in place to manage such "routine processes" as app-based virtual care, arrangement of lab testing and digital results reporting into our app, coordinated communication with family members, and clinical and digital integration with hospital systems, our incredibly caring team members could focus on going above and beyond to deliver a higher level of human-centered coordinated care."

For Chuck DiNardo, personalization doesn't emerge from efficiency; it is a function of product precision and individualized commitment. Chuck, the President of Aesculap Inc., noted, "Our people add human personalization to extremely personalized and precise medical devices. For example, one of our products is a shunt that drains water off the brain of patients suffering from hydrocephalus. After insertion, the shunt occasionally needs reprogramming. During the pandemic, a patient required that service, which a team member could have supported remotely. However, our Aesculap staff member considered how they would want the calibration done if they were the patient. They then took it upon themselves to fly to the patient and be present with the surgeon to ensure reprogramming was successful. To me, everything we do is personal, and I am blessed with a team that pushes us to greater and greater levels of personalization in our products and the way we serve our doctors and patients."

For Tony, Amir, and Chuck, personalization is the aspiration of all their leadership behavior. Tony views personalization as a mass offering. Amir drives efficiency, so clinicians have the freedom to address the personal needs of every patient, and Chuck links precision and personalization to products and human service delivery. Generalized and customized leadership behaviors are necessary to run a business at scale. However, increasingly leaders are appreciating the importance of "making it personal." How about you?

RESILIENCE RECAP

➤ Leadership action, in and out of a crisis, can be viewed as operating on three levels—generalized, customized, or personalized.

➤ The basic level, generalized action, is a *one-size-fits-all* approach.

➤ The middle level, customized action, addresses the wants, needs, or desires of a *segment* of stakeholders.

➤ Personalized leadership behavior targets *individual* needs and preferences.

➤ During the pandemic, leaders reported that they increased their personalized leadership approach.

➤ Remember the law of identification: When something becomes personal, it then becomes important. Ask this question: How must this person feel first so he or she can do what we need that person to do to achieve personal and organizational success?

➤ Fear, by its nature, is profoundly and personally experienced. Understanding how individuals experience fear helps leaders connect.

➤ By taking the time to connect with and address personal needs and values of colleagues, teams report they thrive and are inspired.

➤ Increasingly clients are not content with "off-the-shelf" or slightly modified solutions. Instead, they are searching for options that are personalized to help them survive or reinvent themselves.

➤ When we get personal with our customers, we understand, anticipate, and tailor solutions that help them address short- and long-term needs.

➤ Generalized and customized leadership behaviors are necessary to run a business at scale. However, increasingly leaders are appreciating the importance of "making it personal."

YOUR STRENGTH PLAN

1. Think of your leadership behaviors. Which of them falls into the generalized, customized, and personalized categories?

2. To what degree are you emphasizing personalization? Think of an example where your team has effectively delivered personal care.

3. Are you able to deliver personalized services at scale, or are they "one-offs"? If you are providing personal services broadly, how are you doing it? If not, what is getting in the way?

4. Do you believe customers are looking for more personalization? If so, what do you point to in support of that conclusion? If not, why do you think that is the case?

5. How do you encourage personal interest and support among your team members?

6. Consider asking a personal question of individuals on your team during regular meetings (e.g., their favorite nonprofit) and also inviting an industry partner or customer to your meetings so you can get to know them better.

7. Would your core customers view your business approach as more generalized, customized, or personalized? Why do you think they would say that? Are you content with that answer? If not, what needs to change?

CHAPTER 20

Run Toward the Future

The distinction between the past,
present, and future is only a
stubbornly persistent illusion.
—ALBERT EINSTEIN,
theoretical physicist

STAYING AHEAD OF DANGER

In 1985, the *Economist* magazine shared a quote credited to securities analyst Dan Montano. Many variations of the quote have surfaced since. Dan purportedly said the following at a financial technology conference:

> Every morning in Africa, a gazelle wakes up. It knows it must run faster than the fastest lion or it will be killed. Every morning a lion wakes up. It knows it must outrun the slowest gazelle or it will starve to death. It doesn't matter whether you are a lion or a gazelle: when the sun comes up, you'd better be running.

Everyone in a position of leadership during the pandemic woke up each morning and ran. They ran to ensure the safety of team members and customers, reduce costs, shore up balance sheets, accelerate digitization, drive priorities, communicate more regularly, or pivot in response to rapidly changing conditions.

Some leaders only ran *from* danger, while others also ran *toward* the future. Leaders I spoke with had a mix of metaphors to describe how they split focus between imminent crisis management and future strategic planning. For example, some spoke of wanting to "both win the battle and win the war," while others talked about "not wanting to let a crisis go to waste." For this chapter title and business principle, I decided to go with "Run Toward the Future."

Research conducted by Professor Karam Ghazi for the *Journal of Hotel & Business Management* demonstrates the critical importance of blending both a crisis response (running away from danger) with a future-oriented strategic approach (running toward future success). Professor Ghaz reports:

> Resilience is the ability of an organisation not only to survive but also to thrive, both in good times and in the face of adversity. . . . Through incorporating crisis management into an organisation's strategic planning processes and vice versa, strategies can be developed to take advantage of these "silver lining" opportunities in the midst of crises.

In this chapter, leaders share how they emotionally and practically prepared their organizations for a resilient future. They also offer insights on how to move a company toward an improved future state while actively navigating daily challenges. With an emphasis on digital transformation, integrated learning, product development, innovative marketing, and talent acquisition, interviewees connect us to possibilities and strategies for a postcrisis world. Amazon CEO Jeff Bezos once put it this way, what you "need to do is always lean into the future; when the world changes around you and when it changes against you—what used to be a tail wind is now a head wind—you have to lean into that and figure out what to do because complaining isn't a strategy." Jeff is right—there's no time for complaining, so let's *run toward the future*.

SETTING THE EMOTIONAL TONE AND MINDSET

Amid the pandemic, Nicholas Speeks wasn't complaining about the present or the future; he was communicating opportunities ahead. Nicholas is the President and CEO at Mercedes-Benz USA, a Stuttgart-based German luxury automobile manufacturer with 93 worldwide offices. Mercedes-Benz manufactures its vehicles in 17 countries on five continents.

Nicholas noted, "Leadership is about rallying people to move forward. From the onset of the pandemic, I was reminding our organization that all things pass. Our job in the crisis was to successfully master our challenges, experiment in areas that would make us stronger, and work together to come out on the other side, knowing we stood against a shared burden. I reminded our people that going through this trial by fire together will bring us a renewed sense of community, which will serve us for years to come."

Vala Afshar shares Nicholas's perspective on leaders being in the "move people forward" business, and he frames that forward movement in the context of a "flow-based" mindset. Vala is the Chief Digital Evangelist at Salesforce, a US cloud-based company that provides customer relationship management software and other complementary business management applications. Salesforce's roughly 52,000 employees design and support products used by more than 150,000 businesses worldwide.

Vala noted leaders must understand, "The lifeblood of a group or company isn't capturing resources or ideas but moving them. It is a shift from silos to flows. To quickly react to a crisis and position success afterward, leaders must first develop their own flow-based mindset. They must be willing to share resources across the organization and encourage teams to engage in rapid knowledge sharing. They should take the momentum generated by crisis activity and leverage it toward opportunities that will drive future success."

Both Nicholas and Vala remind us that crises propel movement. You can think of a crisis like a rocket booster that provides the liftoff thrust needed to move a stationary and weighty rocket off the launchpad. Once the spacecraft has fought through inertia, that booster drops off and returns to Earth, and other engines sustain flight. Our job as leaders is to manage the initial force of the booster rockets (the crisis) while investing in sustainment rockets (people, products, and technology) that will propel momentum toward the future.

POSITIONING RESOURCES

Much like the staging of rocket engines, Richard Weil emphasized the importance of adjusting your investment strategy in phases. Richard is the Chief Executive Officer at Janus Henderson Group, a leading global active asset manager, with more than 2,000 employees in 27 worldwide offices. With roughly $295 billion in assets under management, Janus Henderson serves individual, intermediary, and institutional clients globally.

Richard noted, "Most leaders try to plan for crises by creating a strong financial foundation and a robust culture. If that plan is successful, the first hit from the crisis should allow them to stay client-focused and not be reactive in a self-focused way. Their people won't need to worry about themselves and instead can think about their clients first. That initial buffer provides an advantage to take a medium- to long-range perspective from the outset of the crisis. If the crisis holds on, however, it can be difficult to sustain perspective on the longer term, especially as your reserves diminish."

Despite the challenges of a prolonged crisis, Richard warned against cannibalizing future resources. He observed, "Even in those times, you can't do destructive things like eat your seed corn or fire your best talent. To the highest degree possible, you have to put a firewall around some of your resources to make sure you have the right people and tools needed to create success after you escape the crisis. Throughout the pandemic, we've taken this approach to ensure solvent financial leadership with calculated future investments in our business."

John Galloway expands on Richard's message of investing in the future by focusing on innovation across multiple business domains. John, the Chief Marketing and Innovation Officer at GODIVA Chocolatier, said, "When you have a brand that dates back to 1926, you have to leverage your past to drive your future. Our heritage abounds with adaptability and innovation, which fuels our resilience."

John added, "At GODIVA, we built on our foundation of innovation by accelerating breakthrough products, technologies, and marketing tools. On the product side, we launched and iterated our GODIVA Signature Chocolate individually wrapped mini bars, milkshakes, and other items. The mini bars evolved from understanding how consumers break and eat chocolate bars. We also made sharing those bars easier and safer for a pandemic and postpandemic world. Our technology investments have made it possible for rapid product delivery. Let's assume you live in New York City and want to get GODIVA chocolate to a friend the same day in Dallas. Digital integration allows us to fulfill that order from our retail operations in Dallas and not from a more distant fulfillment center. Finally, from a social media front, we have been students of social selling innovations in China and are positioning for future engagement through channels and platforms like livestreaming. We definitely respond to emergent business needs during moments of crisis, but we also attend to important future moments as well."

John reminds us to leverage our organization's history of resilience and invention to springboard future innovation. He also demonstrates the breadth to which those innovative efforts should apply. By suggesting current crisis moments shouldn't interfere with future moments, John offers a view consistent with comedian George Burns. Mr. Burns noted, "I look forward to the future because that is where I am going to spend the rest of my life." Since the future is where all of us will spend the rest of our lives, let's look at how we can use learnings from the past to position us for a better tomorrow.

RAPIDLY LEARNING FROM THE PRESENT

Gail McGovern is a leader poised to integrate crisis learnings to make her organization able to face future challenges. Gail is the President and CEO of the American Red Cross. Founded in 1881, the American Red Cross is a US humanitarian organization that provides disaster relief, emergency assistance, and disaster preparedness education.

Gail shared, "One leadership lesson I've learned anew during this time is the need for adaptability and innovation. The Red Cross has had to make drastic changes across virtually every aspect of our mission delivery over the past months. We are an organization that prides itself on preparedness and our ability to respond to numerous large-scale disasters at once. But I don't think there is any way we could've predicted the full scope of the operational changes we've had to make in such a short time. As we look to the future, it's vitally important that my leadership team and I keep a strong focus on innovation. By doing so, we can be better prepared with the tools, technology, and know-how needed to overcome the unexpected challenges that will most certainly arise in the months and years ahead."

During the pandemic, the Red Cross was asked by the Food & Drug Administration (FDA) to collect and distribute convalescent plasma as part of an experimental treatment for COVID-19 patients. It also navigated significant logistical challenges when conditions required much of the organization's employee base to work from home. Gail viewed those adjustments as learning opportunities for the future, stating, "When people think of an agile organization in today's modern world, they probably don't think of a 139-year-old American institution like the Red Cross. But after each major disaster event, we traditionally develop after-action reports to review everything we've done and determine what worked well and what didn't work. We then incorporate these learnings for the next disaster. While this assessment process is ongoing, there are many lessons we've learned that I believe are already allowing us to fulfill our mission more efficiently and effectively than before. And I'm certain these learnings will help make us a stronger organization in the long run. Ultimately, I believe many of the changes we've adopted will help us become a greener, more environmentally conscious organization with an even stronger focus on the health and well-being of our team members and the people we serve." At 139 years old, the Red Cross is an agile and learning organization, thanks to leaders like Gail. Lessons from the Red Cross also extend to broad, forward-looking sustainability issues like environmental consciousness.

THINKING BIGGER AND BROADER

As a revolutionary social entrepreneur, Blake Mycoskie encourages leaders to factor global economics and environmental impact into their future planning. Blake is the Founder of TOMS Shoes and the originator of TOMS' one-for-one business model, where a product purchase prompts a product donation. Through this approach, TOMS has provided 86 million pairs of shoes, more than 600,000 eyeglasses, and more than 600,000 weeks of safe water to those in need. Blake currently oversees a personal development company Madefor, which he cofounded.

Blake indicated, "When I think of the future, I'm concerned about stakeholders outside of the walls of my business. They are usually invisible and beyond the consciousness of many leaders. The pandemic has been a truth-teller that exposed us to the impact of commerce-driven pollution and to the Earth's ability to heal when we lessen our corporate impact. I want my colleagues to think beyond the bottom line and consider our responsibility for the future of the planet. We need to consider how we are going to come out of and act long after the pandemic. I believe that brands that will emerge from the pandemic the strongest are those with bigger picture thinking."

Mindy Grossman, President and CEO of WW (formerly Weight Watchers), agrees that leaders may become too narrow in their conceptualizations of future success. Mindy suggested, "Based on my experience with other crises, I knew we couldn't spend all our time responding to business fire drills, and I was concerned that we might not be thinking big enough while mired in the pandemic." It's reasonable to think about a future where you accelerate your transition to digital, launch new products, or amplify content platforms, but is that being bold enough when it comes to leveraging the momentum of a crisis?

In response to that boldness consideration, Mindy led a cross-functional visionary team. She advised that group that they were "tasked with big, game-changing ideas. Some of which might not be possible at all, others that will materialize in the distant future, and others we will test now, because now is the perfect time for innovation." While some leaders will postpone innovation until better times, Mindy believes there is no better time than the present to test innovation, especially if that time is a crisis!

PULLING THE CAMERA BACK

Let's imagine you are looking through a telescopic camera lens. As a leader during a crisis, you need to zoom the lens in to manage weekly, daily, or hourly challenges and zoom it out to strategize for the future. The lens of James McElvain, PhD, would zoom far into the past and way beyond what most of us could see. James is the Chief of Police for the Vancouver, Washington, Police Department. When asked about his perspective on leadership, James explained, "Being a leader means you are in the forever business, and I think that that gets lost on a lot of people. Our law enforcement agency existed well before me and will exist well past me. Recognizing that you're in a forever business enables you to see that your real leadership responsibility is for the future of an organization that will survive long past you."

James continued, "Every leader has had to live with the impact of decisions made by prior leaders . . . and future leaders will have to do the same with the decisions we make during the pandemic. If we make decisions only considering short-term goals, we run the risk of handcuffing future leaders. This year is my thirty-fourth in law enforcement, and I've had the pleasure of beating the curve on tenure for police chiefs. As such, I've lived with the impact of many of my earlier decisions, but someday someone else will inherit my choices. I have the responsibility to set those leaders up for greatness and not sell them out for success now." For James, we should run to the future because we are responsible for those who will face it. For him, the future is also less about tactical navigation and more about moral responsibility. Positioning a brand for a better future is not a strategic exercise but a part of the forever role of leaders.

I'll close this chapter with two quotes that relate to how leadership decisions affect future generations. One quote comes from a seventeenth-century physicist and the other from a modern-day business giant. Isaac Newton observed, "If I have seen further than others, it is by standing upon the shoulders of giants." Similarly, Warren Buffet commented, "Someone is sitting in the shade today because someone planted a tree a long time ago." How will you help future generations of leaders see further and find shade? How are you running to the future as a leader of a forever business?

RESILIENCE RECAP

➤ Some leaders only run *from* danger, while others also run *toward* the future.

➤ Companies that blend crisis management and future planning are more resilient and capable of finding the "silver business lining" in the dark cloud of crisis.

➤ Leadership is about rallying people to move forward and developing a flow (as opposed to siloed) mindset.

➤ A crisis is like a rocket booster that provides the liftoff thrust needed to move a stationary and weighty rocket off the launchpad. Once a crisis propels an organization through inertia, leaders must keep the momentum going to expedite future growth.

➤ In prolonged crises, it is tempting to do destructive things like eat your seed corn or fire your best talent. Resist the urge!

➤ Leverage your organization's history of resilience and invention to springboard future innovation.

➤ During a crisis, invest in people, products, and technology that fuel forward-facing success.

➤ Leverage crisis learnings to position future growth.

➤ Future planning sessions should factor in global economic and environmental impact.

➤ Leaders are likely not to think or act big enough when it comes to positioning future success during a crisis.

➤ Leadership is a forever business, and our decisions travel forward in unforeseeable ways affecting the lives of future leaders.

YOUR STRENGTH PLAN

1. Describe some areas where you have helped your team or business run from danger. Similarly, describe some ways you have helped run toward the future.

2. To what degree do your crisis management and strategic planning processes integrate? How has effective crisis management enabled your team or company to pursue the "silver linings" that emerge from crisis?

3. How has a crisis helped your business move through inertia? What has been done to maintain the momentum of the crisis to fuel future growth or distant objectives?

4. What does the phrase "don't eat your seed corn" mean to you, as it relates to future investments? How are you allocating and protecting the money needed for future sustainability and growth?

5. In what ways are you investing in people, products, and technology? How will those investments likely reward future generations of leaders?

6. How broadly are you envisioning the future? Are all your projects incremental improvements, or do you have a mix of conservative and bold, game-changing initiatives?

7. During a crisis, are you able to test future-oriented products or services? If so, how? If not, why not?

8. How have the decisions of past leaders either limited or enabled your success today? What decisions are you making that could restrict or enable future leaders?

CHAPTER 21

Engineer Legacy

*The great use of life is to spend it
for something that will outlast it.*
—WILLIAM JAMES,
psychologist and philosopher

REVERSE ENGINEERING

How do you need to develop so you maximize your leadership impact in times of crisis and beyond? To get a sense of developmental priorities, it helps to imagine you are at the end of your career. It can be a bit odd to think about your professional life coming to an end, but that approach allows you to reverse engineer the steps needed to achieve your desired impact. So imagine, you are looking back on your time as a leader, what legacy do you hope to leave? What do you want people to say about your contribution?

Before you answer those questions, let's look at how a broad cross section of the 140-plus contributors interviewed in this book answered the following:

> Assume the pandemic is sufficiently resolved and people are looking back on the leadership you and your colleagues provided, what do you hope stakeholders will say?

As you will soon see, the answers to that pandemic legacy question reinforce insights from previous chapters. They will also help you craft your legacy statement, which will apply to crisis leadership and beyond.

For years I have been writing and coaching on the importance of declaring a leadership legacy. Upon our departure from leadership roles, people will likely synopsize our impact into a single sentence. If we take the time to think about what we would like them to say, we give ourselves time to develop skills, make decisions, and take actions that will increase the likelihood we will achieve the impact we desire.

As it relates to the pandemic, the desired legacy of leaders fell into three broad areas. They wanted to be known for leading with one of the following:

1. Competence

2. Purpose

3. Character

While some leaders blend elements from these three areas, most have a prominent theme. Where appropriate, I call out subthemes folded into each category. Let's take a look at some respondent comments before you set out to draft a leadership legacy statement.

STUFFING THE TOOLKIT

Many leaders hoped to hear that they and their colleagues demonstrated effort, skill mastery, or execution during the pandemic. I refer to those ability-based outcomes as leading with competence. On the effort front, Brett Schlatterer, the Fire Chief of Pinellas Park, Florida, reported that he hoped he and his leadership team would be seen as "fighting to protect our employees and citizens. We knew things would take turns for the worst despite our best efforts, but we always wanted people to be able to say that we did everything we could on their behalf." Brett's perspective acknowledged that leaders don't control outcomes; they influence them. Leaders, however, do control their diligence. Brett's legacy requires consistently providing a maximal effort.

From a skills perspective, crisis legacy statements indicated a desire to demonstrate communication, goal setting, team alignment, and team productivity capabilities. Consistent with Chapter 6, "Listen Beyond the Words," Matt Renner, President of Enterprise Commercial at Microsoft, noted, "I hope our customers will say we showed up with empathy, technical expertise, and functioned as digital first responders. Optimally, they would also say we listened carefully; cared personally; were consistent, responsive, reliable; and put our best foot forward during the crisis. They would view us as a company that leaned in during the pandemic." Matt wanted the leadership team to be known for listening both for understanding and the emotions behind the words. He wanted to demonstrate that Microsoft leveraged a deep understanding to solve complex customer problems.

While Matt emphasized a legacy of empathic listening, Charlie Acevedo, Senior Vice President of Sales and Merchandising at Costa Farms LLC, hoped employees would find value in his leadership team's honest and regular communication, consistent with Chapter 7, "Seek Carefully and Speak Truthfully." Charlie indicated, "I want people to notice that we were present and communicated consistently and clearly. Hopefully, they saw us as not overpromising or sugarcoating information, and they felt we provided the data they needed to do their jobs." Given the importance of listening and communication skills for Matt and Charlie, it's reasonable to assume they focused on active listening and expressive communication behaviors throughout the pandemic.

Many other leaders talked about priority-setting, mentorship, or team alignment skills as they crafted their crisis legacy statements. In keeping with Chapter 14, "Streamline Productivity," Troy Bader, President and CEO of International Dairy Queen, said he wanted his franchise community to see his leadership team as providing constructive and disciplined direction. Troy added, "Hopefully, they understand the value of our constant focus on a few key objectives and the discipline it took not to get distracted by pursuing a host of well-intentioned projects that would have hampered our effectiveness." Imagine a legacy where the sentence most commonly said about you is: "They kept us on a productive path and helped us avoid unnecessary detours."

Many other leaders focused on the skills needed to help their teams achieve a common goal. Frequently, that achievement linked back to how leaders positioned themselves relative to those teams. For example, Joe Haury, Vice President of Global Logistics at Panasonic North America, wanted to be remembered for effectively "leading from the front" (Chapter 13, "Shift Front, Middle, Back"). Joe stated, "Ideally, my team would have confidence in the strategy I laid out for us. They would sense I was always looking out for their best interest throughout one of the most challenging periods in our journey together."

While Joe shifted his leadership position (front, middle, and back) as situations warranted, I suspect his legacy statement reflects the position from which he is most skilled and most comfortable.

Leaders like Katie Fitzgerald and Brian Gallagher emphasized skills associated with rallying teams to adapt quickly (Chapter 15, "Pivot with Urgency"). Katie Fitzgerald, Executive Vice President and Chief Operating Officer for Feeding America, noted that ideally, her team's actions would be viewed as highly adaptable. Concerning local community partners, Katie hoped they would perceive her and her colleagues as having "helped us all become more agile and more responsive, especially for the front line. They would see us as making daily and weekly changes that gave people greater visibility to community needs. They would acknowledge that we set up systems, made a difference, and grew with intention."

Similarly, Brian Gallagher, President and Chief Executive Officer at United Way Worldwide, hoped his leadership team would cause community members to say, "They moved amazingly quickly to meet our needs. Collectively they innovated solutions. I didn't realize United Way offered all those services. We need their willingness to adapt and their ability to bring communities together." Given how Katie and Brian value adaptivity, it's likely they focused on agile design, scrum, lean, or other iterative technologies. Compare that desired flexibility impact to the disciplined excellence legacy sought by a hospitality leader.

Horst Schulze, the founder of the modern-day Ritz-Carlton Hotel Company and President of Horst Schulze Consulting, noted, "I hope I helped others manage fear during the pandemic so they could sustain their commitment to excellence. Fear does not produce excellence. Dedication, a quest for solutions, and high intent produce excellence. I want to be known as someone who insisted on discipline and the pursuit of excellence even in crisis." While Horst is adaptable, his crisis leadership brand involves the steadfast pursuit of quality standards.

That last set of team-oriented skills frequently included in crisis leadership statements involved mentorship. For example, Carly Fiorina, the Chairman and Founder of Fiorina Enterprises and Former HP CEO, wanted to be known for "helping people develop their leadership talents, see possibilities, and create a better future. I hope people will say that through mentorship and training, I helped them maximize their leadership potential and achieve more than they thought they could." Similarly,

Frank Donchez, Police Chief of the Overland Park, Kansas, Police Department, hoped, "Individuals in my department would see me as someone who developed leaders. Over my career, 12 of my officers have gone on to be police chiefs elsewhere. My greatest legacy in the pandemic hopefully will be that I helped others become ready to lead in future crises." The skillsets and time commitment needed to be an effective coach or mentor are different from those of someone who prioritizes strategic leadership. That's not to say a leader can't do both strategy and mentorship well. It's just that if you want to leave a leadership legacy as a mentor, you will certainly need to hone and practice talent development skills.

Before we move to individuals who emphasized purpose-driven legacies, I will highlight an often-overlooked skill prioritized by Randy Keirn, District Fire Chief at the Lealman, Florida, Fire District. Randy wanted to be known for anticipating and avoiding crises. He said, "People will see how we reacted to the needs of our residents, but I want to leave a legacy as a proactive leader. The impact of our early infection control training with nursing homes isn't something that will get much notice or will be easy to measure, but that's what I value most." Many people errantly interpret the business adage "what gets measured gets done," to mean if something isn't measurable, it is not worthwhile. In Randy's case, his most critical legacy element may be virtually undetectable yet inordinately valuable.

Competence-based legacy statements require leaders to seek mastery of skills in areas like communication, mentorship, or agile design. If you want your impact to be like those mentioned above, your development plan will likely lean toward skills-based learning and behavioral rehearsal. Let's now turn to leaders who primarily wanted to be known for leading with purpose.

STANDING ON PURPOSE

Consistent with Chapters 4, 5, and 10 ("Practice Employee Obsession," "Set Safety Supreme," and "Act Your Culture," respectively), the legacy statement of many leaders emphasized an overarching theme such as safety and employee care or cultural elements like mission or values.

Hans Vestberg, Chairman and CEO of Verizon, emphasized a primary safety focus for all stakeholders in response to the crisis legacy question. Hans noted, "I hope people will look back on this period and say that

Verizon balanced the safety of our employees with our customers' need to stay connected—whether the connection involved hospitals, first responders, teachers, families, or anyone we serve." Jeff Dailey, CEO of Farmers Insurance, by contrast, emphasized employee obsession in his legacy response, "I want to hear that first and foremost, we took care of our people. When we meet their needs, they meet our customers' needs, which in turn takes care of our business." Since a legacy statement captures an individual's (or team's) desired leadership brand, Hans would optimally be known for championing the safety of all, and Jeff would be remembered for employee-centricity. By contrast, many leaders wanted to be associated with leading based on their company's mission or values.

Brian Cornell, CEO of Target, indicated he would like to see Target's leadership viewed as taking action from the outset of the crisis, "guided by our purpose, meaning we helped all families discover the joy of everyday life. Joy looked different throughout the pandemic, but they would say we listened really closely to our guests to understand what they needed from us. Optimally, they would say we met their needs with incredible optimism, inclusivity, connection, inspiration, and drive. In other words, in very challenging circumstances, our company values were on full display, thanks to our team." Similarly, Thomas Tighe, President and CEO of Direct Relief, noted, "I hope our team will be viewed as helping our organization meet its highest purpose. That would mean we were a humanitarian group motivated purely to help people without regard to what they looked like, where they lived, the color of their skin, their religion, or their political affiliation. I hope, in retrospect, that everyone who was part of anything Direct Relief did feels that they were involved in something that mattered."

Lawrence Weathers, Chief of Police for the Lexington, Kentucky, Police Department, crafted his legacy statement connected to purpose expressed across multiple crises. He noted, "As a black police chief in a time of racial turmoil and the pandemic, I hope people would say we treated everyone with respect and stood up to the tasks at hand in the interest of justice, equality, and safety." Leaders who have their legacies connected to organizational purpose tend to make the company's mission, vision, and values a regular part of their communications. They also look for examples of their culture in action and share those stories readily. Let's look at the last common theme among crisis legacy statements—leading with character.

A LEADER'S TEMPERAMENT

Many leaders linked their desired crisis legacy to a character quality such as vulnerability, calm, courage, or compassion. For example, Bracken Darrell's statement incorporates vulnerability elements found in Chapter 9, "Bring Yourself to Work." Bracken, CEO of Logitech, hoped, "People will see we made many mistakes and understand that we were trying a lot of things. We were striving to leverage the best of technology fueled by our humanity, and we routinely asked, 'What more can we do?'" Kevin Clayton, CEO of Clayton Homes, wanted his team's leadership to have a calming impact. Kevin shared, "Hopefully, we will be remembered for being thoughtful. We didn't want to rush to conclusions or solutions. We leveraged experience managing other downturns (with the support of Berkshire Hathaway) to stay calm and grounded." Where Bracken led with vulnerability, and Kevin led with calm, other leaders wanted to be known for leading with courage.

In keeping with Chapter 16, "Decide with Moral Courage," Cathy Lanning, Senior Vice President, Property and Casualty Marketing at Nationwide Insurance, suggested she and her leadership team ideally would be seen as "bold and fearless. I come from a long history of leaders who didn't fear tough decisions. They were visionaries about what protection means to people and businesses. Protection has heightened in its importance today. So, hopefully, people will see our leadership team as being willing to reinvent ourselves and do so fearlessly." It's noteworthy that Cathy frames her team's legacy as a continuation of a lasting impact established by prior generations of leaders.

Consistent with observations made in Chapter 12, "Convey Compassion," many leaders responded to the pandemic with a focus on compassionate leadership. Bradley H. Feldmann, Chairman, President, and CEO at Cubic Corporation, noted, "This legacy isn't about me. It's about my leadership team and the entire organization. It's my fervent hope that when we look back at this unprecedented time in history, we can know that we responded with care for one another, and that people felt a greater sense of security and community. Ideally, they would say we were obsessed with caring for our people and for our customers, and that we stepped up to this moment with compassion."

Joe Duran, CEO and Founder of Personal Financial Management at Goldman Sachs, described compassion in a way not commonly used in business. Joe noted, "I hope people will say love was the driving force for everything we did. Ideally, they would feel we loved our people and our clients. They would also sense that we loved waking up each morning to serve them." Clearly, Joe is not talking about romantic love. From his perspective, love is a passionate approach to work and heartfelt care for the growth and development of those you serve. Given that framework, leading with love may be worth considering as part of your leadership legacy.

IT'S YOUR TURN

Now that you've experienced a variety of crisis legacy statements, it's your turn to craft one of your own. Since it's natural to want to be known for everything, I'd encourage you to keep your statement short and simple. The best impact statements are about a sentence long and focus on one central idea. You can write additional sentences later to unpack your initial idea (but don't add more targets). A good starting point is to decide if you will base your legacy on a competency, a larger purpose, or a character quality. I also recommend making your legacy statement aspirational but realistic based on your strengths and interests. Please take a moment to not only think about your legacy but to write it down. In the final chapter, we will explore ways to bring your legacy to life. We will also outline the next steps needed to leverage ideas shared throughout the book in times of both crisis and calm.

CHAPTER 22

Continuing the Conversation

*Conversation is a catalyst
for innovation.*
—JOHN SEELY BROWN,
organizational researcher

From childhood, I've been fortunate to have had conversations with wise teachers. For example, I learned a lot about coping with adversity by asking my mother how she dealt, at age 13, with the death of her father. Although reluctant to discuss WWII, my dad talked about ways he managed physical pain from the shrapnel that he carried with him from the Battle of Anzio. In adolescence, when I wasn't particularly interested in talking to my parents, I was fortunate to be able to sit for hours on my grandparents' porch and talk with them about ways to manage what seemed like insurmountable teenage angst. Through college, graduate school, and my professional career, I've always found wisdom and comfort in a good conversation.

Then COVID-19 surfaced. Almost instinctively, I turned to the wisest business leaders I knew and asked them for a conversation. Some 140-plus discussions later, I set out to start a conversation with you based on the wisdom they so kindly shared with me. We are approaching the end of this extended conversation, and I hope you will keep the discussion going.

So how might you advance a *Stronger Through Adversity* conversation? In the previous chapter, I encouraged you to create a leadership legacy statement. Hopefully, you took the time to craft that statement and have written it down. What if you took that piece of paper and talked with someone about your optimal leadership impact? What if you asked that person about his or her desired legacy?

I imagine those conversations could lead to more discussions where you encourage one another, commiserate setbacks, celebrate victories, and problem-solve barriers along your path to realizing your full potential as a leader. Possibly, those talks could evolve into a well-rounded leadership development plan that includes specific and measurable objectives and regularly scheduled check-ins.

If you haven't already begun discussing the questions posed in the "Your Strength Plan" sections found at the end of Chapters 2–20, you might find them to be a productive way to engage in conversations with your team or colleagues. Questions in those sections enable appreciative inquiry to fuel personal growth and team-determined change. Hopefully, by sharing responses to those questions, you will prompt follow-up discussions and explore ancillary learning materials.

To further support your journey, my team and I have created a book website at StrongerThroughAdversity.com. The site includes video excerpts from some of the conversations I had with the book contributors and gives a more personal look at the leaders behind the quotes. Stronger ThroughAdversity.com includes curated tools and resources to support and expand leadership development topics covered in the book (e.g., self-care, active listening, empathy skills, authentic leadership, and making decisions with moral courage). Additionally, the site offers a complimentary newsletter that includes tips for effective leadership communication, strategic visioning, and human experience delivery.

I encourage you to take conversations about leadership effectiveness to social media using #strongerthroughadversity. When you write blogs, post to social media, or otherwise offer insights on leadership resilience, my team and I will watch for your tagged content and will reshare helpful input.

You might choose to continue this conversation by making crisis leadership, or this book, a topic for mastermind meetings or regular discussion groups. As my schedule permits, I welcome the opportunity to do a complimentary drop-in for book club discussions of *Stronger Through Adversity*. In my experience, book discussions are a cost-effective way to foster meaningful workplace conversations. They also provide an opportunity to involve all team members in collaborative development (e.g., encourage everyone to lead chapter discussions).

My team and I would be glad to have a virtual coffee conversation with you to talk about your leadership development challenges or human experience design needs. If we don't have a solution, we are more than willing to "leave our island" and reach out to remarkable people in our network. Productive dialogue can only occur when we ask, find, and share wisdom each of us collects along our journey. Those discussions also require persistence and, at times, a willingness to have difficult conversations about fear, insecurity, personal shortcomings, implicit bias, or a host of other topics that often go unspoken.

The pandemic curtailed many forms of human interaction and connection. Handshakes, hugs, and even being within six feet of others, all have brought health risks. However, conversations helped reduce physical isolation. Mediated by technology, people reached out to individuals they hadn't talked to in years. Work teams increased their work-related and non-work-related discussions. Leaders listened more, communicated more, and were emotionally present and vulnerable during discussions. As leaders, we have a responsibility to keep engaging in that type of dialogue so we can help one another and assist those we serve in times of crisis and times of calm.

In her book, *Turning to One Another*, management consultant Margaret Wheatley observed:

> We can change the world if we start listening to one another again. Simple, honest, human conversation. Not mediation, negotiation problem-solving, debate, or public meetings. Simple, truthful conversation where we each have a chance to speak, we each feel heard, and we each listen well . . . Human conversation is the most ancient and easiest way to cultivate the conditions for change—personal change, community and organizational change, planetary change. If we can sit together and talk about what's important to us, we begin to come alive.

As I close my part of this conversation, I ask you to take the time to share your leadership legacy with someone. Hopefully, you will also engage a discussion with a colleague, coach someone, call a mentor, start a conversation online where you share your leadership insights, or take any action that drives leadership effectiveness and resilience. In the process, I trust you will "cultivate the conditions for change" and become even more alive.

Before I go, I will heed guidance offered by others in Chapter 13 and lead from the front. By that, I mean I will show my willingness to do what I've asked of you.

Here's my leadership legacy statement. I want to be remembered as *someone who captured what was right in the world and shared it for the betterment of others.* In this case, I hope I've captured the wisdom of more than 140 remarkable conversations so you will become *Stronger Through Adversity.*

Until our next conversation . . .

List of Contributors

- Acuity Insurance: Ben Salzmann, President and CEO
- Adventist HealthCare: Jonathan Sachs, Vice President of Patient Experience and Foundation
- Aesculap, Inc.: Chuck DiNardo, President
- Airbnb: Christopher Lehane, Vice President, Global Policy and Communications
- Albany, Oregon, Police Department: Marcia Harnden, Chief of Police
- AMB Sports + Entertainment: Steve Cannon, CEO
- American Lebanese Syrian Associated Charities, Inc.: Richard C. Shadyac Jr., President and CEO
- American Red Cross: Gail McGovern, President and CEO
- *Barron's*: Sterling Shea, Global Head of Wealth Management
- Bauer Hockey: Dan Sills, General Manager and Senior Vice President
- BIC Graphic: Barbie Winterbottom, Chief People Officer and Chief Human Resource Officer
- Build-A-Bear Workshop: Maxine Clark, Founder
- CallMiner: Scott Kendrick, VP of Marketing
- Carly Fiorina Enterprises: Carly Fiorina, Chairman and Founder
- Cedars-Sinai: Pattie Cuen, Vice President and Chief Marketing and Communications Officer

- Certified Angus Beef: Brent Eichar, Senior Executive Vice President
- Clarkson University: Kerop Janoyan, Dean of the Graduate School
- Classic Brands: Scott D. Burger, CEO
- Clayton Homes: Kevin Clayton, CEO
- Club Med North America: Carolyne Doyon, President and CEO
- Colorado Women's College at the University of Denver: Ann Ayers, JD, Dean
- ConantLeadership: Douglas R. Conant, Founder and CEO
- Costa Farms, LLC: Charlie Acevedo, Senior Vice President of Sales and Merchandising
- Crown Council and Total Patient Service Institute: Steven J. Anderson, Founder
- Cubic Corporation: Bradley H. Feldmann, Chairman, President, and CEO
- Dayton Flyers Men's Basketball: Andy Farrell, Special Assistant to the Head Coach and Recruiting Coordinator
- DHL Supply Chain: Rob Rosenberg, Global Head of Human Resources
- Direct Relief: Thomas Tighe, President and CEO
- Discount Tire: Mike Bolland, Director of Customer Insights
- DoSomething.org: Aria Finger, CEO
- Edward Jones: Penny Pennington, Managing Partner
- Elevations Credit Union: Gerry Agnes, President and CEO
- Ernst & Young (EY): Karyn Twaronite, Global Diversity and Inclusiveness Officer
- ExPeers: Diane S. Hopkins, CEO
- Farmers Insurance: Jeff Dailey, CEO
- Feeding America: Katie Fitzgerald, Executive Vice President and Chief Operating Officer
- Fitbit, Inc.: Stacy Salvi, Senior Director of Strategic Product Alliances
- Fox Sports: Silver Feldman, Manager, Business Systems

- FTD: Charlie Cole, CEO
- Fund Development Solutions: Kia Croom, Nonprofit Fundraising Executive
- GE Healthcare: Dr. WandaJean Jones, Global Learning Administrator
- Giacopelli Accounting and Giac Capital: James Giacopelli, President and CEO
- Girl Scouts of the USA: Sylvia Acevedo, CEO
- GODIVA Chocolatier: John Galloway, Chief Marketing and Innovation Officer
- GODIVA Chocolatier: Annie Young-Scrivner, CEO
- Gold & Diamond Source, Inc.: Steve Weintraub, Owner
- Goldman Sachs: Joe Duran, CEO and Founder, Goldman Sachs Personal Financial Management
- Goodwill Industries International, Inc.: Steven C. Preston, President and CEO
- Google Inc.: Lily Lin, Vice President, Global Communications
- H&R Block: Jeffrey J. Jones II, President and CEO
- Hanley Wood Media: John McManus, Vice President–Editorial Director
- Hayden Homes: Steve Klingman, President
- High Point University: Nido Qubein, President
- Horst Schulze Consulting: Horst Schulze, President
- Human Rights Watch: Colin H. Mincy, Chief People Officer
- *Inc.* magazine: J. Scott Omelianuk, Editor-in-Chief
- International Dairy Queen, Inc.: Troy Bader, President and CEO
- Janus Henderson Group plc: Richard M. Weil, Chief Executive Officer
- JBF Business Media: Jim Fitzpatrick, Cofounder and President
- Kendra Scott: Kathryn Pace, Senior Human Resources Director
- Kohl's: Michelle Gass, CEO
- Kopplin Kuebler & Wallace: Kurt Kuebler, Partner

STRONGER THROUGH ADVERSITY

- Leading Authorities, Inc.: Rainey Foster, Partner and Executive Vice President
- Lealman Fire District: Randy Keirn, District Fire Chief
- Lexington Police Department: Lawrence Weathers, Chief of Police
- Lexus North America: David Christ, Group Vice President and General Manager
- Logitech: Bracken Darrell, CEO
- Marco's Pizza: Anthony Fontana, VP Company Operations
- Marriott International: Stephanie Linnartz, Group President Consumer Operations
- Mars Petcare: Erica Coletta, Global Vice President of People and Organization
- Mercedes-Benz USA: Nicholas J. Speeks, President and CEO
- Mercy Hospital St. Louis: John Timmerman, PhD, Vice President Operations
- Microsoft: Matt Renner, President, Enterprise Commercial
- Miele USA: Jan Heck, President and CEO
- MindChamps: David Chiem, Founder and CEO
- Mize, Inc: Ashok Kartham, CEO
- Nathan's Famous: James R. Walker, Senior Vice President, Restaurants
- Nationwide: Cathy Lanning, Senior Vice President, Property and Casualty Marketing
- NBA: Kyle Hudson, Director, Team Marketing and Business Operations
- New York Cares: Gary Bagley, Executive Director
- Nurse Leader Network: Chris Recinos, CEO
- One Medical: Amir Dan Rubin, Chair and CEO
- Optym: Vic Keller, CEO
- Overland Park Police Department: Frank Donchez, Chief of Police
- Panasonic North America: Joe Haury, Vice President of Global Logistics

- Pecan Deluxe Candy Company: William "Bill" Barrier, PhD, Chief Strategy Officer
- PGA of America: Suzy Whaley, President
- Pinellas County EMS: Angus M. Jameson, MD, MPH, Medical Director
- Pinellas Park Fire Department: Brett Schlatterer, Fire Chief
- Prosek Partners: Jennifer Prosek, Managing Partner
- PulteGroup: Jay Mason, Vice President for Market Intelligence
- PwC: Ryan Hart, Managing Director, Tokyo Experience Center
- Quest Diagnostics Incorporated: Maria P Ortega, Regional Vice President
- Raymond James & Associates: Tash Elwyn, President and CEO
- Red Robin Gourmet Burgers: Dave Pace, Chairman of the Board
- Rise Consultants: Alberto Brea, Chief Growth Strategist
- Roche Diagnostics: Bryan K. Langford, Vice President, Commercial Operations
- Roche Diagnostics: Randy Pritchard, Senior Vice President, US Marketing
- Royal Bank of Canada: Brien K. Convery, National Director of Early Talent Acquisition
- Saia Inc. and Jack in the Box Inc.: John Gainor, Public Board Director
- Salesforce: Vala Afshar, Chief Digital Evangelist
- San Marino Police Department: John Incontro, Chief of Police
- Siemens USA: Barbara Humpton, President and CEO
- Smartsheet, Inc.: Mark Mader, CEO
- Sonny's BBQ: James S. Yarmuth, President and CEO
- Southwest Airlines Co.: Linda Rutherford, Senior Vice President and Chief Communication Officer
- Spokane Fire Department: Brian Schaeffer, Fire Chief
- Spradley Barr Ford: Bill & Karolyn Barr, Owners
- Starbucks: John Kelly, EVP of Public Affairs and Social Impact

- Starbucks Coffee: Howard Behar, President, Starbucks International (retired)
- Ste. Michelle Wine Estates: Jim Mortensen, President and Chief Executive Officer
- Strategic Horizons LLP: Joe Pine, Cofounder
- StubHub: Sukhinder Singh Cassidy, former President
- Talent Plus, Inc.: Makenzie Rath, President
- Target: Brian Cornell, CEO
- Team One: Mark Miller, Chief Strategy Officer
- Ten Stars Network Inc. (South Korea): Bobby Pang, Founder and Chief Visionary
- The Beverly Hills Hotel: Edward Mady, Regional Director and General Manager
- The Coca-Cola Company: Geoff Cottrill, SVP—Strategic Marketing
- The Humane Society of the United States: Amy Nichols, Vice President
- The Ritz-Carlton Bacara, Santa Barbara: Roberto van Geenen, General Manager
- The Salvation Army: David Hudson, Commissioner and National Commander
- *TIME*: Keith Grossman, President
- *TIME*: Edward Felsenthal, Editor-in-Chief and CEO
- TOMS, Madefor: Blake Mycoskie, Founder TOMS, Cofounder Madefor
- Total Merchant Concepts: Cheri Perry, President
- Truist Financial Corporation: Dontá L. Wilson, Chief Digital and Client Experience Officer
- United Way Worldwide: Brian A. Gallagher, President and Chief Executive Officer
- University of Arizona: Joe Carella, Assistant Dean of Executive Education and Professor of Strategy

- University of Denver: Jeremy Haefner, Chancellor
- University of South Florida Muma College of Business: Moez Limayem, Dean
- University of Tennessee, Knoxville: Ozlem Kilic, DSc, Associate Dean, Academic and Student Affairs
- Vancouver, Washington, Police Department: James McElvain, PhD, Chief of Police
- Verizon: Hans Vestberg, Chairman and CEO
- Volkswagen Group Australia: Jason Bradshaw, Chief Customer and Marketing Officer
- VSP: Don Oakley, President
- Wakefern Food Corp.: Karen Meleta, Vice President of Corporate Communications
- WarnerMedia Entertainment: Natasha Hritzuk, Vice President and Head of Consumer Research
- Wellthy: Lindsay Jurist-Rosner, Cofounder and CEO
- Whole Foods Market: Andres Traslavina, Senior Director of Executive Recruiting
- WordCreate, Inc.: Lior Arussy, President
- WW: Mindy Grossman, President and CEO
- Yale School of Management: Abigail R. Kies, Assistant Dean of Career Development
- Yale University: Ronnell Higgins, Director of Public Safety and Chief of Police
- YMCA of the USA: Kevin Washington, President and CEO
- Zappos.com: Tony Hsieh, CEO
- Zeiss: Cheryl Vescio, Senior Director, Retail Sales Group
- Zimmer Biomet: Ivan Tornos, Group President

Notes

Chapter 1

"Ex-heavyweight champion Mike Tyson . . . punched in the mouth.'": Mike Berardino, "Mike Tyson explains one of his most famous quotes," *SunSentinel*, November 9, 2012, https://www.sun-sentinel.com/sports/fl-xpm-2012-11-09-sfl-mike-tyson -explains-one-of-his-most-famous-quotes-20121109-story.html.

"Author Napoleon Hill . . . equal or greater benefit.'": Napoleon Hill, *BrainyQuote*, https://www.brainyquote.com/quotes/napoleon_hill_121336.

"One of the transformational leaders . . . that is strength.'": Mahatma Gandhi, *Simple Reminders*, https://gomcgill.com/strength-does-not-come-from-winning-by -mahatma-gandhi/.

PART I

"A house built on granite . . . to pull down.": Haile Selassie, *AZ Quotes*, https://www .azquotes.com/quote/728986.

Chapter 2

"If your compassion does not . . . it is incomplete.": Jack Kornfield, *Everyday Power*, https://everydaypower.com/self-care-quotes/.

Chapter 3

"Asking for help . . . honesty and intelligence.": Anne Wilson Schaef, *Enkiquotes*, https://www.enkiquotes.com/quotes-about-asking-for-help.html.

"Unfortunately, many leaders lose perspective . . . 'No man is an island, entire of itself.'": John Donne, *Brainy Quote*, https://www.brainyquote.com/quotes/john _donne_101197.

"On March 18, the leadership . . . are significant employers.'": *Leadership 18*, http:// leadership18.org/americas-charities-request-60-billion-infusion-of-support -to-help-the-most-vulnerable.

Chapter 4

"Everyone talks about . . . build one with your employees first.": Angela Ahrendts, *Inc.*, https://www.inc.com/partners-in-leadership/31-quotes-from-great-leaders -to-improve-workplace-satisfaction-for-employees.html

"As you might guess . . . 'put the customer first,'": Dan, *Satalytics*, "Amazon & Customer Experience: 13 Quotes from Jeff Bezos," November 6, 2016, https://www.satalytics .com/jeff-bezos/.

". . . while the founder of the Virgin Group . . . they will take care of the clients.'": Richard Branson, *Goodreads*, https://www.goodreads.com/quotes/7356284 -clients-do-not-come-first-employees-come-first-if-you.

"Well into the pandemic . . . additional publicly available data.'": "The CEO Leaderboard: COVID-19 Reputation Rankings," https://www.groupsjr.com/ceoleaderboard/.

"Hans Vestberg ranked 4th . . . roughly 135,000 employees.'": Ezequiel Minaya, *Forbes*, "The Forbes Corporate Responders New Ranking of Nation's Top Em- ployers' Responses to Pandemic," May 26, 2020, https://www.forbes.com/sites /ezequielminaya/2020/05/26/the-forbes-corporate-responders-new-ranking-of -nations-top-employers-responses-to-pandemic/#4a15d83b4a51.

Chapter 5

"The purpose is . . . safety with solvency.": Dwight D. Eisenhower, *BrainyQuote*, https://www.brainyquote.com/quotes/dwight_d_eisenhower_112049.

"One of Cicero's maxims . . . safety of the people be the highest law.'": Marcus Tullius Ci- cero, *BrainyQuote*, https://www.brainyquote.com/quotes/marcus_tullius_cicero _118644.

PART II

"The ear of the leader . . . voices of the people.": Woodrow Wilson, *Your Dictionary*, https://quotes.yourdictionary.com/author/quote/193305.

Chapter 6

"The most important thing . . . what isn't said.": Peter Drucker, *BrainyQuote*, https:// www.brainyquote.com/quotes/peter_drucker_142500.

"For this chapter . . . as much as we speak.'": Epictetus, *BrainyQuote*, https://www .brainyquote.com/quotes/epictetus_106298.

"Kia is the Nonprofit Fundraising Executive . . . people in underserved communi- ties.'": *Fund Development Solutions*, https://funddevelopmentsolutions.com.

"Paul Tillich, the philosopher, . . . is to listen.'": Paul Tillich, *BrainyQuote*, https:// www.brainyquote.com/quotes/paul_tillich_114351.

Chapter 7

"Transparency, honesty, kindness . . . businesses at all times.": John Gerzema, *BrainyQuote*, https://www.brainyquote.com/quotes/john_gerzema_556880.

"In 1938, while working . . . the way I do.'": Maria Popova, "How Steinbeck Used the Diary as a Tool of Discipline, a Hedge Against Self-Doubt, and a Pacemaker for the Heartbeat of Creative Work," *Brain Pickings*, https://www.brainpickings.org /2015/03/02/john-steinbeck-working-days/.

"Han Fei, a Chinese philosopher . . . be proved is an imposter.'": Han Fei, *QuoteFancy*, https://quotefancy.com/quote/1599249/Han-Fei-He-who-claims-to-be-sure-of -something-for-which-there-is-no-evidence-is-a-fool.

Chapter 8

"Take advantage of every opportunity . . . emotions to affect other people.": Jim Rohn, *BrainyQuote*, https://www.brainyquote.com/quotes/jim_rohn_165073.

"Author and former presidential speechwriter . . . language of leadership.'": James Humes, *BrainyQuote*, https://www.brainyquote.com/quotes/james _humes_154730.

"Southwest is one . . . and company spirit.'": Leonard Evans, *Panmore Institute*, "Southwest Airlines Co.'s Mission Statement & Vision Statement (An Analysis)," May 30, 2019, http://panmore.com/southwest-airlines-vision-statement-mission -statement-analysis.

"In the words of . . . people make meaning.'": Chris Cavanaugh, *QuoteHD*, http:// www.quotehd.com/quotes/chris-cavanaugh-quote-storytellers-by-the-very-act -of-telling-communicate-a-radical-learning.

Chapter 9

"Vulnerability is a . . . Anne Truitt": Maria Popova, "Artist Anne Truitt on Vulnerability, the Price of Integrity, and What Sustains the Creative Spirit," *Brain Pickings*, https://www.brainpickings.org/2016/01/21/anne-truitt-turn-art/.

"Brené has summarized her findings . . . Ignite creativity": Brené Brown, *Dare to Lead: Brave Work. Tough Conversations, Whole Hearts*, October 9, 2018, and Patrick Lencioni, *The Five Dysfunctions of Team: A Leadership Fable*, April 11, 2002.

"In her book . . . fear and disconnection.'": Brené Brown, *Daring Greatly: How the Courage to Be Vulnerable Transforms the Way We Live, Love, Parent, and Lead*, February 2013.

"'He's doing it . . . had run out.": John McManus, *Builder*, "A Builder Call to Action as Economies Reboot Efforts to Dig Out from COVID-19 Shutdowns," April 26, 2020, https://www.builderonline.com/builder-100/leadership/a-builder-call-to -action-as-economies-reboot-efforts-to-dig-out-from-covid-19-shutdowns_o.

"In the words of . . . do so much.'": Helen Keller, *BrainyQuote*, https://www .brainyquote.com/quotes/helen_keller_382259.

PART III

"Without a mission statement . . . the wrong building!": Dave Ramsey, *QuoteFancy*, https://quotefancy.com/quote/1377749/Dave-Ramsey-Without-a-mission -statement-you-may-get-to-the-top-of-the-ladder-and-then.

Chapter 10

"Vision without action . . . can change the world.": Joel A. Barker, *BrainyQuote*, https://www.brainyquote.com/quotes/joel_a_barker_158200.

"Children's author Lewis Carroll . . . will get you there.'": Lewis Carroll, *BrainyQuote*, https://www.brainyquote.com/quotes/lewis_carroll_165865.

"Until the pandemic . . . go together.'": African Proverb, *Quotespedia*, https://www.quotespedia.org/authors/a/african-proverbs/if-you-want-to-go-fast-go-alone-if-you-want-to-go-far-go-together-african-proverb/.

"As thought leader Ralph Buchanan . . . collide with destiny.'": Damien Thomas, *Your Positive Oasis*, "25 Quotes to Help You Live Your Purpose," July 1, 2020, https://yourpositiveoasis.com/25-quotes-to-help-you-live-your-purpose/.

Chapter 11

"Strive not . . . be of value.": Albert Einstein, *BrainyQuote*, https://www.brainyquote.com/quotes/albert_einstein_122232.

"Let's look at . . . in all situations.": *BusinessDictionary*, http://www.businessdictionary.com/definition/values.html.

"Contrast that with . . . to pay for it.": *BusinessDictionary*, http://www.businessdictionary.com/definition/value.html.

"For now, I'll . . . what they want.'": Zig Ziglar, *BrainyQuote*, https://www.brainyquote.com/quotes/zig_ziglar_381984.

Chapter 12

"Our human compassion . . . for the future.": Nelson Mandela, *BrainyQuote*, https://www.brainyquote.com/quotes/nelson_mandela_447262.

"Maybe that is why . . . a dealer in hope.'": Napoleon Bonapart, *BrainyQuote*, https://www.brainyquote.com/quotes/napoleon_bonaparte_106371.

Chapter 13

"The art of life . . . to our surroundings.": Okakura Kakuzo, *Quotes.net*, https://www.quotes.net/quote/20648.

"In her book, *Leadership Beyond Measure*, . . . pace set by her.'": Jude Jennison, *Leadership Beyond Measure: Profound learning with horses to transform leaders and business*, May 2015.

"Other times it . . . walk beside them.'": Lao Tzu, *Goodreads*, https://www.goodreads.com/quotes/10627-to-lead-people-walk-beside-them-as-for-the.

"Robert Greenleaf, founder . . . become leaders?'": Robert Greenleaf, *QuoteFancy*, https://quotefancy.com/robert-k-greenleaf-quotes.

"Put simply by . . . as all of us.'": Ken Blanchard, *Goodreads*, https://www.goodreads.com/quotes/56863-none-of-us-is-as-smart-as-all-of-us.

"As you practice . . . appreciate your leadership.'": Nelson Mandela, *BrainyQuote*, https://www.brainyquote.com/quotes/nelson_mandela_393048.

PART IV

"It's not enough . . . what are we busy about?": Henry David Thoreau, *BrainyQuote*, https://www.brainyquote.com/quotes/henry_david_thoreau_153926.

Chapter 14

"Great leaders are . . . everybody can understand.": Colin Powell, *BrainyQuote*, https://www.brainyquote.com/quotes/colin_powell_144992.

"Management consultant Peter Drucker . . . the right things.'": Peter Drucker, *BrainyQuote*, https://www.brainyquote.com/quotes/peter_drucker_134881.

"About four months . . . to 'very high' range.": Lorrie Lykins, *i4cp*, "I4CP: The COVID-19 Hit on Productivity Is Accelerating in Most Companies," March 19, 2020, https://www.i4cp.com/coronaviri/i4cp-the-covid-19-hit-on-productivity -is-accelerating-in-most-companies.

"Let's imagine your . . . sharpening the axe.'": Abraham Lincoln, *BrainyQuote*, https:// www.brainyquote.com/quotes/abraham_lincoln_109275.

"In their book *Effective Crisis Communication* . . . its high-priority goals.": Robert R. Ulmer, Timothy L. Sellnow, & Matthew W. Seeger, *Effective Crisis Communication: Moving from Crisis to Opportunity*, December 26, 2017.

"Steve Jobs once noted . . . you can move mountains.'": Steve Jobs, *Goodreads*, https:// www.goodreads.com/quotes/915331-that-s-been-one-of-my-mantras-focus -and-simplicity.

"Bill Gates once . . . magnify the inefficiency.'": Bill Gates, *BrainyQuote*, https://www .brainyquote.com/quotes/bill_gates_104353.

"Apple CEO Tim Cook . . . about empowering people.'": Tim Cook, *BrainyQuote*, https://www.brainyquote.com/quotes/tim_cook_843436.

"Chinese inventor and philosopher . . .elimination of nonssentials.'": Lin Yutang, *BrainyQuote*, https://www.brainyquote.com/quotes/lin_yutang_107810.

"As overwhelming as that may seem . . .and focused effort.'": Paul J. Meyer, *BrainyQuote*, https://www.brainyquote.com/quotes/paul_j_meyer_393225.

Chapter 15

"An organization's ability . . . ultimate competitive advantage.": Jack Welch, *BrainyQuote*, https://www.brainyquote.com/quotes/jack_welch_173305.

"Entrepreneur and author . . . revision and change.'": Richard Branson, *QuoteFancy*, https://quotefancy.com/quote/899399/Richard-Branson-Every-success-story -is-a-tale-of-constant-adaption-revision-and-change-A.

"Psychologist Abraham Maslow . . . as if it were a nail.'": Abraham Maslow, *Goodreads*, https://www.goodreads.com/quotes/13932-i-suppose-it-is-tempting -if-the-only-tool-you.

"Minister and civil rights activist Martin Luther King . . . keep moving forward.'": Martin Luther King Jr., *eNotes*, https://www.enotes.com/homework-help/you -cant-fly-then-run-you-cant-run-then-walk-you-343193.

"Whenever I hear . . . unexpected in common hours.'": Henry David Thoreau, *BrainyQuote*, https://www.brainyquote.com/quotes/henry_david_thoreau _163655.

Chapter 16

"Courage is not simply . . . the testing point.": C. S. Lewis, *BrainyQuote*, https://www .brainyquote.com/quotes/c_s_lewis_100842.

"The actor and writer Christopher Reeve . . . out in the ocean.'": Christopher Reeve, *BrainyQuote*, https://www.brainyquote.com/quotes/christopher_reeve _167081.

"They also align with . . . he who conquers that fear.'": Nelson Mandela, *BrainyQuote*, https://www.brainyquote.com/quotes/nelson_mandela_178789.

"That policy change, posted . . . the next 12 months.": *StubHub*, "Statement Regarding StubHub's Event Cancellation and Refund Policy, in Light of Coronavirus (COVID-19)," March 12, 2020, https://www.stubhub.com/live/stubhub-event -cancellation-and-refund-policy-light-coronavirus-covid-19.

Chapter 17

"Alone we can . . . do so much.": Helen Keller, *BrainyQuote*, https://www.brainyquote .com/quotes/helen_keller_382259.

"As first lady, Abigail Adams . . . ardor and diligence.'": Abigail Adams, *BrainyQuote*, https://www.brainyquote.com/quotes/abigail_adams_124585.

"Eighteenth-century Scottish philosopher . . . aid me tomorrow.'": David Hume, *AZ Quotes*, https://www.azquotes.com/quote/555896.

PART V

"The most reliable . . . future is to create it.": Abraham Lincoln, *AZ Quotes*, https:// www.azquotes.com/quotes/topics/creating-the-future.html.

Chapter 18

"Gratitude unlocks the fullness . . . confusion to clarity.": Melody Beattie, *BrainyQuote*, https://www.brainyquote.com/quotes/melody_beattie_177949.

"In their book *Appreciate* . . . monumental tasks without praise?'": David Sturt, Todd Nordstrom, Kevin Ames, and Gary Beckstrand, *Appreciate: Celebrating People, Inspiring Greatness*, August 14, 2017.

"The poet William James . . . craving to be appreciated.'": William James, *BrainyQuote*, https://www.brainyquote.com/quotes/william_james_125466.

"This commitment to social . . . networks across the country.'": Anthony Myers, *Confectionery News*, "GODIVA partners with Tenet Healthcare Corporation to distribute chocolates across the US," April 30, 2020, https://www.confectionerynews .com/Article/2020/04/30/Godiva-partners-with-Tenet-Healthcare-Corporation -to-distribute-chocolates-across-the-US.

"Primatologist Jane Goodall . . . difference you want to make.'": Jane Goodall, *Goodreads*, https://www.goodreads.com/quotes/511077-you-cannot-get -through-a-single-day-without-having-an.

Chapter 19

"We must establish . . . no work can occur.": Peter Block, *AZ Quotes*, https://www .azquotes.com/author/38092-Peter_Block.

"Steve Jobs put it . . . realize it themselves.'": Steve Jobs, *QuoteFancy*, https://quote fancy.com/quote/911620/Steve-Jobs-Get-closer-than-ever-to-your-customers -So-close-that-you-tell-them-what-they.

"Zappos procured 300 devices . . . diagnoses of COVID-19.'": Adrian Swinscoe, *Forbes*, "You Can Call Zappos to Ask for Help on Anything—One Doctor Did and Was Able to Help 300 COVID-19 Patients," April 20, 2020, https:// www.forbes.com/sites/adrianswinscoe/2020/04/20/you-can-call-zappos-to -ask-for-help-on-anything-one-doctor-did-and-was-able-to-help-300-covid -19-patients/#74d905046d28.

Chapter 20

"The distinction between . . . stubbornly persistent illusion.": Albert Einstein, *BrainyQuote*, https://www.brainyquote.com/quotes/albert_einstein_148814.

"In 1985, the *Economist* . . . you'd better be running.": Dan Montano, *Economist*, "The other dimension: Technology and the City of London: A survey," page 37, July 6, 1985.

"Research conducted by Professor Karam Ghazi . . . in the midst of crises.": Karam Ghazi, *Journal of Hotel & Business Management*, "The Impact of Strategic Planning on Crisis Management Styles in the 5-Star Hotels," February 2018, https://www .researchgate.net/publication/331940469_The_Impact_of_Strategic_Planning _on_Crisis_Management_Styles_in_the_5-Star_Hotels.

"Amazon CEO, Jeff Bezos . . .isn't a strategy.'": Jeff Bezos, *BrainyQuote*, https://www .brainyquote.com/quotes/jeff_bezos_591677.

"Mr. Burns noted . . . the rest of my life.'": George Burns, *BrainyQuote*, https://www .brainyquote.com/quotes/george_burns_189717.

"Isaac Newton observed . . . the shoulders of giants.'": Isaac Newton, *BrainyQuote*, https://www.brainyquote.com/quotes/isaac_newton_135885.

"Similarly, Warren Buffet . . . a tree a long time ago.'": Warren Buffet, *BrainyQuote*, https://www.brainyquote.com/quotes/warren_buffett_409214.

Chapter 21

"The great use of life . . . that will outlast it.": William James, *BrainyQuote*, https:// www.brainyquote.com/quotes/william_james_101063.

Chapter 22

"Conversation is a catalyst for innovation.": John Seely Brown, *QuoteFancy*, https://quotefancy.com/quote/1702150/John-Seely-Brown-Conversation-is-a-catalyst-for-innovation.

"In her book, *Turning to One Another* . . . to come alive.": Margaret Wheatley, *Turning to One Another: Simple Conversations to Restore Hope to the Future*, February 2, 2009.

Index

About the Author

Dr. Joseph Michelli is the CEO of The Michelli Experience (TME) and is certified as a customer experience consultant, professional speaker, and virtual presenter. TME helps business leaders develop and communicate a transformational strategic vision and provides customized solutions to ensure you drive customer engagement, loyalty, and referrals.

To achieve measurable outcomes, Dr. Michelli offers virtual and in-person:

- Leadership and management coaching
- Keynote speeches
- Workshop presentations
- Customized training tools
- Strategic visioning sessions
- Journey mapping and experience design
- Resilience resources

Dr. Michelli has been recognized globally for his thought leadership on customer experience design, as well as his engaging speaking skills and influential impact on service brands. In addition to *Stronger Through Adversity*, Dr. Michelli is a *New York Times, Wall Street Journal, USA Today*, and *Businessweek* bestselling author who has written:

> *The Airbnb Way: 5 Leadership Lessons for Igniting Growth, Community, and Belonging*

> *Driven to Delight: Delivering World-Class Customer Experience the Mercedes-Benz Way*

> *Leading the Starbucks Way: 5 Principles for Connecting with Your Customers, Your Products, and Your People*

> *The Zappos Experience: 5 Principles to Inspire, Engage, and WOW*

> *Prescription for Excellence: Leadership Lessons for Creating a World-Class Customer Experience from UCLA Health System*

> *The New Gold Standard: 5 Leadership Principles for Creating a Legendary Customer Experience Courtesy of The Ritz-Carlton Hotel Company*

> *The Starbucks Experience: 5 Principles for Turning Ordinary into Extraordinary*

> *The MindChamps Way: How to Turn an Idea into a Global Movement*

> *Humor, Play, and Laughter: Stress-Proofing Life with Your Kids*

Dr. Michelli also coauthored *When Fish Fly: Lessons for Creating a Vital and Energized Workplace* with John Yokoyama, the former owner of the World Famous Pike Place Fish Market in Seattle, Washington.

For more information on how Dr. Michelli can present virtually or in person at your event, provide training resources, or help you elevate your culture and/or customer experience, visit www.josephmichelli.com.

Dr. Michelli is eager to assist you in growing *Stronger Through Adversity*. You can reach him via email at patti@josephmichelli.com, or by phone at 727-289-1571.

Also by **Joseph Michelli**